The Church Universal and Triumphant

Religion and Politics

Michael Barkun, *Series Editor*

The Church Universal and Triumphant

Elizabeth Clare Prophet's Apocalyptic Movement

Bradley C. Whitsel

SYRACUSE UNIVERSITY PRESS

First Edition 2003

03 04 05 06 07 08   6 5 4 3 2 1

The paper used in this publication meets the minimum requirements
of American National Standard for Information Sciences—Permanence
of Paper for Printed Library Materials, ANSI Z39.48–1984.∞™

Library of Congress Cataloging-in-Publication Data

Whitsel, Bradley.
The Church Universal and Triumphant : Elizabeth Clare Prophet's
apocalyptic movement / Bradley Whitsel.— 1st ed.
p. cm.—(Religion and politics)
Includes bibliographical references (p.) and index.
ISBN 0–8156–2999–0 (hardcover)—ISBN 0–8156–3000-X (pbk.)
1. Church Universal and Triumphant. I. Title. II. Series.
BP605.S73 W45 2003
299'.93—dc21   2002151303

Manufactured in the United States of America

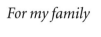

For my family

Bradley C. Whitsel is a political scientist at Pennsylvania State University (Fayette campus).

Contents

Illustrations

Preface

As one of the most prominent of the new religious movements to blossom in America in the 1960s and early 1970s, the Church Universal and Triumphant (CUT) has for some time attracted the attention of both scholars and the media. In its colorful history, the event generating the greatest fascination with the controversial New Age church was its mobilization for a global disaster in early 1990. This drama was precipitated by the movement's spiritual leader, Elizabeth Clare Prophet, who urged CUT's adherents in the United States and abroad to flock to church-built emergency shelters in Montana in order to survive an imminent nuclear war. While several thousand panicked members of the group converged in Park County, Montana, to prepare for the catastrophic event, news crews from all over the world arrived in the mountainous and sparsely populated region to cover the unusual occurrence. When Prophet's predicted time frame for the crisis passed, CUT entered into a new period in its history defined by organizational turmoil, mass defections, and overall decline.

The lack of a close examination of the Church Universal and Triumphant's route to apocalyptic panic in 1990 remains as a significant gap in the field of contemporary millennial studies. This omission is strange, since scholars displayed much interest in several other high-profile cases of apocalypticism that occurred in the 1990s. These incidents are, by now, well-known, and each was somehow associated with loss of life. They include the 1993 Branch Davidian standoff, the 1994 and 1995 mass suicides and ritualistic murders of members of the Solar Temple, Aum Shinrikyo's campaign of millennial violence in 1995, and the group suicide of Heaven's Gate members in 1997. What set the CUT incident apart from these other cases was the nonviolent character of its period of millennial excitement, which, when compared to episodes involving human tragedy, may explain why the group's desperate survivalist efforts in the Montana Rockies have been largely forgotten.

CUT's preparations for a world disaster did not occur in isolation from its past. The church was formed in 1958 as religio-political organization synthesizing superpatriotic beliefs with millennial yearnings for the birth of a new golden age civilization. Its leaders infused the movement with the conviction that conspiratorial forces were succeeding in their plans to destroy America and preached that a sweeping cataclysm would soon take place, demonstrating God's judgment against those responsible for the country's troubles. These fears led the group to adopt a separatist existence that placed believers at some distance, both psychologically and geographically, from the larger society surrounding it. Ultimately, this strategy brought CUT to its communal ranch in southwestern Montana, a location thought to offer safety from the nuclear nightmare Elizabeth Clare Prophet envisioned. Although the group acquired weapons to survive in the postapocalyptic world, CUT's theology steered its members away from a violent encounter with outsiders during the agitated period of waiting for the expected disaster.

As the spate of apocalyptic activity in the 1990s illustrated, End of the Age ideologies have proven capable of invigorating the imagination of some contemporary counterculturalists. The underexamined history of the Church Universal and Triumphant gives us insights into how a millennial community might receive and act upon such ideas. CUT's path to disaster panic draws attention to the perceived pressures and strains felt by millenarians believing themselves to be struggling against the dangers posed by a threat-filled world.

This project originally began as a political science doctoral dissertation. As a political scientist, I have naturally approached the subject from a perspective informed by my own field. Thus I have primarily examined the politicized aspects of CUT's millennial outlook and the group's interactions with the political environment. Throughout, I concentrate upon the relationship between CUT and the outside world, which grew more contentious as the group matured. Since my focus is on the larger movement as the singular unit of analysis, CUT is generally presented as a unified social organization whose institutional beliefs guided collective action. The terms "group" and "organization" are often used in the book for purposes of convenience, but it is not lost upon me that social movements are comprised of individuals with a wide range of attitudes, some of which may deviate from the official position of the institution to which they belong.

The interviews I conducted with members of the Church Universal and Triumphant were undertaken mainly during two separate field studies at the organization's Royal Teton Ranch. However, additional telephone and face-to-face interviews (along with correspondence) with current and former group members continued until summer 2000. As the book neared completion, I conducted telephone interviews with several CUT defectors specifically to gain information concerning the group's period of millennial excitement in early 1990 and to provide an alternative view to the church's well-documented management changes. The onetime CUT members with whom I spoke had all served at some point on the church's staff, and most had been involved in the organization's period of apocalyptic mobilization.

The first of my visits to the Royal Teton Ranch took place in August 1993. Church officials permitted me to begin preliminary research on the organization several months prior to my initial visit to the group's ranch headquarters. During this "pilot study" phase of my research, I conducted interviews with three members of the permanent ranch staff, including a key CUT officeholder. At this time, I also interviewed several representatives of CUT's Glastonbury colony. In 1994, I made arrangements to attend CUT's annual summer conference held at the ranch between June 25 and July 4. Officials of the church waived my registration fee and provided me with housing at a reduced rate on the Glastonbury property. In addition, a secretary working for the church kindly assisted me in arranging times for several group members to participate in interviews.

While at the conference, I conducted twenty-six full-length interviews with group members. However, my communications with church members were not limited to these formal interviews. The informal discussions I had with group members greatly exceeded the number of full-length interviews I had time to conduct. Among the persons interviewed were several church ministers, administrative personnel on the ranch, and church members entrusted with the task of dealing with reporters and scholars, such as public relations officials. The interviews were semistructured, with subjects being given the opportunity to respond to questions in as much detail as they desired. It was made clear to the subjects that they were free to decline my request or to withdraw at any time from the interview. In several cases, subjects indicated their reluctance to have their names appear in this study. In accordance with their preference, I have omitted their names and used their statements anonymously. In three cases, at the request of the subject, I have used a pseudonym.

Although the majority of the interviews I conducted at CUT's summer conference were with members of the permanent ranch staff, I also interviewed eight subjects who were either residents of Glastonbury or church members living in other regions of the United States. My interview with Elizabeth Clare Prophet took place at her home on the evening of July 3, 1994. This opportunity was a surprise since I had been informed earlier by CUT officials that Prophet would be unable to meet with me. The interview with Prophet lasted approximately ninety minutes.

Acknowledgments

During the considerable time required to research and write the book, I have had the good fortune of receiving help from a number of people. I owe a debt of deep gratitude to Michael Barkun, whose comments on all phases of this work were most helpful. His own pathbreaking work on millennial belief was a source of inspiration to me. Peggy Thompson (Syracuse University), David Bennett (Syracuse University), Allen Sapp (Central Missouri State University), and Amanda Porterfield (University of Wyoming) also provided important suggestions, as did the anonymous readers who evaluated the manuscript for Syracuse University Press. In addition, conversations with scholars who shared an interest in CUT, including Rob Balch (University of Montana), Susan Palmer (Dawson College), and Tim Miller (University of Kansas) helped me to better understand aspects of its recent history. In order to acquire information on the church's early years, it became necessary to spend time at the Institute for the Study of American Religions at the University of California at Santa Barbara. J. Gordon Melton, director of the institute, provided invaluable help in locating specific materials relating to CUT's teachings and its communal history. I also want to express my appreciation to the library staff at the Pennsylvania State University (Fayette campus) for their help in acquiring materials through interlibrary loan.

While this book is not an ethnography, I conducted approximately forty full-length interviews with both members and former members of CUT. Most of these interviews were conducted during two separate field visits to the organization's Royal Teton Ranch in August 1993 and in June and July 1994. Discussions with the interviewees were always enlightening, and I appreciated the patience and thoughtfulness of all those who participated. In particular, I thank Moira Prophet, Theresa Kitajewski, Cheri Walsh, and Barbara Hopkins for taking the time from their busy schedules to accommodate me. Despite her other obligations during the church's 1994 annual summer conference, Elizabeth Clare Prophet agreed to meet with me and to be interviewed at her home on the Royal Teton Ranch. I believe this to be the only interview she has given to an academic researcher.

The ranch administrators were receptive to my request to interview whom I chose and permitted me access to the church's archives, comprising the organization's published literature housed in a converted trailer. The administrators also graciously granted me access to an on-site copier to reproduce documents on church teachings, provided me with several videotapes of Elizabeth Clare Prophet's lectures, and waived my attendance fee for the 1994 summer conference. Prophet's recent incapacitation from Alzheimer's disease gave court-appointed custodians the responsibility of handling her affairs. They kindly granted me access to her student records, and these materials would not have been located had it not been for the efforts of Scott Sanders and the archival staff at Antioch College.

Research was facilitated by aid from the Syracuse University Maxwell School's Roscoe-Martin Fund and a Syracuse University Creative Research Project Grant. Generous support from the Pennsylvania State University's Commonwealth College in the form of a faculty development grant allowed me the time to undertake additional research and to bring the book to completion. Special thanks go to Mary Gergen, social science division head of the Commonwealth College, Sandra Gleason, associate dean for faculty and research at Commonwealth College, and James Ostrow, former director of academic affairs at Pennsylvania State University (Fayette campus), for their part in supporting this project.

My deepest appreciation, however, goes to my wife, Laurie, and our children, Amy and Christian, for their patience, love, and understanding.

I gratefully acknowledge permission from the editors of *Nova Religio, Communal Societies,* and *Studies in Conflict and Terrorism* to use brief passages from my work previously published in these academic journals, and from the *Los Angeles Times, Calgary Herald,* and *Billings Gazette* for the use of photographs.

The Church Universal and Triumphant

1

Escape to the Mountains

In the early evening of March 15, 1990, several thousand adherents of the Church Universal and Triumphant (CUT) braced themselves for the onset of a cataclysmic nuclear war. Members of the Montana-based religious movement were responding to Elizabeth Clare Prophet's warnings that the world had entered upon a "danger period of accelerated negative karma" that made likely the arrival of a Soviet first strike upon the United States. The politicized theme of the envisioned crisis was rooted in the church's history; from the time of its founding in 1958, the organization had incorporated strident anticommunism in a syncretic religion that blended Theosophical doctrine, New Age ideas, apocalypticism, and superpatriotism. Prophet, who by 1990 had served for seventeen years as CUT's lone spiritual leader, urged all those associated with her New Age sect who could to flee their homes and find safety at the network of underground shelters the group constructed in anticipation of the missile attack. Her warning was not a matter to be taken lightly. Prophet was acknowledged within the ranks of the church to be the sole appointed "Messenger" of the Ascended Masters, a post she had inherited from Mark L. Prophet, the movement's founder and her husband, following his death in 1973. As Messenger, she was believed to be in communication with the pantheon of spiritual entities that the church attributed with guiding the destiny of the universe.

For months prior to the prediction, frightened believers streamed into the Paradise Valley region, the ironically named swath of mountainous Park County just north of Yellowstone National Park, where the church's vast Royal Teton Ranch was situated. The newcomers came from many regions of the United States as well as from a number of other countries. Once in the area, they rushed to secure spaces for themselves and their loved ones in shelters on CUT-owned property or in emergency structures church members who lived near the ranch had built. In many cases, those belonging to the panicked flock exhausted their financial resources in a desperate effort to acquire enough survival equipment, food, and other supplies to weather the expected nuclear event, which they believed would necessitate an underground stay lasting anywhere from months up to seven years. As the group hurriedly stocked up on provisions, media crews from all over the world descended on Park County to cover the story. News that two church members had been arrested for conspiring to buy a large stockpile of assault weapons in the summer of 1989 attracted reporters to the site and ratcheted up the fears of local residents that CUT was a doomsday cult planning to declare war on outsiders. Word that Prophet's most highly devoted followers had been practicing emergency drills at the ranch's $3 million main shelter did nothing to calm the nerves of edgy local Montanans observing the activity.[1]

As the outside world followed the story, CUT's apocalyptic mobilization finally concluded but with little drama. On the morning of March 16, after having spent the previous night in fallout shelters scattered throughout the region, the emotionally drained contingent reemerged from the earth after realizing that the attack had failed to take place. The nonappearance of the predicted event caused many to reevaluate their beliefs. A large proportion of those who had made the trek to Montana were financially broke after having quit their jobs and channeled every available resource into the survivalist initiative. With their faith in Prophet shaken, about one-third of the membership immediately severed ties with the church. However, most of those who came to wait out the effects of the Soviet attack retained their convictions. The Messenger's declaration that the group's prayers had helped avert the crisis may have struck outsiders as a rationalization to explain the nonmaterialization of disaster, but for CUT's core following the explanation validated the significance of the church community's preparations and the work of the faithful in forestalling a nuclear Armageddon.[2]

By the time CUT had embarked upon its survivalist strategy in the late 1980s, it had become one of the most controversial nontraditional religious movements in America. As a consequence of its period of heightened millennial excitement, problems continued to plague the group into the next decade. Shortly after the disconfirmation of the prophecy, the Justice Department and the Internal Revenue Service focused attention on the group's activities. The well-publicized arrest of two CUT members for their part in attempting to acquire an arsenal of firearms to be used for emergency purposes led to a protracted investigation of the church. After determining that CUT had for years been secretly involved in purchasing weapons to defend its community in the event of a crisis, the Justice Department recommended that the IRS strip the church of its tax-exempt status as a religious organization; the tax agency did so in 1992, following an audit that revealed the acquisition of illegal weapons by church leaders. In its efforts to overturn the IRS decision, CUT's attorneys argued that the group had been the target of a sustained campaign of religious bigotry led by the media and the organization's critics.[3]

CUT would soon have its tax-exempt status restored, but the 1994 out-of-court agreement that settled the matter hinged upon a tragedy. On April 19, 1993, after a lengthy standoff between federal authorities and David Koresh's Branch Davidians, the Federal Bureau of Investigation employed forceful tactics to extricate members of the obscure apocalyptic sect from their Mt. Carmel compound on the outskirts of Waco, Texas. Davidians believed their leader, Koresh, to be the messiah, whose interpretation of the Bible (particularly the Book of Revelation) would reveal to his 130-member community the events of the "Last Days." The tiny millennial group had emerged from the numerous schisms that occurred since the 1940s within the Seventh Day Adventist Church, but Koresh's prophecies were of his own making. In order to prepare the faithful for the nearing battle with the Antichrist, the charismatic thirty-three-year-old leader of the Branch Davidians oversaw the militarization of the cheaply built, wooden-framed Mt. Carmel facility, a labor that involved stockpiling weapons and constructing fortified emplacements in the compound for self-defense. When news of the sect's significant purchases of arms led agents of the Bureau of Alcohol, Tobacco, and Firearms to gather outside the commune on February 28, 1993, its residents believed that the prophesied war brought on by the forces of Babylon had begun. In terms of the result, it had. BATF's initial "dynamic entry" raid against the heavily armed group on February 28 resulted in the deaths of four agents and five Branch Davidians.[4]

The authorities' decision to use aggressive measures on April 19 to end the fifty-one-day standoff that by this point had captured public attention brought the law enforcement siege of Mt. Carmel to a conclusion but not in the way officials orchestrating the plan had hoped. The disastrous outcome of the operation, which was watched by an international television audience, seemed almost surreal. The fiery deaths of seventy-four Davidians, brought on by the total incineration of the compound, set off a national debate on the events at Waco and led to a congressional investigation of the raid. The hearings shed light on major mistakes the on-scene authorities had made, including mischaracterizing the case as a standard "hostage-barricade situation" and using a stress-escalation strategy against the Branch Davidians that only strengthened their resolve.[5] The revelations that most directly impacted CUT had to do with the FBI's reliance during the siege on anticult experts and the effect this might have had on law enforcement operations.

Throughout the Waco standoff, the FBI depended upon professional anticultists for much of their information. These selected experts called into question the legitimacy of nontraditional religious organizations, and they were successful in advancing their interpretation, which downplayed the strength of the Branch Davidians' convictions. Given the perspective their consultants held, it is no surprise that authorities paid little attention to the theological beliefs of Koresh's following. Instead, Koresh came to be narrowly portrayed as a cunning "operator" holding his "cult" members against their will by the use of psychological coercion, an assessment generated by the FBI's advisers and accepted without scrutiny by the media.[6]

Since much of CUT's legal defense in its case with the IRS revolved around the claim of religious persecution at the hands of anticult activists, the Waco episode and the attention surrounding the anticult network gave the church's arguments a measure of plausibility. Despite the Justice Department's findings, Prophet's church regained tax exemption but with several stipulations the IRS demanded concerning the group's weapons and taxable assets.

The favorable out-of-court settlement did not halt the decline afflicting CUT in the years following its preparations for nuclear war in 1990. Mass defections, in particular, damaged the church's overall health. While CUT has made a practice of not revealing its numerical size,[7] it is likely that it could claim as many as twenty-five thousand members (of varying degrees of association with the church) in the late 1970s when the group was located in southern California.[8] This figure had substantially declined by the late 1990s. Interestingly enough, another source of difficulty for CUT stemmed from changes in the world political order. As a movement imbued with superpatriotic sentiments from its earliest days, the church built its doctrine on a religiopolitical foundation supported by spiritually energized visions of America as a chosen nation and steeped in the mind-set of the Cold War between the United States and the Soviet Union. For Mark and Elizabeth Clare Prophet, whose visceral cold warrior attitudes filtered into their organization, the American-Soviet struggle represented a cosmic battle between the forces of light and darkness. CUT's nationalistic underpinnings remained a powerful subcurrent in the movement until shortly after the group's descent into the Montana earth.

But when the Soviet foe disintegrated politically in 1991, Prophet's church was left without the historic enemy against which the group's spiritual battle for world freedom was conducted. The conclusion of the Cold War effectively stripped from CUT a long-standing part of its theology and left the organization ideologically rudderless.

In late 1997, the church announced that Elizabeth Clare Prophet was in failing health and had contracted an unknown neurological disorder. The affliction, which was later identified as Alzheimer's disease, was rapidly incapacitating Prophet, who was forced to severely limit her church activities. The diagnosis came as a shock to CUT members, who viewed the appointed Messenger as nearly inseparable from the group's divine Ascended Masters for whom she spoke. Since the role of Messenger had been central to group doctrine throughout CUT's forty-year history as a charismatically led religion, Prophet's illness raised uncomfortable questions about the organization's future. It had once been expected that succession to the post of Messenger would follow the family-line precedent established in 1973 upon Mark Prophet's death, but when Elizabeth Clare Prophet became ill, none of her four adult children were any longer associated with the church.[9] In addition, the emergence in 1996 of a new Ascended Master splinter group suggests that Prophet's ill health may have become the occasion for further defections. The new movement, the Temple of the Presence, is led by former CUT members who claim to be the "true" Messengers for the Ascended Masters. Based in Chelsea, Vermont, the Temple of the Presence claims about one thousand members (many of whom left CUT), and observes a virtually identical theology to that of its "parent" organization.[10]

In recent days, CUT has made clear that it is preparing for existence without the now-retired Elizabeth Clare Prophet, who remains affectionately referred to as "Mother" by the membership. Framing her increasingly phased-out status in the best possible light, church administrators have embraced a new leadership plan for the organization that seeks to modernize CUT. The strategy involves transforming its image to that of a New Age corporation, with attention directed to further developing its approximately two hundred small teaching centers and study groups in the United States and abroad and to loosening the authoritarian leadership style and crisis planning used in the past.[11] In 1999, faced with mounting financial and morale problems, CUT sold to the government (or placed in conservation easements) approximately half of its twelve-thousand-acre Royal Teton Ranch for $13 million.[12] Selling the property was part of an effort to downsize the cash-strapped organization, which was also forced to eliminate all but seventy-five of the six hundred staff positions it had formerly maintained on the ranch. The layoffs and the sale of ranch property, once considered the church's "holy land," signified obvious setbacks for CUT, which less than a decade earlier scholars had estimated to be one of the more successful of the twentieth century's new religious movements.[13]

Much can be mirrored in seemingly small events, and this is perhaps the most illuminating way in which to understand the implications of CUT's fixation upon catastrophe during the years leading up to the group's preparations for nuclear war. Born as a religio-political group with its countercultural ideology firmly in place, CUT followed a path of development that might well have been predicted. Perceptions of besiegement, conspiracies, and the psychological strains they elicited within the organization were all powerful factors in forging a distinctive, movement-specific outlook; but underlying the fears was the anticipation of life in a perfect, postapocalyptic age. This group-held image of renewal was fed by the certainty that the old, degraded world was dying, a revelation that was received by the movement in its early days but that fully absorbed believers during the period of heightened millennial excitement in Montana.

CUT's doctrine led its membership to prepare for the destruction of human civilization, which it believed to be corrupted beyond hope for redemption by the time Prophet warned of a looming nuclear Armageddon. Since this book takes the form of a case study of crisis belief in a religion-inspired social movement, attention is given to the group's disaster-focused cosmology and the way that it stimulated a period of apocalyptic fervor. Because social phenomena as complex as millennial activity require detailed theoretical analysis, this chapter attends to studies that offer interpretive frameworks by which the church's path to its apocalyptic mobilization in the northern Rocky Mountains may be understood. Chapter 2 serves both as an introduction to the groups in the Eastern occult/metaphysical tradition from which CUT evolved and as a general institutional history of the organization until the time of its relocation to Montana. The discussion of the Eastern alternative religious lineage makes clear the philosophical currents influencing the development of CUT. Chapter 2 also concentrates on the group's transition from a small splinter growth of the I AM religious movement in the late 1950s to its maturation as a well-known alternative spiritual organization in the New Age orbit. Following chapters will focus more directly on the church's period in

California beginning in the mid-1970s and, thereafter, on its experiences in Montana. In chapter 3, I discuss the ways in which CUT's efforts to create a separatist community of elect helped shape a distinctive organizational ideology. During its years at the Camelot headquarters near Malibu, California, members of the organization developed an increasingly conspiratorial outlook. These convictions were strengthened by the various pressures CUT experienced and ultimately led to Prophet's decision to geographically separate her following from a surrounding culture believed to threaten the church's existence. Chapter 4 examines CUT's relocation to Montana and discusses the catastrophic fears that led the membership to prepare for a nuclear disaster. Chapter 5 details the membership's response to the nonmaterialization of the disaster prophecy and seeks to explain why the period of millennial agitation unfolded without violence. Chapter 6 investigates the major changes that took place within CUT following the failure of its prophecy as well as examining the challenges that it presently faces. The short epilogue discusses the most recent developments affecting CUT's future.

Millennial Doctrine and Theories

From its inception in 1958, the Summit Lighthouse (later renamed the Church Universal and Triumphant) exhibited tendencies commonly associated with millenarian social movements. Mark Prophet's small following of spiritual seekers gradually attracted new members throughout the early 1960s while the group was located in the Washington, D.C., area. The organization's complex cosmology was derived largely from two sources: the late-nineteenth-century metaphysical doctrine Theosophy and the I AM religious movement, a depression-era offshoot of the Theosophical belief system. Theosophy provided Mark Prophet with the esoteric basis for his group's theology, which included belief in the existence of divine spirit beings (Ascended Masters) who governed the course of life on earth.[14] However, it was Theosophy's doctrinal relative, I AM philosophy, that created the Summit Lighthouse's political orientation—a perspective defined by patriotism and staunch anticommunism.

The I AM movement blended Ascended Master spirituality with right-wing political ideology to form a religio-political social movement in opposition to the New Deal policies of the Roosevelt administration. After a number of organizational setbacks, including the death of its charismatic founder, Guy Ballard, the Chicago-based group began in the 1950s to dissolve into several splinter factions. Mark Prophet was associated with one of these factions, the Bridge to Freedom, for which he served as a spiritual communicator, or Messenger, to the Ascended Masters.[15] His relationship with a branch of the I AM movement established an ideological linkage between the millennial visions of Guy Ballard's patriotic metaphysical group and those of the Summit Lighthouse. Mark Prophet's following inherited the underlying concepts fortifying the I AM movement's conviction in the arrival of a new golden age. These beliefs included currents of thought possessing both religious and political overtones.

According to I AM teachings, the Ascended Masters designated the United States as the place where a new golden age civilization would begin.[16] Through prayers and other devotional activities, this race of "Lightbearers" in America was to turn back the tide of negative karma thought to be preventing humankind from attaining its destined state of godly existence. For the I AM movement, as for the Summit Lighthouse, the negative powers impeding human transformation rejected God and the vision "for the Perfection of Life."[17] Like Guy Ballard's organization, the Summit Lighthouse observed a doctrine that fused theology with strands of political thought. In Mark Prophet's worldview, the agents of darkness at work in the world were most clearly apparent in their guises as left-wing political groups, elite power brokers in global society, and the forces of world communism.

The fusion of political ideology and religion in the Summit Lighthouse reflects a pattern of thinking regularly found in millennial movements. In *Disaster and the Millennium,* Michael Barkun draws attention to the synthesis of religion and politics that takes place in groups inspired by millennial beliefs. According to Barkun, these movements (which sometimes are described as "chiliastic" or "messianic" in character) do not separate the components of their guiding cosmologies into "political" and "religious" categories. Rather, their visions provide believers with a system of universal order that defies "neatly packaged" and artificial distinctions between politics and religion.[18] In this sense, the millenarian weltanschauung is totalistic. Such groups are galvanized by the conviction that they alone possess an all-encompassing truth that dictates the order of the world.

As James Rhodes argues in *The Hitler Movement,* clear distinctions between the divine and the secular are difficult to discern in social movements of a millennial character. Using the example of the Nazi movement, Rhodes points to the interchange between religious and political beliefs that marked

National Socialist ideology. Although ostensibly a political organization, the Nazi Party displayed the characteristics of a religious mass movement in its millennial goals. Rhodes draws parallels between the apocalyptic thought motivating medieval religious groups, such as the Crusaders and the Anabaptists, and the ideology of the National Socialists. Among the abundant ideological characteristics they shared, Rhodes argues, were their perceptions of themselves as "victim" groups and their dreams for elect salvation. Rhodes therefore maintains that Nazi radicalism represented a form of millennialism with clear political overtones.[19]

From the time he founded the Summit Lighthouse, Mark Prophet preached to his followers that times of troubles had befallen the nation and that the decay afflicting society threatened to send America "down into the dark night."[20] Observing the world as beset with problems wrought by humankind's failure to accept the Ascended Masters' "Perfect Divine Plan for the Earth," Mark Prophet's fold turned away from the depraved environing culture and focused on the objective of creating a better way of life.[21] Provided with evidence from Mark Prophet's invisible spiritual mentors that communism, human wickedness, and social degeneracy imperiled the land, the organization constructed a millennial worldview in which religious and political beliefs were inextricably joined.

Until this point, I have dealt with the concept of millennialism in a limited way as an ideology that blends group-specific views of religion and politics. The result of such a synthesis is the creation of a totalistic belief structure that provides adherents with an explanation for worldly problems. It is now appropriate to delve more deeply into the foundations of millennial thought and to address the salvific and transformative basis of its outlook.

Undergirding all millenarian ideologies is the expectation of the sudden conclusion of earthly history, an event that is to be followed by the arrival of a thousand-year glory period for the elect. The term *millennium* has its roots in the New Testament Book of Revelation. In its biblical context, the millennium denoted the epoch of Christ's triumphal reign on earth. As Catherine Wessinger notes, however, scholars no longer strictly adhere to the original, biblically inspired usage of the term. In its more current usage, *millennialism* refers more generally to the conviction in a divine plan for earthly salvation.[22]

Wessinger's essay "Millennialism with and without the Mayhem" offers some new insights into the study of millennial movements. Recognizing the prevailing tendency for scholars to adopt traditional terminology to differentiate between millenarian movements as premillennial or postmillennial, Wessinger argues that more dynamic categories need to be developed. Until recently, scholars have often used the premillennial and postmillennial distinction to subdivide Christian millennialism into readily recognizable forms. This distinction is used as a means to point to when believers expect the earthly return of Christ. Postmillennialism reflects the more optimistic of these concepts and is based upon the belief that Christ will appear following the church's establishment of the millennium through human deeds, an achievement involving prayer and spreading the word of the gospel. Premillennialism, on the other hand, anticipates Christ's arrival before the millennium and connotes the destruction of the earthly order by divine force prior to the establishment of the millennial kingdom.[23] Scholars have applied these categories to non-Christian millennial movements when communities of believers have displayed either premillennial tendencies of pessimism about the future or postmillennial characteristics of optimism. The extrapolation from a Christian millennial framework has been, however, something of a forced fit for many groups.

Wessinger maintains that millennial thought can be made more understandable if the categories *catastrophic* and *progressive* are used in place of terms derived from Christian millennialism. In addition to providing scholars with a means of more accurately categorizing non-Christian millennial activity, the suggested terms help clarify the essential attributes of End Time belief to the general public. According to Wessinger, catastrophic millennialism represents a universal religious pattern of thought based upon a pessimistic view of society and emphasizes the downward progression of history. This outlook is driven by the conviction that evil is ascendant in the world and only the total destruction of the corrupted earthly realm by a divine act can purge it of its affliction. In the mind-set of the catastrophic millennialist, it is necessary that this period of cleansing destruction take place before the world can be created anew. For those subscribing to a progressive millennial view, however, the emphasis is upon the constant improvement of worldly conditions. Progressive millennialism harbors a belief in human progress, to be realized through humanity's cooperation with a divinely orchestrated plan for earthly salvation.[24] Unlike scholars who distinguish between apocalyptic and millennial beliefs, Wessinger argues that apocalypticism is an accurate and recognizable synonym for catastrophic millennialism. Rejecting the view that apocalyptic believers are differentiated from millennialists by their narrow concern with events leading to the end of human history,[25] she suggests that apocalyptists see in the expected catastrophe a form of salvationism connected with the unfolding of a sweeping disaster. Both outlooks, in this respect, are grounded in the anticipation of a cataclysm that will destroy the world and bring about the millennium.[26] Since both catastrophic millennialism and apocalypticism point to the arrival of an imminent disaster, I use the terms interchangeably throughout this book.

In his work *The Pursuit of the Millennium,* Norman Cohn argues that the cataclysm foreseen by millennial movements symbolizes their hope that the world will be reborn and, in the process, transformed and redeemed.[27] For Cohn, millennial communities view salvation in a group-centered context: "The Heavenly City is to appear on this earth; and its joys are to crown not the peregrinations of individual souls but the epic exploits of a chosen people."[28]

The millennial dream for group renewal is, thus, exclusive. Terrestrial and collective salvation are perceived within the millennial movement as "rewards" for believers in the faith. Cohn associates the presence of this conviction with groups throughout history that have embraced "militant, revolutionary chiliasm." Such movements see history being brought to its consummation by a final struggle of transcendental importance between the forces of Good and Evil.[29]

As I shall argue, CUT's millennial outlook was dominated by visions of earthly catastrophe. This is not to say, however, that the group was solely absorbed with perceptions of disaster. The church's doctrine of human transformation to the godhead, a route to divinity with roots in Theosophical and I AM teachings, underscores the salvific basis of the organization's belief system. Group members viewed this concept of human ascendance as the ultimate objective to which they devoted their lives. Nonetheless, the church's teachings on attaining a more exalted state of spiritual being did not prevent it from evolving into a catastrophic millennial group. The foundations of CUT's theological system, as well as its esoteric understanding of salvation, are addressed in chapter 2. What merits attention at this point is the group's apocalyptic worldview and the ways in which this view shaped organizational behavior.

Beginning with its resettlement from the Washington, D.C., area to Colorado Springs in 1966, the church undertook a series of moves designed to give the community of believers some measure of safety from a surrounding society thought to be on the verge of collapse. These relocations took the group to southern California, where it remained for about ten years, and ultimately to Montana in the mid-1980s. By the time the church had established its headquarters in Colorado Springs, Mark and Elizabeth Clare Prophet had become established in the membership's eyes as prophetic seers whose exclusive connection to the Ascended Masters gave them semidivine status as leaders of the proto-New Age organization. Although the co-Messengers for the Ascended Masters stressed the possibility of their flock's ascension to godhood, the group's teachings more regularly pointed to the arrival of the End Times, a period believed to be linked with the close of the Piscean Age.[30] This era, according to group doctrine, spanned the previous two millennia of earthly history and became more dangerous as the transformation to the new Aquarian Age unfolded.[31]

It was during the group's stay in Colorado Springs that its theology fused with survivalism. Anticipating that the growth of negative karma (brought about by the approaching end of the Piscean Age) would lead to troubled times, the membership began its preparations for the approach of a period of great social distress. The church's pursuit of communal safety involved, notably, the acquisition of a small arsenal for self-defense and the teaching of basic survival skills to members. These steps were taken to protect the church against the collapse of American society, a scenario Mark Prophet envisaged that included his following's persecution by the armed forces of the state.[32] See chapter 2 for a discussion of Mark and Elizabeth Clare Prophet's fears during the time the group was in Colorado.

The catastrophic impulse underlying the group's perspective on the future derived from the extreme stress developing in the movement as a result of its frustrations with worldly conditions. Mark Prophet and his following saw their hopes for the creation of a perfect world order, led by the Ascended Masters, foiled by a host of problems brought on by humanity's depraved state of being. In response to the degradation it perceived in the larger society around it, the group organized as a millennial movement seeking to construct a more satisfying culture. While I maintain that the organization was born as a social movement seeking cultural revitalization, this desire became more visible as the church matured. However, its members came to believe that a coterie of enemies were combating its goal of instituting a group-specific vision of earthly perfection, foes that, by the time the church moved to Colorado, had grown to include the government, mainstream religions, and extraterrestrials.[33]

Theosophy and the I AM belief system formed the philosophical template within which Mark Prophet's organization functioned. Each cosmology provided the group with a set of ideas that served as a perceptual lens allowing it to see itself, and the dominant social order, in ways familiar to the church's esoteric forebears. Yet beyond this inheritance acquired from its doctrinal precursors, Prophet's church was the product of its leaders' fixation on ideas bred in the cultural underground of society. The Summit Lighthouse was born into the strange history of esoteric movements that shared a generalized style of countercultural thought, one that British sociologist Colin Campbell has described as "the cultic milieu." This concept describes the ideological universe in which social communities with heterodox beliefs function and thrive apart from the prevailing currents of thought in the dominant societal culture. Representing all ideas, norms, and values at odds with mainstream cultural orthodoxies, the cultic milieu is the natural home for adherents of society-rejecting beliefs and is comprised of the constellation of fringe and unconventional ideas that provide sustenance for the existence of an alternative, subterranean culture.[34] In his classic essay, "The Cult, the Cultic Milieu, and Secularization," Campbell argues that cults (as opposed to sects and churches) tend to be ephemeral and unstable. According to Campbell, cults exist in a specific ideological orbit defined by esoteric thought and are governed by a life-cycle process. In this respect, cults are seen as religious or quasi-religious collectivities that organize around countercultural ideas; yet they ultimately fade away and, in doing so, give birth to new cultic movements. This continual process of cult birth and death suggests that the generalized cultic milieu is a permanent aspect of society, while the individual cult is only a transitory entity.[35]

Mark Prophet's movement of spiritual seekers eagerly responded to the organization's countercultural appeal. Reassured of their group's chosenness by the Messenger, the members came to perceive themselves as spiritual adepts whose possession of divine truth distinguished the community of believers from outsiders. Prophet instilled this view by making use of the rejected knowledge of the cultic thoughtworld as a means to vitalize his movement. As a consequence, the most luxuriant alternative conceptions of reality became embedded in the group's collective worldview. Themes with links to science fiction, such as UFOs, extraterrestrials, and semihuman "mechanized men" descended from the "Forces of Darkness,"[36] were intertwined with grand reformulations of history and visions of a catastrophic future to establish the foundation of the group's alternative reality. The latter had roots in Mark Prophet's fascination with Atlantean mythology, legendary secret societies, and the prophetic works of Edgar Cayce, the Kentucky-born mystic who foretold geological disasters in the many "psychic discourses" he gave from the 1920s through the 1940s.[37]

That the group advanced these heterodox beliefs in its early days is not at all surprising. These notions provided the membership with a sense of detachment from the mundane quality of mainstream life. The adoption of a weltanschauung saturated in the mystical and fantastic might be thought of as an attempt to escape from the universe of reason.[38] But these beliefs were also much more: they formed the basis of the community's vision of renewal. Believing that the world brimmed with decadence and corruption, and that Armageddon was at hand,[39] the membership's esoteric, private world gave it hope in the millennial dream.

As the group became increasingly convinced that its efforts to usher in the new golden age were being thwarted, its outlook on the future took on more pessimistic overtones. Although the community persisted in its devotional attempts to improve humanity's condition, the spiritual war with the forces of darkness became the dominant theme in the church's teachings. Ultimately, the group came to see prospects for worldly improvement tied to the arrival of a major disaster. This view became ascendant in the church following its 1986 move to Montana, a place believed to offer the community safety from "the world emergency" it anticipated in the near future.[40] Thus the church's expectation of disaster became linked with its image for the creation of a new way of life, a vision that mobilized the organization's elect for the apocalypse.

2

History and Beliefs of the Church Universal and Triumphant

Several eclectic belief systems with long histories comprise the lineage of the Western occult/metaphysical tradition. This chapter begins with a more general discussion of the spiritual counterculture. This review provides some necessary perspective on the development of those Western ideas that formed an alternative theological path to more orthodox understandings of religion. Traced chronologically, this brief exploration of alternative religious movements provides a useful analysis of group beliefs running counter to the dominant ideas of Judeo-Christianity. More directly, however, this discussion helps make clear the larger philosophical currents from which the modern-day Church Universal and Triumphant developed. Emerging from a religious heritage outside the Western Judeo-Christian tradition, CUT has its roots in the community of religions that historically operated on the periphery of mainline beliefs. The second part of the chapter takes the form of an institutional history of the church until the time of its relocation to Montana.

As an outgrowth of religious activity initiated by a cluster of late-nineteenth—and early-twentieth-century metaphysical groups, CUT evolved from a comparatively recent expression of alternative spirituality. Its spiritual philosophy descends most clearly from two streams of thought within the Western alternative spiritual milieu: the Theosophical tradition and New Thought. The group's moorings in these beliefs, as well as its direct philosophical linkage to the I AM movement (itself an offshoot of Theosophy and New Thought) will be discussed below. Although my account of CUT's development as a major new religious movement is far from exhaustive, I have attempted to examine its maturation in some detail, concentrating especially on its gradual transition from a small splinter growth of the I AM religious activity in the 1950s to its status as a well-known spiritual organization in the New Age orbit.

Western Alternative Spirituality

By the close of the nineteenth century, a wave of metaphysical/occult activity in Europe and North America had shaped a popular spiritual movement whose influence on Western culture remains visible today. Rejecting many of the tenets of orthodox Christianity, the various groups within this metaphysical community formed an early spiritual counterculture to the dominant tradition of Christian thought. These groups, empowered by a new intellectual climate challenging established religious "truths," collectively sought to move beyond accepted understandings of religion by constructing an alternative spirituality based upon the new science of the day. Bound together by a common rejection of the old paths of Christian theology, the Western metaphysical community came to adopt the prevailing scientific critique of supernatural religion, observed its Darwinian emphasis on evolution, and maintained an open-minded attitude toward novel visions of spirituality.[1]

This new system of religious thought appearing in nineteenth-century America had its metaphysical antecedents in spiritual philosophies blending scientific belief with conceptions of the divine. Among the most important figures in the early stages of the metaphysical movement were two scientifically trained Europeans. Emanuel Swedenborg (1688–1772), a prominent Swedish mathematician and metallurgist, and Franz Anton Mesmer (1733?–1815), a German physician, laid the foundation for the popularization of a Western metaphysics grounded in "scientific religion." Swedenborg's metaphysical ideas, many of which were directly adopted by later generations of metaphysicians and occultists, employed empirical analysis in the pursuit of ultimate knowledge.[2] Rejecting the thinking of Enlightenment rationalism, Swedenborg acknowledged the reality of two planes of existence, the material and the spiritual, and claimed communication with the latter during his dreamlike trances. His teachings gained a small but devoted following in portions of Western Europe and America, partly because of their optimistic assessment of humankind's place in the universe. The Swedenborgian religion was different from the hellfire doctrine associated with the Christian tradition in that it pointed to the existence of a benign God who did not require atonement for human sin.[3] Recasting Christianity's image of a three-tier universe consisting of heaven, earth, and hell, Swedenborg's vision of earthly and spiritual realms reconfigured the orthodox Christian cosmology.[4] In particular, however, it was Swedenborg's claims of "correspondence" between the material and spiritual worlds that generated popular interest. His "scientific law" of correspondence laid out a theory of communication with figures who had moved into the spirit realm and paved the way for the establishment of later metaphysical doctrines.[5]

Like Swedenborg, Franz Mesmer's metaphysical explorations grafted elements of science with a divine vision to create a new religious outlook. Mesmer concluded through his investigations that a universal magnetic field surrounded the human body and maintained that skilled "manipulation" of this force could cure patients of illnesses. This practice involved placing the patient under hypnotic trance, at which time the manipulator (or "sensitive") would attempt to remove those obstacles responsible for the cessation of the natural flow of the magnetic force.[6]

Ostensibly a therapeutic exercise, mesmerism also clearly embodied religious components that were thought to explain the mysteries of the spirit world. Mesmerism influenced a collection of subsequent spiritual followings. It established basic philosophical tenets that were passed on to later outgrowths of alternative religiosity.

Gaining a somewhat wider following than Swedenborgianism, mesmerism's claims of healing power and the existence of a universal "life force" suggested the presence of uncertain powers governing humanity. However, for those seeking to penetrate the shroud of life beyond, it was the hypnotic trance Mesmer's students experienced that was most alluring. Mesmerist trances pointed to the connection between the earthly and the spiritual and involved the patient's "travel" to the ethereal realm where communication with the dead and looking into the future were possible.[7]

The metaphysical and occult precepts of Swedenborg and Mesmer were soon absorbed in the form of a generalized spiritualism observed by an American following. By the mid-nineteenth century, Spiritualist "associations" began to surface in considerable numbers in the United States. Influenced by the metaphysical Christianity of Emersonian transcendentalism, as well as by Swedenborgianism and mesmerism, the American Spiritualists synthesized these teachings in a movement organized around the objective of communicating with the dead.[8]

Like its European antecedents, Spiritualism in America included a scientific element. Spiritualists considered trained "mediums" to be the mechanism for contacting the deceased and claimed that their ability to connect with the departed proved the existence of an afterlife. Constructing a "supernatural science" from the earlier theories of Swedenborg and Mesmer, Spiritualism was met with widespread enthusiasm despite the occurrence of occasional hoaxes perpetrated by charlatans claiming mediumistic powers.[9]

The Spiritualist phenomenon of the second half of the nineteenth century stimulated a surge of other metaphysical organizations seeking answers from supernatural sources. Among these were the "mental healers," who extrapolated from Spiritualism's occult science and rejection of mainstream Christianity. Although its initial activities can be traced prior to the Civil War, the mental healing community remained numerically marginal (even by the standards of esoteric movements) until the 1870s. Early mental healers looked to the ideas of Mesmer to cure bodily disease but added a psychological dynamic by introducing the use of "positive thoughts" to ward off illness.[10] Advancing the ideas of what became known as "the New Thought Activity," Phineas Parkhurst Quimby (1802–66), an artisan of Portland, Maine, combined this scientific framework with mystical beliefs. Quimby's therapeutic prescriptions acknowledged the presence of a universal life force that the mind could tap into. Quimby's metaphysical system provided a totalistic explanation for human suffering that blended science, health, and religion in an esoteric thought structure.[11]

Among the heirs to Quimby's "mental medicine" was Mary Baker Eddy (1821–1910), whose ideas on health and religion led her to the development of Christian Science. Although almost certainly influenced to some degree by Quimby's therapy, which she experienced directly as one of his patients, Eddy claimed a revelation of divine law that became the basis of her religious movement. Eddy rejected the mesmerist conception of magnetism, however; her healing was predicated on the primacy of the mind. Within her Christian Science framework, disease and all forms of human trouble were viewed as a product of erroneous thought. These negative human impulses were to be combated by a philosophy conceiving of a neutral, harmonic order of the universe that promised personal salvation if only humanity could overcome its carnal desires. Ascribing humankind's problems to materialistic illusions, Eddy proclaimed that healing necessitated the renunciation of these thoughts in order to become worthy of Christ.[12]

In contrast with her predecessors in the scientific healing movement, Eddy's Christian Science espoused a reform element that directed its energy toward solving the problems of humanity. Eddy's movement applied its belief in "universal harmony" to the sins and sicknesses afflicting humankind and trained "practitioners" of the doctrine to teach others its concepts.[13] In this reformist sense, Christian Science became the exemplar for all New Thought activity. Pointing to the mind's power to defeat evil in all its manifestations, Eddy's doctrine built on the optimistic (and scientific) foundations for faith common to the new nineteenth-century religions. The philosophy conveyed the implicit message that "heaven on earth" was attainable with positive, disciplined thought and a desire to follow Christ's example. Christian Science tapped into a receptive audience hungry for esoteric divinity. Growing steadily despite being plagued by controversies,[14] the Church of Christ, Scientist, numbered nearly 100,000 members by the time of Eddy's death in 1910.[15]

Ancient Wisdom Belief

As historian of religion J. Gordon Melton observes, the end of the nineteenth century witnessed the rise of a distinct group of occultists whose beliefs diverged from those of early Spiritualists.[16] Melton distinguishes this religious activity from New Thought and its Swedenborgian/mesmeric roots and locates these organizations in the "ancient wisdom family," a category of religious bodies with a similar occult orientation. The groups comprising this religious tradition formed a branch of esotericism separated from the ideas of New Thought religious expression by their focus on obtaining secret knowledge.

Groups in the ancient wisdom tradition built upon the Spiritualists' conviction in an afterlife but advocated a different conception of universal truth. Among the ancient wisdom groups of the late nineteenth century, the notion of hidden, or occult, knowledge assumed the doctrinal core of the movement.[17] This attachment to secret understandings and the relearning of mysterious "lost truths" was clearly exemplified in the ideas of the Theosophical movement. Theosophy was energized by popular culture's growing passion for the occult, and its ideas were eagerly received by an audience of esoteric seekers who sought novel approaches to psychic growth.[18] Taking the organizational name of the Theosophical Society, which was founded in 1875 by Helena Petrovna Blavatsky (1813–91) and Henry Steel Olcott (1832–1907), the circle became the period's most significant expression of ancient wisdom belief. In comparison to Spiritualism, Theosophy was based on a complicated and syncretic metaphysics that, as its practitioners claimed, eclipsed the provincial concerns of shallow "phenomena."[19]

Blavatsky personified the era's occult fervor. Her colorful and controversial career began in Russia. She rejected the propertied social circle of her aristocratic family in favor of a bohemian existence early in her life.[20] While little is known of Blavatsky's life between 1851 and 1871, it is thought that she spent much of this time in restless, worldwide travel.[21] A lifelong student of the occult and an early follower of Spiritualism, Blavatsky's interest in psychic phenomena led her to pursue a path of esoteric wandering that culminated in the birth of the Theosophical Society. Together with Olcott, a gentlemanly lawyer fascinated with the spiritual world, Blavatsky organized the group as an association dedicated to the study of comparative religion, science, and the unexplained laws of nature.[22] Yet beyond these genteel "investigations," the Society displayed an activist agenda propelled by the charismatic Blavatsky. As the movement's central figure and its leading expositor of ideas, Blavatsky used the organization as a vehicle for spreading the group's new vision. She saw herself as a teacher of mystical truths passed on to her by spiritual guides, which made her stewardship of the Theosophical Society indistinguishable from her role as the doctrine's chief pedagogue.[23]

While originally intended to be an open forum for discussion of a broad range of esoteric subjects, the founders of the Theosophical Society gradually steered it in new metaphysical directions. In her two-volume manifesto *Isis Unveiled* (1877), a work commonly viewed as the Theosophical bible, Blavatsky laid out the doctrine's formal principles.[24] Underscoring Theosophy's eclectic qualities, *Isis Unveiled* affirmed that "ancient wisdom" could be gained from diverse mystical sources, a point that conformed to the Theosophical belief in the interconnection between the world's faiths.[25]

Although drawn from a number of esoteric sources, Theosophy (in the broadest sense) represented an alternative reality detached from both the linearity of "crude science" and the rigid orthodoxy of the established churches. Its thoughtworld combined elements of Eastern and Western mysticism, "secrets" derived from arcane texts, and a heavy dose of Spiritualism. The Theosophical quest, however, involved the search for a universal truth believed to reside in the religious teachings of all peoples.[26] Theosophy credited history's secret societies as being the bearers of archaic knowledge and maintained that the mysteries of the universe could be understood by those who studied its esoteric origins.[27] Looking to the Knights Templar and the Order of the Masons, among others, as groups of elect possessing an eternal (and closely guarded) divine wisdom, Theosophical thought fostered a sense of chosenness and intrigue among its followers.

Theosophy's labyrinth of secret societies must have been alluring for those in the movement, but the actual key to its worldview was the Theosophical conception of highly evolved entities governing the evolution of the earth. Fascinated with what they considered to be the universal wisdom associated with religions of the East, Blavatsky and Olcott spoke of an Occult Brotherhood of Eastern Adepts.[28] These beings (or Masters) were said to dwell on a higher plane than that of material humanity and were believed to provide disciples with the knowledge necessary to lead humanity to a more elevated state of spiritual evolution.

While its founders conceived of a hierarchy of masters representing the philosophies of all ancient cultures, the Theosophical system attached particular significance to India and Tibet. The link to the region reflected Theosophy's detachment from conventional Western religious thought as well as the Society's romanticized image of the East. For early Theosophists, the East represented hallowed ground that served as the access point to transcendent being. The attraction to the Asian subcontinent, and especially to enigmatic Tibet, embodied the movement's thirst for arcane and occult lore.[29] Although Blavatsky and Olcott traveled to India to establish the Society's headquarters at Adyar in 1882, the "journey to the East" for most Theosophists took the form of a psychological pilgrimage. Those in the movement saw the region as the dwelling place of the Masters and took on a symbolic meaning that resonated with spiritual enlightenment.[30]

Perhaps the most compelling aspect of the Theosophical system for the initiate was its positive vision for humankind's evolutionary development. Rejecting Darwinian evolutionary theory ("from monkey to man") as merely one part of a larger growth process, Theosophical doctrine viewed humanity as involved in a continuing struggle to attain spirit form.[31] For Blavatsky, this ongoing evolution located man on a lengthy, upward progression, the end point of which was to be the realization of divine status. Pointing to spiritual possibilities unrealizable through the paths of conventional religious faiths, Theosophy presented a theory of personal growth with cosmic-level implications. Since the doctrine asserted that humanity was possessed with the ability to become godlike, it offered adherents an optimistic message for spiritual advancement. This conception of humankind's upward urge to divinity was joined with the

Eastern idea of reincarnation in Theosophy's complex cosmology. Reincarnation was viewed by Theosophists as an educative process and suggested the unfolding of a cosmic plan in which human beings were given repetitive cycles of opportunity to overcome the tendency to seek lower planes of being.[32]

A new generation of metaphysical/occult movements inspired by Theosophical teachings emerged in America during the first few decades of the twentieth century. Among these doctrinal offshoots, two are of particular importance, both for their absorption of key Theosophical beliefs and for their leaders' successes in forming new alternatives to the Theosophical Society.

The metaphysical philosophy taught by Alice Bailey (1880–1949) elaborated on Blavatsky's ideas. Encountering opposition within the Theosophical Society due to her insistence that she was receiving messages from the Masters, Bailey's claims challenged Blavatsky's historic role as amanuensis for "the invisible brotherhood."[33] Bailey was removed from office in the society for her transgression and shortly thereafter established the Arcane School in 1923 for the purpose of creating a less autocratic alternative to the post-Blavatsky Theosophical Society. Interestingly, Bailey's departure prefigured what would later become a common practice of defectors slurring the esoteric religious movement to which they had belonged. Following her separation from the Theosophical Society, she alleged that they made false claims and pointed specifically to "the extraordinary control" over the group's members by its leader, Annie Besant.[34]

The Arcane School was founded to prepare its students for "receivership" of the Masters' messages and took the shape of an esoteric assembly devoted to the advanced training of a new world religion. Bailey's group clearly absorbed much of the Theosophical tradition, which included the adoption of its perspective on evolution and the fusion of Eastern and Western thought. However, while both groups shared a general vision of history as an evolutionary process involving humanity's upward march to divinity, Bailey's Arcane School emphasized the imminent earthly reappearance of Christ as signaling a collective and terrestrial salvation. Christ's return, in this sense, signified to the Arcane School's membership the advancement of human spiritual evolution to that point where a perfect brotherhood on earth was achieved.[35]

Unlike the Theosophists, whose view of humankind's lengthy evolution occurred without the sudden reappearance on earth by the Masters, Bailey's eschatology envisioned the arrival of the messiah as a near-term event. In contrast to Theosophy's long view of evolutionary ascendance, Bailey's writings suggested the approach of a forthcoming "New Age"[36] brought about by the spiritual yearnings of humanity.[37] Emphasizing the importance of psychic energy in expediting Christ's reappearance, Bailey promoted the practice of "full moon meditation" to prepare for this occurrence. This practice was designed to harness spiritual energies from the divine realm, and the lunar festivals reflected the Bailey following's missionary spirit.[38] As perceived intermediaries between the divine hierarchy of the Masters and the masses of human civilization, the followers of Bailey's new world religion planned to spread its teachings worldwide in anticipation of a New Age of universal harmony.[39]

The practice of communication with spiritual masters in groups deriving from the ancient wisdom tradition continued when Guy Ballard (1878–1939) founded a religious movement whose philosophical roots extended directly to Theosophy. Claiming to have received divine revelations from the "Ascended Master"[40] Saint Germain in 1929, Ballard organized a small group in Chicago for the purpose of delivering these messages to interested spiritual seekers. In time, Ballard's communications with the Ascended Masters expanded to include contact with not only Saint Germain, a legendary figure in metaphysical/occult lore,[41] but with all the cosmic beings Blavatsky declared steered the course of world evolution.[42]

Taking the name "I AM Activity," a title derived from the group's belief that the presence of God resides in each individual,[43] the organization prospered throughout the 1930s under the direction of Guy Ballard and his wife, Edna. As the first of the Theosophical offshoots to embrace a particular political agenda, the I AM movement occupies a different place in the history of alternative religious movements than its predecessors. Blending Ascended Master teachings with a high level of patriotic fervor, Ballard's movement expressed a belief in America's "cosmic destiny," an idea synthesizing elements of Theosophy and American nationalism. Ballard maintained that Saint Germain "adopted" America as a fitting location in which to begin the development of a new civilization to serve as the model for the entire human race. The popularity of the I AM's occult and nationalistic beliefs was reflected in the number of its believers and the appearance of its churches throughout a number of major American cities in the 1930s. Although some estimates of the period put the group's membership size in the hundreds of thousands, a more reasonable figure would be in the high tens of thousands.[44]

According to the I AM movement's detractors, Guy and Edna Ballard used patriotism as a convenient cover to disguise the group's darker motivations. By

1940, allegations arose concerning the organization's early attempts to recruit William Dudley Pelley, the leader of the fascist Silver Legion of America, for a leadership post in the movement. Although the group's chief accuser (former member Gerald Bryan) asserted that Pelley refused the offer, Bryan maintained that the Ballards were successful in attracting some of the Silver Legion's members, including its treasurer.[45] In his attempt to make explicit the linkage between the groups, Bryan claimed that, furthermore, Edna Ballard had secretly been a devoted follower of Pelley's mystical philosophy before the founding of the I AM movement.[46]

Bryan's 1940 expose of the group, *Psychic Dictatorship in America*, let loose a broadside of charges against the Ballards. Bryan argued that the two were "pee-wee Hitlers" who played on group-induced fears. According to Bryan, who charged the leaders with "brainwashing" their following, the Ballards sought to psychologically reprogram the I AM membership for the purpose of creating a political movement capable of toppling a spiritually impure American government. As unsubstantiated as the brainwashing allegations were, some of the group's practices reveal that its patriotic sentiments were quite bizarre. Consistent with the conspiratorialism that pervaded the movement's worldview, Guy Ballard frequently received and conveyed messages from the mysterious Ascended Master K-17, "Director of the Inner Secret Service." Appearing through Ballard to report foreign mischief and to alert the group about diabolical plots American leaders had undertaken, the dramatic urgency of K-17's information further reinforced both the sense of chosenness and persecution felt throughout the organization.[47]

While some unusual commonalities existed between the I AM movement and the Silver Legion, not least of which concerned the Ballards' success in winning to their group a sizeable number of Pelley's students, the theological ideas of the I AM movement had no precise parallel with those of other metaphysical/occult organizations.[48] Although anchored in the Theosophical framework, I AM Activity was differentiated from other manifestations of metaphysical spirituality both by its political orientation and in its view of more direct interaction with the Brotherhood of Ascended Masters.

As was the case with Theosophy, the role the Brotherhood assumed remained the key to the I AM belief system. Within their respective cosmologies, each religious system shared roughly similar conceptions of the spiritual order of the universe. Residing at the highest level of both groups' belief structures was God. Known as the Cosmic Logos to Theosophists and as "The Mighty I

AM Presence" in the Ballard movement, God was seen in each as the omnipotent, universal force from which a considerable number of somewhat lesser cosmic beings extended downward to the human race in a descending hierarchy.[49] Groups in the Theosophical tradition perceived these beings as divine intermediaries between the godhead and mankind whose role was to guide the evolutionary course of earth.

The Ballards retained the Theosophical emphasis on the role of the Brotherhood,[50] but adopted a theology that focused on close personal association with the Ascended Masters. Whereas previous manifestations of Brotherhood activity tended to view the cosmic beings as involved in an impersoanl, gradual process of guiding the universe, the I AM system embraced a more activist conception of the spiritual hierarchy. Members of the group considered the dynamic Ascended Masters to be "tangible and real beings" who functioned freely in the world and performed supernatural acts.[51]

The Ballards further activated the energy of I AM thought by introducing the use of "decrees" or "calls" in the organization. Having some basis in the affirmations New Thought groups practiced, the point of these exercises was to initiate constructive change by making forceful commands. While approximating Christian prayer, the I AM use of decrees more closely paralleled the mental medicine orientation given it by its early practitioners, Phineas Parkhurst Quimby and Mary Baker Eddy.[52] In this context, the act of decreeing was based on a mind over matter concept whereby one's mental vision was believed to dictate events in the physical realm. In their I AM form, the decrees were undertaken (either individually or collectively) in order to bring into action the power of the Ascended Masters. The exercises were observed as a crucial devotional activity that set in motion group visions for change.[53]

Espousing powerful nationalist sentiments, the I AM movement's spiritualism assumed a political character that set it apart from other metaphysical/ occult groups. With the exception of Pelley's Silver Legion, whose unusual blend of esoteric metaphysics, clairvoyance, and political ideology compared in striking ways to the Ballards' syncretic philosophy,[54] only the I AM worldview had incorporated a clear political agenda in its belief structure. The movement's conservative position was inherited from the Ballards' personal political convictions. Firmly opposed to labor strikes, communism, and the New Deal policies of the Roosevelt administration, the superpatriotic group became a vigorous defender of the status quo.[55]

Guy Ballard's belief in a special destiny for America, a central aspect of the

I AM worldview, was filtered throughout the group's membership in its books and other publications. In the first of several works Ballard wrote under the pseudonym Godfre Ray King, his 1939 book *Unveiled Mysteries* exhibits the author's conception of America as the kingdom of God on earth. The volume recounts Ballard's personal meeting with the enigmatic Saint Germain and reveals the heavy strains of American exceptionalism characterizing the I AM philosophy. In the story, Ballard was escorted by the Ascended Master on a mystical journey to places with great spiritual importance[56] and was taught about the Brotherhood's special relationship with America, a nation said to play the key role in the divine plan of God.[57]

Following Guy Ballard's death in 1939, I AM Activity encountered a series of setbacks that gradually began its disintegration. Already beset by a number of public embarrassments, including charges of fraud by former members and criticism by the press for I AM's authoritarian style,[58] Ballard's demise generated considerable stress in the organization. Since he, along with his wife and son, had attained the distinguished status of the group's earthly Messenger of the Ascended Masters, it was widely felt that Ballard would not die but rather would physically make his "ascension" and join the Brotherhood. As news of his death (brought on by heart disease) spread within the movement's ranks, many followers began to question the credibility of the departed leader.[59] To compound the confusion, Edna Ballard, who immediately took control of the organization, attempted to explain away the controversy in ways that appeared to contradict I AM teachings.[60]

Soon after Guy Ballard's death, the movement experienced another serious crisis. In 1940, after being sued by a number of former members, the organization was targeted by the federal government on charges of mail fraud. Edna Ballard and her son, Donald, were initially convicted in federal court for using the mails to solicit money for a fraudulent religion. However, the case was subsequently reviewed and overturned by the 1944 Supreme Court decision *United States v. Ballard.* Although the Court ruled that alternative religions need not "prove" the validity of their faith to a jury as a condition for their practice, the lengthy legal battle proved damaging.[61] The legal proceedings tarnished the group's reputation, and it never regained its once-considerable popularity. Despite the Ballards' acquittal on the fraud charges, the ban on the movement's use of the mails remained in effect until 1954. Shortly thereafter, the organization regained its tax-exempt status.[62]

The I AM movement's public image problems provided the opportunity for Ascended Master splinter groups to emerge in the 1950s. These groups adhered closely to the religious framework the Ballards established, observing both the ancient wisdom beliefs associated with the Theosophical tradition and the strongly patriotic ideas embodied in the I AM system. The first of these outgrowths was initiated in the early 1950s by one-time I AM member Geraldine Innocente, who began to deliver "dictations" from various Ascended Masters. Innocente claimed that her organization, the Bridge to Freedom, was the bearer of a new dispensation of truth passed on to her by the Ascended Masters Saint Germain and El Morya.[63] The reason for the formation of the new organization had to do with the contentious issue of publishing the I AM material in other languages.[64] Bridge to Freedom adherents maintained that the exclusive use of English prevented the I AM message from being received by a wider audience. In order to remedy the problem, the New York City-based Bridge following, a sizeable portion of which was comprised of Spanish-speaking immigrants, translated teachings into other languages. Despite the formal separation from the Ballard group, the Bridge to Freedom continued to observe I AM doctrine with only minor alterations. However, in an interesting departure from the high-profile visibility of the Ballards' leadership style, Innocente avoided public attention as the Bridge movement's Messenger. She published the Ascended Masters' messages under the pseudonym of Thomas Printz, which kept her identity a secret to all except a small circle within the group.[65]

Organized at nearly the same time as the Bridge movement, the Lighthouse of Freedom was founded as a separate religious activity also following in the I AM tradition. Directed by Francis Ekey, a former member of the Bridge movement in Philadelphia, the Lighthouse also devoted its efforts to circulating the messages of the Ascended Masters. Ekey's group adopted an educational mission similar to that of the Bridge to Freedom. Its program involved establishing formal classes of Ascended Master instruction in 1954 as a means of enlightening new students to the teachings.

Ekey's newsletter for the movement, *I AM the Lighthouse of Freedom*, featured the writings of an anonymous figure who received messages from the Ascended Masters.[66] The deliverer of these communications was Mark L. Prophet (1918–73), an Army Air Corps veteran from Chippewa Falls, Wisconsin, and former railway worker whose lifelong interest in the esoteric eventually led him to the teachings of the Ascended Masters. Prophet was raised in a Pentecostal family, and his working-class roots and lack of formal education distinguished him from the gentrified backgrounds of some Theosophical mystics. But his self-proclaimed metaphysical experiences with the Ascended Masters echoed the grandiosity of earlier accounts by Blavatsky and the Ballards. Reportedly, Prophet was approached by the Ascended Master El Morya when the youthful railroad hand was driving spikes on the line near his Chippewa Falls home. When the cosmic being asked him to serve the cause of the Ascended Masters, the startled laborer initially refused, and only after thoughtful deliberation accepted El Morya's offer.[67]

Prophet was one of the more prominent competing Messengers appearing in the vacuum left by the post-Guy Ballard leadership controversy. His preoccupation with personal spiritual seeking as a young man absorbed his time and made him less than financially successful. While searching for metaphysical enlightenment, Prophet sold household products door-to-door to make ends meet, all the while flirting with Rosicrucian teachings and other esoteric ideas before becoming the amanuensis of the Ascended Masters.[68] While continuing to cooperate with Ekey for some time in his role as Messenger, Prophet severed his ties with the Lighthouse of Freedom in 1958. Having been "appointed" by the Ascended Master El Morya to start a new teaching activity, Prophet by this time had founded the Summit Lighthouse in Washington, D.C., where he relocated from Wisconsin in the mid-1950s with his wife and children to find better job opportunities.

Prophet's residence in the Washington, D.C., area became a major source of controversy between the fledgling Summit Lighthouse and Ekey's group. Confused by the relatively close names, the Lighthouse of Freedom's Washington, D.C., membership (at least for a short period) unknowingly contributed monetary donations to Prophet's splinter group.[69] The early friction between the rival organizations subsided, however, as the Summit Lighthouse emerged as a fully independent religious body. Prophet worked at making the group a successful outgrowth of I AM spirituality and devoted his time to teaching and publishing the words of the Ascended Masters. While little is known of his early experiences in Washington, D.C., it is apparent that he dedicated his efforts to legitimizing the Summit Lighthouse as the "true" extension of Ascended Master activity.[70]

From the Summit Lighthouse to CUT

While located in Washington, D.C., the Summit Lighthouse began the publication of dictations from the Ascended Masters in order to provide its small circle of followers with written records of the teachings. Messages Prophet received from the Masters were printed in the group's first publication, *Ashram Notes,* and regularly mailed to a membership residing almost exclusively in suburban sectors of the nation's capital. The Summit Lighthouse's initial prospects for growth appeared less than encouraging due to the retirement-age membership of its following. The likelihood of organizational collapse was averted, however, when Mark Prophet met and subsequently married Elizabeth Clare (Wulf) Ytreberg in 1963. At the time of their first meeting, Ytreberg was enrolled as an undergraduate at Boston University. Herself a devotee of esoteric thought, the twenty-one-year-old student had much in common with the Messenger of the Summit Lighthouse. Like Prophet, whose wife and five children lived in Washington, D.C., Ytreberg was also married and resided in Boston with her new spouse, a Norwegian-born law student. Following a brief courtship, which began with Prophet's April 1961 visit to Boston University during a stop on the Messenger's speaking tour at several northeastern colleges, the two had their previous marriages annulled and started life anew.[71]

Elizabeth's parents were émigrés to the United States. Her father, Hans Wilhelm Wulf, had been a German submarine commander in World War I and, later, as an American citizen, privately ran a small construction business. Her mother, Freida Enkerli, was born in Switzerland and worked as a governess for wealthy families in Red Bank, New Jersey, a small community within an hour's drive of New York City. The couple's only child was raised with attention to her education, including instruction from her mother in Christian Science.[72]

The Wulf family squeezed out a middle-class existence in Red Bank, but financial strains and her parents' unhappy marriage made life difficult for Elizabeth. While she excelled in school, and ranked near the top of her public high school class, the youngster experienced mild epileptic seizures that concerned her parents and aggravated the serious and goal-directed "Betty Clare." Religion seemed to be an outlet for her frustrations about her medical condition and a less-than-satisfying home life. Even before matriculating at selective Antioch College in Yellow Springs, Ohio, in 1957, she immersed herself in the study of Christian Science and attributed her understanding of the doctrine with "changing her outlook and solving the problems in her life."[73]

Just as Mark Prophet had turned away from the strict Pentecostal teachings he learned as a youth, Elizabeth also ultimately rejected the Christian Science beliefs observed in her family.[74] Nonetheless, her quest for esoteric enlightenment remained a source of inspiration during her days as a student, first at Antioch, and later at Boston University where she completed her undergraduate degree in political science. Furthermore, the two shared similar beliefs about the spiritual vacuousness of mainline religions and sensed the increasing corruption of America's political condition.

Interestingly, while Mark Prophet's patriotism and belief in a special destiny for America probably extended directly from his exposure to I AM splinter movement teachings, Elizabeth came to this same position by way of more personal experiences. From the time she enrolled at Antioch in 1957, Elizabeth expressed an interest in finding a career in the diplomatic service. An "Autobiographical Sketch" she wrote for admission that year indicated her desire to "contribute to world peace" and to "do a small part in the great task of establishing the true brotherhood of man."[75] But, when working as a student intern at the United Nations while attending Antioch, the young political science major soon lost her faith in the value of international politics. She became disgusted with what she saw as "the self-serving and corrupt nature of politicians and bureaucrats," and walked away from her U.N. internship convinced "that only God could save America."[76]

In 1962, the Prophets moved the Summit Lighthouse's headquarters from Washington, D.C., to nearby Fairfax, Virginia, where a teaching center was established in their home. After purchasing a mechanized printing press to increase the production of *Ashram Notes,* the organization greatly expanded its publication operation. In addition to its reinvigorated printing efforts, which permitted a wider distribution of the dictations, the Summit Lighthouse also announced the creation of a special inner circle within the group. At the direction of El Morya, Mark Prophet organized this devotional society, named the Keepers of the Flame Fraternity, and made available its teachings to students who desired "advanced training" from the Ascended Masters.[77]

The Keepers of the Flame quickly became the spiritual core of the Summit Lighthouse. Consisting of seven secret lessons and special decrees reserved for devoted followers, members of the church's inner circle of initiates pledged "to be their brother's keeper" by sustaining the flame of God within the self and by working for the enlightenment of humanity.[78] This elite body of Summit Lighthouse members was said to have descended from a legion of cosmic beings led by the Ascended Master Sanat Kumara, who came to Earth from Venus to save the soul of humanity from self-destruction.[79] Volunteering to serve mankind until the flame of life (literally God) was rekindled in men's hearts, the extraterrestrial contingent came on a valorous mission. As the legend had it, the heroes remained on earth to nurture the spiritual fire in humankind.

The theme of a cosmic destiny for America was a central motif in the fraternity. Throughout its early days, nationalist rhetoric suggesting a unique spiritual role America held characterized much of the literature published specifically for the inner circle of members. The special teachings and decrees issued for Keepers of the Flame were marked by archconservative social and political statements and disclosed an unmistakable anxiety over the group's perception of America's rapid decline. Particularly evident in the Keepers' materials of the period were indications that the Ascended Masters' divine plan for America was being jeopardized by "Dark Forces" or "Fallen Ones."[80] Becoming the object of much of the fraternity's literature by the mid—to late 1960s, these adversaries were cast as agents of evil who plotted to divide and conquer the American people. The fraternity viewed the Dark Ones' campaign against the Brotherhood of Ascended Masters' (or Great White Brotherhood) conception of America as an unfolding conspiracy against the children of God.[81] Unquestionably, those belonging to the Summit Lighthouse without dual membership in the fraternity were also made aware of such ideas, largely through the more widely circulated *Ashram Notes.* However, cryptic statements would occasionally surface in the movement's publications suggesting that general Summit Lighthouse members were not privy to the "sensitive" information disseminated within the ranks of the inner circle.[82]

Mark Prophet's initiation of the Keepers of the Flame compares closely with the Ballards' inner organization, the "One Hundred Percenters." His possible motive to duplicate the voluntary devotional group employed within the larger I AM movement seems conceivable given the structural similarities between the subgroups. Just as the Ballards' One Hundred Percenters represented the spiritual core of the I AM Activity,[83] the Keepers of the Flame (at least in its early form) were also portrayed as deeper initiates of the group's teachings. Although the fraternity eventually took on an entirely different and much more inclusive character, the concept of separate inner societies within the larger organization was passed on to the Church Universal and Triumphant.[84]

For five years (1961–66), Elizabeth Clare Prophet "trained" under the direction of her husband and the Ascended Masters El Morya and Saint Germain to become the group's co-Messenger. While Elizabeth gradually assumed a visible leadership presence and periodically delivered dictations from the Ascended Masters, the organization was largely operating under the stewardship of her spouse.[85] Following a brief relocation to Vienna, Virginia, in 1965, Mark Prophet moved the Summit Lighthouse headquarters to Colorado Springs. The organization's westward migration corresponded with major developments taking place in the movement's institutional strategy for growth. Supplanting the *Ashram Notes* as the mouthpiece of the Ascended Masters was a new weekly publication called *Pearls of Wisdom,* which was mailed free of charge to all interested readers. The production of *Pearls of Wisdom* helped spread the group's teachings to a much wider body of spiritual seekers from which the Summit Lighthouse could recruit members. The move to Colorado also became the occasion for the organization's adoption of nationwide conferences, known as Ascended Master Conclaves, which united members of the Summit Lighthouse from all parts of the country. These regularly held gatherings took place on a leased two-hundred-acre ranch on the outskirts of Colorado Springs and became a central activity in the life of the growing religious movement.[86]

The organization's purchase of a stately nineteenth-century mansion in the heart of Colorado Springs represented the development of a more communal style within the Summit Lighthouse. The spired three-story mansion, which the Prophets named "La Tourelle," served as the group's headquarters and was situated on a two-acre tract in this scenic town at the foot of the Rocky Mountains.[87] The church's westward move, however, also signified an important turning point in the psychological worldview of the group. As opponents of what they saw as the decadent and depraved interests of the eastern monied class, the Prophets' brand of populist, New Age religion was not well-suited to Washington, D.C. The two were distrustful of politicians and wary of the birth of an "International Capitalist/Communist Conspiracy" designed to subvert the American way of life,[88] and it is probable that the church's relocation symbolized the coleaders' suspicions about eastern political culture and the existence of a shadowy power elite controlling the country.

While the images of the political enemy remained much the same as that the I AM movement observed, the Summit Lighthouse began to recognize more unusual foes by the time it migrated to Colorado. Adding to the air of impending crisis that circulated in the group, the organization's literature revealed concerns about the alleged endeavors of extraterrestrial beings. Mark Prophet's belief concerning the existence of alien enemies poised to interrupt humankind's path to spiritual perfection was made clear in his 1965 book, *The*

Soulless Ones. "Dictated" to the Messenger by "Master R" to uncover a startling truth unknown to humanity, *The Soulless Ones* recounts the story of ancient astronauts from a distant star system who came to earth in order to conduct genetic experiments on human beings. Claiming that these malevolent visitors created a counterfeit race of soulless automatons designed to control "the real people of earth," the book revealed a diabolical, cosmic-level conspiracy.[89] In it, the Messenger warned that the genetic experiments spawned a race of evil mutations disguised as humans who often "worked in high places,"[90] a point that buttressed nicely the populist spirituality of the Summit Lighthouse. While probably influenced in part by the UFO theories of amateur archaeologist and active I AM member George Hunt Williamson, Mark Prophet's account of the aliens' motivations carried more ominous overtones. Whereas Williamson made the case that extraterrestrials were "space brothers" helping usher humankind into a new Age of Aquarius,[91] Prophet's interpretation conveyed the message that the visitors were would-be conquerors of Earth.

Although the movement may have had only about one thousand committed members nationwide by 1970, the figure increased substantially in the next several years as word spread about the Prophets' New Age church. According to sources who belonged to the Summit Lighthouse when it was based in Colorado Springs, the organization's membership numbers were impossible to confirm with precision. Peter Arnone, one of forty permanent "staff" members who resided at La Tourelle in 1971, indicated that Mark Prophet routinely inflated the group's numerical size by claiming that each issue of *Pearls of Wisdom* was being passed on to several nonmembers, who in turn were said to be inspired to join the movement.[92]

The Colorado Springs headquarters attracted the group's most committed members, who arrived from all parts of the country to devote their lives to the teachings of the Ascended Masters. The influx of believers created some problems for Mark and Elizabeth Clare Prophet since available space in the communal mansion was limited. The Prophet marriage had produced four children by this time, and, with the co-Messengers and their offspring absorbing most of La Tourelle's space, members of the Summit Lighthouse staff were faced with finding cramped living quarters in the attic and basement of the building. Arnone estimates that the Summit Lighthouse had one hundred on-site staff members by 1972, which caused the Prophets to permit some of the group's following to find lodging away from the headquarters. Whether living at La Tourelle or nearby, the church's elite staff members experienced a highly regi-

mented existence consisting of an arduous work schedule that offered little or
no financial compensation, frequent decree sessions, and mandatory attendance at all group functions.[93]

Reaping the dividends associated with both a burgeoning membership
and an intriguing spiritual vision that pointed the way to divine union with
God, the group's Colorado years proved highly successful. In part, some of the
organization's growth was attributable to good timing. The Summit Lighthouse tapped into early societal expressions of New Age thought, thus facilitating a connection between its spiritual system and subcurrents of alternative
religious belief becoming more visible in American culture. Propelled by a
popular perception that mainstream religions were restricted in scope and up-
held outmoded, formal, and decayed principles of faith, the New Age vision
sought to transcend the limitations of conventional forms of spirituality.[94]

The eclectic components of New Age thought, including Eastern mysticism, the occult, and astrology, appealed to a considerable following among
both the bored and the divinely discontented. The first traces of the phenomenon, which eventually evolved into a mass spiritual movement, began to appear in the late 1960s as Western interest in Asian religions combined with
transformative visions for society. New Age philosophy engendered a sense of
community for those thirsting for a new view of the world; at the same time, its
central message was based on a fundamental concept of human transformation. In this sense, the essence of the New Age was largely personal and predicated upon the individual's "awakening" to new realities within the realm of the
self. The epiphany often involved the "discovery" of one's psychic abilities and
"new potentials," which allowed the New Age experience to fill a spiritual void
for those disenchanted with the historic religions of the West.[95]

The Summit Lighthouse's eclectic system of beliefs corresponded with
some fundamental aspects of the New Age vision. Perceiving its mission as that
of directing seekers to the ultimate truth, the Summit Lighthouse emphasized a
process of self-change whereby the soul's upward evolution led humanity to
higher states of spiritual being.[96] This path to individual union with God,
viewed as the goal of human life, conveyed a message of universality and easy
approachability. Yet beneath this superficial connection with New Age univer-
salism lay a highly structured and complex belief system. The Summit Lighthouse mixed components of Christian doctrine, Eastern religions, and I AM
doctrine, whose combination permitted the organization to perceive itself as
"the true Church" of Jesus Christ, Gautama Buddha, and the Ascended Mas-

ters.[97] While acknowledging the supremacy of one God, the "I am that I am," the group's early literature made clear its observance of a wide array of "humanity's teachers" who functioned as agents of God's purpose. Led by the Ascended Master El Morya, this Council (or Great White Brotherhood) of spiritually illumined beings was credited by the Summit Lighthouse with serving the cause of God.[98]

The Summit Lighthouse taught that the sizeable contingent of cosmic beings comprising the Great White Brotherhood operated in a "behind the scenes" manner as sponsors of a new age of self-transformation. These emissaries of God were defined as those who have balanced at least 51 percent of their karma and, as a consequence, have become immortal.[99] In addition to Saint Germain and El Morya, there were many other divine beings among the legion of Ascended Masters, some of whom had especially notable backgrounds. A few among them were Serapis Bey, once a priest on the "lost continent" of Atlantis; Kuthumi, who was credited (along with Helena Blavatsky) with having founded the Theosophical Society; the Goddess of Liberty, Godfre, who walked the earth as Guy Ballard; Jesus Christ; and Gautama Buddha.[100] Also viewed as part of the spirit of the Great White Brotherhood were those "unascended" beings who successfully balanced the majority of the karma they incurred during previous earthly embodiments. Having rendered themselves free of most of their karma, the Prophets (as co-Messengers for the Great White Brotherhood) occupied an elevated place in the group's ascending hierarchy of being. As the exclusive representatives for the Ascended Masters, the Prophets assumed an intermediary position between the membership and the group's pantheon of spiritual deities.[101]

From Eastern mysticism the Summit Lighthouse acquired a predilection for the conception of karma and reincarnation. In contrast, however, with the pleasantly amorphous New Age quality of these ideas, the group viewed the concepts in a much more serious and doctrinaire manner. Attributing to mankind's "free will" the power to make or mitigate karma, the Ascended Masters (through the voice of the Messengers) made clear to their students that individual actions and behavior determined spiritual destiny.[102] In order to stem the accumulation of one's "negative karma," the organization adopted a course of discipleship for its members to follow. This practice involved cautioning students against unpredictable tests of their worthiness orchestrated by the Great

White Brotherhood and encouraging followers to "behave as Christ" in order to overcome individual karma.[103] Within the group, attaining "the Christ consciousness" signified the individual's transformation from selfhood to a more exalted state of being.[104]

The Summit Lighthouse's route to discipleship also included the mastery of decrees, which group members recited to mitigate karma and which became an important aspect of the initiate's training. Structurally similar to the prayers of the rosary, decreeing was a statement of faith that called forth the reality "commanded" by the reciter. Students were taught to utter decrees rapidly so that maximum benefit could be derived from the spiritual energy they were believed to produce.[105] Although the membership used decrees for a variety of purposes, their central function was to destroy all manifestations of evil and attune the planet to the power of light (God) in the universe.[106]

From Colorado to California

While based in Colorado Springs, the Summit Lighthouse acted on plans aimed at expanding its teaching mission outside the United States. In a series of excursions taken between 1969 and 1972, the co-Messengers went to Latin America, the Middle East, India, Europe, and several African countries to convey the group's philosophy to foreign audiences.[107] The Prophets' efforts sowed the seeds for what became in later years a modest international following, perhaps numbering up to several thousand members. The work applied to building a worldwide movement would take time to materialize, but other institutional plans proved more immediately successful. In 1970, the Prophets founded Montessori International, a nontraditional school whose curriculum included both secular and spiritual learning for the children of parents who lived and worked near the organization's headquarters. The program was based on the education theories of Maria Montessori, a pioneer in the field of cognitive learning,[108] and offered parents in the Summit Lighthouse an alternative to a public school system that the Ascended Masters blamed for "promoting a godless atheism." [109]

In an effort at laying out the spiritual philosophy of their movement, the Prophets coauthored the book *Climb the Highest Mountain* in 1972. As the first comprehensive exposition of the organization's eclectic cosmology, *Climb the Highest Mountain* attempted to make clear the previously unrecorded "truths" of the Great White Brotherhood. Directed by this cosmic assembly to reveal its teachings to humanity, the Prophets provided their insights into spiritual law and the route to higher consciousness.[110] But within the Messengers' mystical treatise there also appeared strong signs of a dualistic worldview that clearly separated the world into camps of Light and Darkness. Stressing the need for "students of higher truth" to remain vigilant in their watch against "the Laggards and the Luciferians," the leaders of the Summit Lighthouse devoted a significant portion of their book to describing the misdeeds these "manipulators of man" had undertaken.[111] While never clearly identifying the agents of evil who walked the earth, the Prophets addressed their perceived strategies for mankind's manipulation and cautioned that the unknowing would be influenced by the plots of earth's "archdeceivers."[112]

The Summit Lighthouse met with an unexpected setback on February 26, 1973. Mark Prophet's death, brought about by a sudden seizure, presented the group with its first major crisis. Having been the lesser of the co-Messengers throughout the previous decade, Elizabeth Clare Prophet, at thirty-three years of age and the mother of four children, became the sole leader of the Summit Lighthouse. Taking over her late husband's position may have been a daunting task, at least initially, for Elizabeth. Evidence in the form of tape-recorded dictations made immediately after Mark Prophet's death reveals that the youthful widow was unsteady in her delivery and, perhaps, insecure about her new role.[113] While the immediate transition period presented an unprecedented challenge to the growing movement, Elizabeth soon capably filled Mark Prophet's position as amanuensis for the Ascended Masters and, thus, ensured the stability of the Summit Lighthouse.

In a repeat of Edna Ballard's declaration of Guy Ballard's "ascension" following his death, Elizabeth immediately announced that Mark Prophet had assumed Ascended Master status as "Lanello," the Ever-Present Guru. The leadership transition ushered in an era of change in both the institutional structure and philosophy of the organization. Both direct attention to Elizabeth's ideas for movement growth as well as to her own personal ambitions. When Mark Prophet was leading the group, Ascended Master teaching took on a masculine tone, due largely to his own forceful, charismatic persona. In order to establish herself as the legitimate leader of the group, Elizabeth reconstructed the Summit Lighthouse along new lines.

The first step in the organization's restructuring involved an effort to introduce a feminine quality to its leadership style.[114] Elizabeth emphasized for the first time the importance of the feminine Mother as the counterpart to God the Father and employed a gender distinction to initiate her stewardship of the movement. Serving to solidify her personal charismatic authority, as well as providing an observable separation with her late husband's leadership style, Elizabeth's self-projection as "Divine Mother" enabled her to create a distinctive leadership role. The position of Divine Mother had its roots in the deification of Mary, mother of Jesus. Under Elizabeth's direction, Mary became identified as "the Mother of the Flame,"[115] whose divinity resided in the new Messenger. With the archetype of Mary prominently included in the group's spiritual vision after the leadership transition, Elizabeth acted as the personification of the holy figure and later assumed new titles of authority that reflected her elevated status within the organization.[116]

The second step in Elizabeth Clare Prophet's attainment of a psychological severance from the heritage of "Mark's flock" took place through the institutional reconfiguration of the movement. Called by Jesus in 1974 to found "the Church Universal and Triumphant," Elizabeth broke up the old institutional structure and formally incorporated its successor. With bylaws and a board of elders appointed by the new leader in her capacity as the proclaimed "Vicar of Christ," the Church Universal and Triumphant became the renamed continuation of the Summit Lighthouse. Shortly thereafter, the church designated the Summit Lighthouse as its publishing arm. From this point onward, Church Universal and Triumphant, Inc., was defined by a dual structure with each division in the nonprofit organization having separate responsibilities and functions. Other changes involved the start of a new program aimed at establishing teaching centers in a number of American cities, including Minneapolis, Washington, D.C., and New York City, to help boost the church's visibility.[117]

In the aftermath of Mark Prophet's death, the church also reformulated the structure of its membership hierarchy. The revamped organizational framework featured five separate membership categories, each representing the member's progress along the path to the church's spiritual truth. In addition to the reconstituted Keepers of the Flame (now the first, most accessible category), which by the early 1970s had become the membership core of the Summit Lighthouse, the new levels included in ascending order: Communicants (the first step at which one became a full member), Sons and Daughters of Dominion, Council of the One Hundred and Forty-Four, and Elders of the church. Under the redesigned groupings, only the Keepers of the Flame were not required to tithe their income. As the student advanced to the higher classes, however, a different set of obligations and privileges were observed. For example, in the class designations beyond the Keepers of the Flame, prospective members were required, along with tithing, to submit a written petition to the Messenger for acceptance.[118] Admittance to the upper membership classes was accompanied with specific responsibilities, including church-service-related duties such as volunteer work at meetings and helping disseminate literature and information material, but various benefits were associated with higher rank. Among the privileges for upper-level initiates was access to special church services, held at both the teaching centers and at larger conference gatherings.[119]

Having earlier established in 1969 a regional teaching center known as "the Motherhouse" in Santa Barbara, California, the church had been positioned for an eventual move to the region. Even during the years immediately prior to the leadership change, it appeared as if southern California was intended to serve as something more than merely a regional extension of the Colorado Springs headquarters. By 1971, Mark Prophet was already using the Santa Barbara Motherhouse as the site for Ascended Master University, an intensive two-week training session for church members seeking more advanced knowledge of the Great White Brotherhood. The course regimen at Ascended Master University exposed students to the church's spiritual teachings as conveyed by Mark Prophet, the program's featured lecturer.[120]

In 1973, Elizabeth fortified the church's teaching mission by making more rigorous the learning experience at the Motherhouse. Taking over the principal teaching duties Mark had held, she expanded the sessions from a two-week period to a twelve-week experience. Her central role in the instruction undertaken at the sessions, renamed Summit University, reveals some insights into the energy and determination that came to mark her personal leadership style. She taught three twelve-week sessions per year in Santa Barbara, where she and her children resided full time beginning in 1973, as well as handled her obligations at the church's headquarters in Colorado Springs. In the process, she quickly established herself as a dynamic spiritual leader in the eyes of church members.

As a result of the church's growing appeal during the early 1970s, the enrollment at the Summit University sessions rapidly outgrew the facilities at Santa Barbara and, for a short time, had to be conducted at Colorado Springs.[121] By 1976, however, Prophet found the opportunity she had been seeking to relocate the organizational headquarters to southern California. Finding an available site in Pasadena at the former Nazarene College, the

The grounds at Camelot in 1980 with the administrative buildings in the background.
Courtesy of the *Los Angeles Times.*

church's board entered into a leasing agreement to use the defunct institution's facilities as an administrative base of operations. This move turned out to be short-lived. By 1977, Elizabeth was considering a relocation to a site near Malibu on the Mulholland Highway where a property being leased by Saint Thomas Aquinas College had recently been put up for sale. Originally owned by the razor manufacturer King Gillette, the beautiful estate and its buildings were acquired in the early 1950s by the Claretian Fathers who used it as a Catholic monastery. When the Catholic order phased out its monastery in the mid-1970s, the estate was temporarily leased to the small private college. After purchasing the 218-acre property for $5.6 million, the church redesignated the site as "Camelot," a legendary name derived from Prophet's interest in Arthurian lore.[122]

In California, the church's relations with both the media and local officials first became a major problem. These difficulties emanated mainly from two issues: questions about CUT's observance of local zoning laws on its campus property and negative reports coming from church defectors. The frictions be-

The chapel at Camelot.
Courtesy of the *Los Angeles Times*.

tween the church and the surrounding community were exacerbated by the growth of a popular anticult position various special interest groups adhered to throughout the 1970s. Formed as a grassroots movement by families whose children had been "lost to cults," the anticult movement advanced an agenda that aimed at publicly discrediting the new religious groups. Often successful in its attempt at winning support, the anticult movement emerged as a powerful lobby whose opposition to new religions nourished public fear and confusion about the propagation of alternative spiritual groups in the 1970s.[123]

Despite the problems the church encountered after its move to the Malibu site, Elizabeth Clare Prophet's organization prospered throughout the mid—to late 1970s, by which time it counted in its worldwide ranks some twenty-five thousand members.[124] Through concerted efforts at recruiting new adherents, the church widened its membership base by attracting a New Age audience interested in the unfamiliar aspects of Ascended Master teachings. Traveling by private bus throughout the country, Elizabeth and her entourage made frequent visits to towns and cities on extended lecture tours. At these stops, the Messenger claimed that a world transition from the Age of Pisces to the Aquarian era was on the horizon and that a "revolution" in higher consciousness was about to occur.[125] The Aquarian epoch was said to be especially significant because it represented the coming of a new golden age and symbolized for the church the realization of the consciousness of God in the world. Although the Messenger declared the dissemination of this message to be the primary mission of the church at the organization's 1976 Freedom Conference, the revolution in higher consciousness had been discussed earlier in *Climb the Highest Mountain.* Cast in a more sobering light in the text, the future revolution carried connotations of struggle and conflict that pointed to the possibility for sweeping changes, including "the destruction of sovereign governments" to take place in the secular world.[126]

Survivalism and Separation

Throughout the 1970s the church stressed the need for its membership to be prepared for uncertain events, but this became especially evident in the period directly following Mark Prophet's death. The group's worries about a future disaster contributed to the growth of a survivalist outlook, which surfaced occasionally in both church publications and as an important theme at major organizational gatherings. The first visible evidence of the church's gravitation toward survivalism emerged at the 1973 annual conference in Colorado Springs. Featured at the meeting were group sessions designed to inform members of the earthly dangers associated with humankind's misdeeds. Ranging from personal selfishness and vanity to the misguided laws of sovereign governments, humanity's shortcomings were viewed by the church as the catalysts for future disasters.[127] In an attempt to prepare its following for the difficult times ahead, the church made survival equipment available to its members. Sold under the label "The Exodus Series," [128] the name itself carried interesting symbolic overtones. Using the Old Testament story of the Israelites fleeing Egypt as a metaphor applicable to the modern world condition, the organization's advertising literature emphasized the need to prepare for earthly calamities and displayed a deep concern with what were called "the rapidly moving events" of the era.[129]

Elizabeth Prophet's own fears about a near-term catastrophe led her to undertake an all-out survivalist plan to ensure the safety of the church. The new Messenger's declaration of "Operation Christ Command" in 1973 was orchestrated to alert her movement to the likelihood of a future war with the Soviet Union, a scenario that was believed would provoke the collapse of the U.S. government and send the country into anarchy. In a prelude to a similar group scare that would occur fifteen years later, Prophet pointed to the church's vulnerability in the event of either a Soviet missile attack or land invasion. The organization's close proximity to what she saw as two likely strategic targets, the North American Aerospace Defense Command (NORAD) near Colorado Springs and the Rocky Flats Nuclear Weapons Storage Facility outside Denver, alarmed her and may have factored into her eventual decision to move the church to California. The Messenger's fear was that her following was not adequately prepared for the reality of this emergency, and therefore she set out to mobilize the membership for the coming of desperate times. In order to make ready for the disaster, the church opened a small survival food processing business in Colorado Springs whose products (along with survival equipment) the organization recommended to its members for purchase.[130]

Operation Christ Command also set in motion two major developments in the church. The first was the decision some high-ranking members made to purchase a sizeable cache of firearms to be used for security purposes. This arsenal, which was largely financed by a wealthy officeholder in the group, included an array of high-powered hunting rifles and semiautomatic, assault-style weapons. The $100,000 investment in firearms was officially made by a joint-stock company (the Rocky Mountain Sportsmen Club), which was comprised of a small handful of inner-circle church members who sought to provide the tax-exempt organization, and Prophet, with plausible deniability of the venture. Few rank-and-file members were made aware of the existence of the weapons, which were stored on church grounds but later moved to other sites to avoid detection.[131] The other development Operation Christ Command precipitated was a very short-lived attempt to locate a suitable tract of isolated property where the movement could survive the envisioned crisis. A few months after Mark Prophet's death, Elizabeth and her closest advisers planned to develop a self-sustaining church community on several hundred acres arranged to be leased near Coeur D'Alene, Idaho. Prophet's hope was for the tract to become the full-time home for the membership since its location in the mountainous, rugged terrain of the Northwest offered protection from the foreseen troubles associated with the collapse of American society. Plans for the establishment of the survival community abruptly ended, however, when southern California was determined to be a preferable site for the church's development.[132]

Prophet's leadership demonstrated strong traces of her desire to separate her organization from the enemies she believed were plotting to subvert world governments. She inherited this conviction from her late husband, whose patriotic, anticommunist views had a profound effect on the group's worldview. Influenced to a large degree by the pro-American sentiments of the I AM group, Mark Prophet built on the civil religion that pervaded the philosophy of Guy and Edna Ballard. The church's early expressions of Americanism drew upon I AM patriotic beliefs and corresponded with a religious framework that placed the country in a divine role.[133] While CUT often reverted to conspiratorial explanations for humanity's failings and the perceived "gains" made by America's foes,[134] the real struggle against the "Luciferian Rebellion" was invariably cast as a total war between the forces of good and evil. The contest took the form of a timeless engagement pursued on all fronts simultaneously until God's "army" emerged victorious. As Mark Prophet envisioned it, the common enemy of the people was the power of Darkness. The relentless nature of the foe, often controlling those at the highest levels in society, allowed the children of God little option for withdrawal from the conflict.[135] Yet soon after Elizabeth took charge of the church, this is the direction she seemed intent on taking her following.

It is imperative to distinguish at this point between the meaning of withdrawal as a collective retreat and the way in which Prophet likely viewed it as a strategy for protecting her flock against its visible and invisible adversaries. Quite clearly, her position on the necessity to pursue the conflict with the forces of Darkness paralleled that of Mark Prophet. In fact, some of the dictations she gave shortly after his death conveyed an urgency about group "self-defense" that seldom surfaced in her husband's teachings. In a dictation from the Ascended Master K-17, Agent of the Cosmic Secret Service, the Messenger revealed to her group the need to remain vigilant in preparation for possible future struggles with the Dark Ones: "And so I say to you, those of you who have considered nonresistance to violence, think well. For to allow the hordes of Darkness to take command of this planet and turn it over to a one-world government under Lucifer, to allow this to take place when you know better, is fraught with grave consequences."[136]

For the new Messenger, leading the church into uncertain times necessitated a "break," manifested both in terms of psychological and geographic space, with an outside world that appeared increasingly threatening.[137] Although it was during Elizabeth Prophet's tenure that CUT's actual turn toward separation took place, it was Mark who placed CUT on a course that made its eventual withdrawal an inevitability.[138] Undertaken in progressive steps, the church's ultimate rejection of a decaying culture can be traced to the formation of the Summit Lighthouse. By the time Elizabeth assumed its leadership, the image of the church as the New Jerusalem (uncontaminated by the vile forces of secular society) was firmly set in the outlook of its membership.

While Mark Prophet had earlier employed anticommunism, opposition to elite-led one-world government, and extraterrestrial threats as conceptual vehicles to build group cohesion against perceived foes,[139] Elizabeth fortified the power of the church's enemies by making them the entities against which the organization defined itself. This process involved elevating the threat of world communist domination to new heights in the group's teachings. Under her guidance, CUT organized as a spiritual bastion of the Chosen defending against the communist presence in America. The foundations of the communist threat, as she viewed it, were inextricably tied to "the Satanic lie" originated in the Garden of Eden.[140] Through the temptation of Eve, all hope was lost that mankind would ever again walk so near to God. Eve's transgression, from Elizabeth's perspective, ushered into history the moral relativism that was thought to characterize modern life. As a result of the loss of absolute standards of good and evil, humankind came to overinflate its station in the universe and a host of dark philosophies grew that celebrated man as the essence of religion. Elizabeth sought to educate her following about communism's misplaced view of humanity and the "doctrine of hatred" it advanced against God. In an effort at awakening the group to its dangers, she exhorted the membership to read Marx and Engel's *Communist Manifesto* in order to understand "The Great Red Dragon" of world communism.[141]

Elizabeth's declaration of spiritual warfare against communism was not the only means by which she inculcated in the church a sense of apocalyptic angst. There were at least two other representations of evil that were also used to justify an organizational strategy of calculated withdrawal from an impure outside world. The first appeared in the form of an international power elite said to be in league with the "Nephilim," a Hebrew biblical term the Messenger often used to refer to those who were cast down from the heavens.[142] This clique was regarded as an elite group of international "powerbrokers" that operated secretly in order to gain control of the world's major economic and political systems. Ascribing to this exclusive body a hidden agenda aimed at destroying democratic government, Prophet saw such organizations as the Council on Foreign Relations and the Trilateral Commission as agents of political intrigue bent on gaining global power. She felt that such groups were responsible for hatching a diabolical plot against the children of God aimed at subjugating all nations to the authority of these figures and their "banking houses." [143]

Elizabeth also relied on a threat of extraterrestrial origin to further her designs on removing the church from the environing society. The appearance of menacing foes from space flowed logically into CUT's outlook on the world. Mark Prophet's 1965 book *The Soulless Ones* laid the groundwork for Elizabeth's later practice of demonizing the extraterrestrial entities believed to be visiting earth. Like communists and the international power elite, the Messenger saw the alien presence as part of a Luciferian conspiracy that moved to extinguish the flame of God residing in humanity. In at least one sense, however, the threat from space posed an even greater danger to the safety of the church. Whereas the other enemies remained partially visible to the discerning eye by their trademark efforts at creating a one-world government, [144] the aliens were more difficult to monitor. Each of these foes emanated from the same "seed" of the Evil One (Lucifer), but the church associated the extraterrestrials more closely with the direct powers of Darkness. The space visitors assumed a more highly distilled "otherness" as nonhuman genetic marauders thought to be engaged in the "manufacturing" of simulated people who would infiltrate society and carry out their creators' plans to promote wickedness in the world. Increasingly, Elizabeth's statements about the aliens' activities revealed obvious traces of alarm. In a 1980 passage she wrote on the extraterrestrial plot, the Messenger revealed that "the robot creations" were already walking the planet while alien ships stood by in orbit. [145]

Exodus to Montana

Elizabeth's stewardship of the church was notable in two respects. First, she successfully established her legitimacy as the group's religious leader, a major feat given both her relative lack of leadership experience and the legacy of Mark Prophet against which she had to compete. Second, she succeeded in defining the organization's world outlook to an extent that further refined the ambiguous qualities of patriotic Americanism and group elitism her husband had established. Her use of a renewed and reinvigorated organizational dualism was an essential component of this leadership strategy. Since she required a new position to set herself apart from the legendary status group members accorded to Mark Prophet, Elizabeth took the founding Messenger's formative ideas to heightened levels of expression. Her effort to take the movement's historic worldview to an ultimate ideological endpoint resulted in an irrepressible urge for CUT to gain separation from an environment thought to be hostile and dangerous.

While the organization was based in Malibu, serious efforts were made at moving to an area offering greater possibilities for safety and seclusion. Beginning in 1981, CUT began to acquire large tracts of land in southwestern Montana near Yellowstone National Park. The decision to move its headquarters to Montana was not arbitrary. The impressive Teton Mountains were located near the church's property purchase and had always held a special importance for spiritual groups following in the I AM tradition. Believing the Tetons to be the hollow dwelling place of Saint Germain, portions of the I AM following routinely visited the site in the 1930s and 1940s in the hope that the opening of the mountains would allow the faithful to ascend to the ethereal plane on which the Great White Brotherhood resided.[146] CUT representatives initially purchased a twelve-thousand-acre ranch formerly owned by publishing magnate Malcolm Forbes and continued to buy available property in the surrounding Paradise Valley region throughout the mid-1980s until its land holdings exceeded twenty-four-thousand acres. The group's exodus from California was finalized in 1986 when CUT's headquarters formally moved to the Montana site after the Camelot estate was sold for $15.5 million to a group of Japanese investors representing the Nichiren Shoshu Buddhist sect.[147]

Also significant as a reason for the relocation to Montana was the group's perception of impending disaster. In *Prophecy for the 1980s,* a short volume CUT published in 1980 that blended religious doctrine with apocalyptic predictions, Prophet discussed the strong possibility that the decade would be marked by catastrophic events. She argued that the prospects for international warfare, revolution, and natural disasters (such as earthquakes and floods) were increasing, and pointed to the 1980s as "the most challenging decade man might ever face."[148]

Organized as a cloistered spiritual community, the establishment of the church's Royal Teton Ranch was the culminating act in Elizabeth's quest for group separation. The move to Montana represented a psychological break with the troubles the group saw in secular society and symbolized a new vitality in the organization's life. Devoted members were permitted to serve as staff members at the ranch and soon the site became the permanent home for approximately six hundred followers of the Ascended Master religion. As a devotional standard for those choosing to live on the ranch, it was required that individuals be standing members of Keepers of the Flame and hold Communicant status in the church.[149] The rigors associated with life in the rustic spiritual community proved trying for those deciding to follow the church to Montana. Unlike the Malibu site, where a preestablished college campus offered a relatively comfortable home for CUT's headquarters, the Montana property was rugged and required hard work to make it suitable as a communal home.

Even before its official relocation, the church began to encounter voices of opposition that declared that the group exploited its membership and practiced brainwashing.[150] These allegations were often fueled by charges defectors made against CUT. Accusing Prophet of accumulating great financial wealth by expropriating the resources of members, the regional media in California focused on the disparities between the austere existence of ordinary CUT members and the group leader's lavish lifestyle, which was said to have provided Prophet with servants catering to her needs and frequent luxury vacations.[151] Equally damaging to the organization's reputation were charges that the group had used mind-control techniques to separate members from their families and to foster a high degree of loyalty and allegiance to CUT. Once targeted by the media in California as a "brainwashing cult," these accusations followed the group to Montana where the media there continued to look at Prophet's organization with a suspicious eye.

In part, the skepticism about Elizabeth Clare Prophet and her church extended from the media's loose association with the growing anticult movement. Dedicated to exposing new religious groups as coercive and manipulative, the anticult movement came to fruition in the 1970s in response to the increased presence of marginal religions in America. The movement was comprised of former members of these new religions, who (along with their supporters) sought to impart their agenda to a wider public audience. Due to the anticultists' activism, they generally received the full endorsement of media representatives. The movement's program presented media with a new possibility for offering spectacular headlines by making public anticult allegations.[152]

Observing no distinctions among new religious groups, the anticultists pursued a policy of discrediting all organizations that deviated from the religious mainstream. For this reason, the Church Universal and Triumphant became a tempting target for their attacks. Anticultists subscribed to anachronistic theories of mind control and psychological coercion.[153] Anticultists were particularly energized by the media's coverage of the mass suicides in the Rev. Jim Jones's Peoples Temple community in 1978, an event that provided a wide audience in America eager to embrace the anticult viewpoint, which perceived many alternative religions as threats and sought their elimination.[154]

The purchase of the Montana property marked the onset of a protracted series of disputes between CUT and the local community. Concerned that ranch members would mobilize as a political force in sparsely populated Park County (pop. 14,000), fears circulated among locals that the group might attempt a political takeover of the region. A well-publicized precedent for this scenario occurred in the early 1980s when a religious sect led by the Bhagwan Shree Rajneesh, an Indian-born mystic and philosopher, founded a separatist spiritual community in Antelope, Oregon. Named "Rajneeshpuron" by the Bhagwan, the utopian town existed until 1986, when its founder's personal legal problems put an end to the communal experiment. The controversial group had engineered a strategy for gaining political power in the region, a plan that involved the recruitment of homeless people to Rajneeshpuron in order to increase the community's voting numbers in the remote area.[155] The "Antelope issue" loomed large in the perspective of Montanans residing near CUT's new headquarters. Natives feared that the organization would make a deliberate attempt to engineer a political uprising against the local government. In retrospect, the concern proved unwarranted. Although the Bhagwan temporarily succeeded in his efforts at leading a small-scale "coup" in Oregon (leading to a short-lived legal incorporation of the sect's personal town), Elizabeth Clare Prophet was contemplating no such plan.[156]

Far more significant as a source of trouble than the group's misperceived political ambitions was the bitter dispute brewing over environmental issues. The question of CUT's physical impact upon the Yellowstone ecosystem sparked controversy in the region dating from its purchase of the Forbes ranch. Prior to the purchase, Malcolm Forbes had been negotiating with the U.S. Park Service to sell the expansive property as an addition to the Gallatin National Forest. The failure of these negotiations became the occasion for CUT's acquisition of the land. Following the transaction, local environmental interests, which had hoped to turn the ranch into public property, voiced opposition to the group's use of the tract.[157]

The development of CUT's Royal Teton Ranch took several forms, most of which placed the organization at odds with officials from neighboring Yellowstone National Park and local residents. In order to make the site habitable for its permanent staff, the organization embarked upon a series of work projects. The first of these included placing trailer housing and a sewer system on the property, replacing old boundary fences, and constructing storage facilities for foodstuffs, tools, and small machinery. Both legislators and park representatives reacted with alarm to CUT's efforts at development and feared that the group's activities would result in environmental damage to the Yellowstone region. In particular, Yellowstone Park officials expressed frustration with the church over the issue of wildlife migration. According to park officials, man-made structures on the ranch interfered with the natural migratory patterns of grizzly bears, elks, antelope, and bison, which previously moved unhindered through Paradise Valley.[158]

The fear that CUT would harm the ecosystem of the nation's oldest national park also ignited debate outside Montana. In early 1981, U.S. Representative Wayne Owens (D-Utah) threatened to introduce legislation that would allow the government to claim the church's property and return it to public use. Citing the threat posed to the park by the group's construction work, Owens proposed that the federal government first attempt to buy the ranch from the church. However, in the event that CUT proved unwilling to sell, Owens suggested that the government could use eminent domain to expropriate the property.[159] Owens' charges against CUT failed to attract much political support but nonetheless highlighted what many in the nature lobby perceived as the group's careless disregard for the Yellowstone region. More than anything else, this sentiment was fueled by concerns that the church's newly acquired tract would become the base for a de facto city in the midst of the environmentally sensitive region.

In short time, other significant rifts would occur between Prophet's millennial church and outsiders following the relocation of CUT's headquarters to the new ranch site. But throughout most of the 1980s, locals generally continued to see the church merely as a strange "California cult" invading native soil.[160] Since little was known outside the organization about its apocalyptic beliefs, or the reasons for the group's move to Montana, Prophet's plans for the development of her survival community remained a closely guarded matter. By the end of the decade, this would change as the disaster-focused beliefs enmeshed within CUT's theology boiled over in a massive demonstration of millennial enthusiasm.

Camelot and Group Separatism

Without question, CUT's defensive posture toward the outside world can be traced to before its 1977 purchase of the Claretian Fathers estate in the Santa Monica Mountains near Malibu. Evidence shows, for example, that officials in the organization had purchased a sizeable arsenal of weapons in 1973 that was stored on church property.[1] CUT officials intended to use the guns for defense when a perceived future social collapse would trigger widespread anarchy in America.[2] Additionally, it becomes apparent that some of Mark Prophet's early writings (particularly his book *The Soulless Ones*), reflected the group's alienation from the surrounding culture. Prophet's belief in a conspiracy led by "counterfeit man" (literally, soulless agents of the Antichrist), helped direct his movement on a psychological path toward separatism. In actuality, the fears that led to both the stockpiling of weapons and the warnings against "spiritual wickedness in high places"[3] were inextricably linked. By laying the foundations for a group outlook steeped in conspiracy and feelings of besiegement, Mark Prophet established a mode of thinking about the outside world that led to deepening concerns about the church's security. These attitudes crystallized in Elizabeth Clare Prophet's spiritual movement by the time its communal headquarters were established near Malibu. As the events of this period in CUT's history bear out, the group increasingly saw itself as being threatened by forces in the larger society.

The organization's problems in California stemmed from two immediate causes, location and defections, each of which became the source of considerable friction between the church and the outside. In order to accommodate its burgeoning membership, in 1977 CUT purchased the 218-acre Claretian Theological Seminary. While according the group a number of amenities unavailable at previous sites in Santa Barbara and Pasadena, including plentiful housing and office space, the church's relocation almost immediately sparked conflict. Despite an ambitious $33 million plan to further develop the scenic property, CUT was forced to put this goal on hold due to the interest that the National Park Service had in the property. Situated in a location that the Park Service had targeted for acquisition as part of the Santa Monica Mountains Recreational Area, CUT's "Camelot" site was eagerly sought by the government.[4]

The property dispute became the occasion for investigative reporting by the media. In growing numbers, stories appeared in regional newspapers alleging that the church had hidden caches of firearms on its property and that its leaders encouraged members to break family ties.[5] Many of the reports came from defectors, whose statements were seized upon by reporters as proof of the group's dangerous proclivities. Although some of these accounts may have been sensationalized, on occasion revelations were made about the church and its activities that proved accurate. Of these, two stand out mainly for the implications they would have on future organizational thinking. First, rumors that CUT had been actively involved in training some of its members in survival skills turned out to be true when leadership members of the group acknowledged the activity in an interview with the *Los Angeles Times*.[6] Although the church's representatives "categorically denied reports of munitions," defectors revealed to the media that the organization had been secretly hoarding weapons and ammunition since its days in Colorado Springs.[7] Throughout its stay in Malibu, CUT was faced with accusations that it was a "paramilitary cult." Rumors circulated about the group's alleged ties to military strongmen in Ghana and Liberia (where it had established teaching centers in the late 1970s) and about supposed efforts at smuggling arms and precious metals into the United States.[8] While there was little evidence at the time to show that the church was engaged in such activities, developments periodically surfaced that suggested that the group was preparing for an uncertain future.

Boundary Control

In order to grasp how the church perceived the outside world in the years leading up to its Montana relocation, it is useful to consider the strains weighing upon the group's "boundary control" mechanism. This concept has been widely used to describe the way that social systems protect themselves from outsiders.[9] The boundary control function in social units simply acts to differentiate between those who are group members and those who are not. There is, however, a corollary process at work in the environing social system surrounding the group. Just as the self-contained group raises its defenses against the perceived encroachments of the outside, the surrounding society forms a reciprocal set of attitudes that is hostile toward the insulated social system.[10] By the time CUT was in Malibu, a number of events occurred that caused it to become more concerned with boundary control.

The church's public relations problems were partly responsible for its growing defensiveness. Regional newspapers certainly cast suspicion on CUT, but the icy response to the group's move to Malibu Canyon might have been expected given Elizabeth Clare Prophet's declarations about her intentions for the new site. Just before the move to Malibu, Prophet told the media that the recently purchased property was to stand apart from the rest of the local community. She informed the *Los Angeles Times* that Camelot was a tract of holy ground where men and women were "taking responsibility for self-government." In her view, the task of building the settlement required "sacrifice and disciplined effort in defense of truth and honor," as well as a commitment to the teachings of the Ascended Masters.[11] Her clarification of Camelot's purpose, while not defiant, underscored her intention to establish a self-reliant community with a monastic atmosphere.

Because of the efforts of the *Los Angeles Times,* whose reporters had been covering the church since it arrived in California, CUT was not an unknown entity to the press. Although hardly out of place in the alternative religious milieu of southern California, CUT attracted an unusual degree of attention from journalists for its unique blend of Ascended Master spirituality and scientific inquiry. Its meetings and events on topics such as the dangers of genetic engineering, problems with the Federal Reserve system, and the potential for nuclear war, reflected the organization's concerns with concrete worldly issues, a characteristic that separated CUT from the stereotypical "airiness" of the New Age.[12] While the region was heavily represented by offbeat religious groups, the church began to stand out for its fixation on these and other more esoteric themes.

Shortly following the purchase of Camelot, the conspiratorial and apocalyptic traits in CUT's organizational outlook resurfaced. The cause was the gradual escalation of stress coming mainly from sources inside the group. Since the time of its founding, the movement had followed a standard pattern whereby its spiritual leaders articulated their visions of the future to which the membership responded. The group's initial move westward, from the Washington, D.C., area to Colorado, was the first step in this process. Mark Prophet's increasingly strident populist mysticism launched the movement in search of new frontiers safely distant from the tentacles of the one-world government conspiracy he saw unfolding around his following.[13] The second major step in the group's pursuit of self-preservation came with its adoption of survivalism in the aftermath of Mark Prophet's death in 1973. Defectors have revealed that this period of leadership transition was accompanied by membership concerns about geological catastrophes and a growing fear of both world communism and the federal government.[14] Randall King, a church staff member whose marriage to Elizabeth Clare Prophet lasted from shortly after Mark Prophet's death until their divorce in 1980, referred to the church's days in Colorado Springs as "a paranoid phase" in CUT's history.[15]

The church's construction of a defensive psychological perimeter around itself was thus part of a long-standing institutional practice. But, in distinction from its previous attempts at stress reduction, CUT's experiences in Malibu involved some new variables. Whereas the church had enjoyed a relatively quiescent existence in the past, this was no longer the case by the time it migrated to California. Spurred into action by anticultists, whose network of concerned citizens, psychologists, and social workers sought to "deprogram" the converts to new religions,[16] investigative journalists focused stories on the brainwashing allegations levied against these groups. As it happened, CUT's relocation to Malibu took place just as the anticult-driven media frenzy reached its peak. CUT was, for the first time, subjected to lawsuits against it by former members, which further focused public scrutiny on church practices. Worst of all for the church, the timing of its move roughly coincided with the November 1978 Jonestown disaster, an event that transfixed the American public and resulted in the growth of anticult sentiments.

Compounding the problems brought about by anticultists' claims, in the early to mid-1980s CUT faced legal difficulties in the form of personal injury lawsuits brought against the organization by former members. In 1983, in a suit eventually settled out of court, Randall King filed an action against CUT claiming involuntary servitude, fraud, and emotional distress.[17] Following the church's settlement with King, a verdict was reached in a 1986 case by a former member that further damaged the group's faltering image. In an attempt to recover a $37,000 loan extended to Gregory Mull, CUT brought suit against the defendant for repayment. Mull, who had briefly served as a church staff member at Malibu, countersued for fraud, involuntary servitude, and extortion.

Mull alleged that the church practiced mind control on the membership. Arguing that the highly regimented and harsh lifestyle associated with participation on the staff had caused him emotional distress, Mull's lawyers convinced the jury that their client had been subjected to brainwashing. The case, which was heard in Los Angeles Superior Court, was decided after a four-week trial during which CUT's theology became the major subject of examination. In an outcome damaging to CUT's reputation, the jury found against the organization and Elizabeth Clare Prophet and awarded Mull $1.5 million in compensatory damages.[18]

The mass suicide at Jonestown also had harsh consequences for CUT. News coverage of the grisly event at the Rev. Jim Jones's Peoples Temple had a chilling effect on television viewers. Jones, a charismatic minister who had established a separatist commune in the jungles of Guyana in 1974, sought safe haven for his multiracial movement from the economic and racial oppression he saw in the capitalist system of the United States. Reports coming from the community's defectors, however, indicated that Jones was becoming psychologically unstable and entertained visions of apocalyptic doom.[19] Reacting to news that the nine-hundred-member community had shut off communication with the outside world, U.S. Representative Leo Ryan (D-Calif.) and a fact-finding team flew to Guyana to investigate. After touring the colony and meeting with Jones, Ryan and his entourage departed from the settlement along with a number of group members who chose to defect. As Ryan's team was preparing to board its plane at the isolated airfield near the settlement, a squad of men dispatched from the Peoples Temple shot and killed most of the entourage, including Ryan. Following the massacre, Jones and his flock ritualistically ended their lives by drinking a cyanide-laced beverage.[20]

The macabre events of Jonestown resulted in the reinvigoration of the anticult movement. As a consequence of the disaster, both Senate hearings and a House investigation were held to look into the circumstances of Ryan's death and to assess the possibilities of similar episodes taking place among other new religious movements.[21] The wave of anticult opinion after Jonestown was also felt in other ways. Books and articles on the dangers cults presented, some of which were written by former members, appeared with regularity in the wake of Jonestown. Capitalizing on prevalent anticult opinion, these writers tended to use Jonestown as the exemplar for all new religions and advanced the stereotypical image of the destructive cult.[22]

With such a pervasive anticult atmosphere in America after the Jonestown incident, the Church Universal and Triumphant was destined to face scrutiny when it arrived in Malibu. It was here that the frictions building between the group (insiders) and the surrounding social order (outsiders) locked into a cycle of intensifying conflict. As more charges were made against the church, the group responded by tightening its boundary controls. Given CUT's hierarchical leadership structure, the organization's defensive strategy started at the top.

Prophet, as the singular focus of religious authority in the movement, issued the directives that placed CUT in its defensive posture. Her leadership function extended to virtually every aspect of the group's existence, including the way the outside world was perceived.

CUT's efforts at maintaining boundary control were severely tested in 1980. Emboldened by the Jonestown affair, local media began to aggressively monitor the organization. Since Jonestown, a sea change of public opinion had taken place over the issue of cults. No longer popularly viewed as merely eccentric, small and short-lived movements constructed around a charismatic leader, the term "cult" became an attack word used to discredit new religions that were thought to dupe followers and to lack legitimate spiritual motives.[23] The local press seized upon reports families of group members made that CUT was practicing mind control, and began to devote its attention to finding evidence of the group's alleged misdeeds. While the protracted media investigation unearthed nothing that was illegal, some of the accounts about CUT's activities were surprising. In addition to revealing that the organization was in solid financial health (members had contributed more than \$3.7 million between July 1977 and April 1979), the church owned a number of properties and businesses, some of which were located outside California. What appeared strange, however, was the church's apparent fixation with precious metals and the degree to which it had become involved in their purchase, storage, and sale. CUT became involved in this activity in 1973 when it formed Lanello Reserves, Inc., a private, profit-making stock corporation dealing in the production, sale, and holding of gold bullion and silver coins, as well as the manufacture of processed emergency food supplies. The enterprise, whose board of directors was headed by Elizabeth Clare Prophet, took its name from the title given Mark Prophet at the time of his ascension.[24]

Marketed as a prudent investment in a period of economic uncertainty and possible future food shortage, Lanello Reserves products were to be a hedge against the difficult times the church anticipated.[25] While the early advertisements for Lanello Reserves made it clear to group members that famine and other environmental disasters "might take place at any time,"[26] great emphasis was also placed on the need to procure gold and silver. Advertising literature for the business resonated with a populist distrust of the federal government and urged members to immediately convert their financial holdings into coins and bullion.[27] The call for members to invest in precious metals carried with it a religio-political message, one that imbued the valuable commodities with a spiritual purity. Concerned with the manipulation of the money supply by "the Federal Reserve and the international bankers," Prophet gave a speech at Camelot on New Year's Day 1980 that castigated "these controllers and destroyers" of the American people.[28] Prophet's lecture laid out her ideas for a "God-ordained economy" based on the gold standard. Paramount among the reasons to prevent the "nation's power elite" from demonetizing gold, she argued, was the danger this act would hold for the church's spiritual mission. Citing the problems of civil unrest and social breakdown associated with runaway inflation, Prophet told her audience that their goal of "integration with God" would be compromised if Congress did not abolish the Federal Reserve system.[29]

Prophet's warnings about the United States's economic disintegration and the need to support the dollar with a national gold supply were millennial in nature. As opposed to the more secularized concerns about gold that have mobilized some economically issue-oriented social movements on the outer fringe of American culture (such as the John Birch Society and other nonreligious tax-resistance groups),[30] CUT blended populist economic convictions with conceptions of the ultimate. The result of the synthesis was a group-conceived "Golden Age economy"[31] with philosophical roots extending from both a conception of an idealized American past devoid of threats from the Federal Reserve and a New Age vision for humanity's divinity.

The group's atavistic notions about a gold-based economy were not an idiosyncrasy. Rather, CUT's efforts to convince members to invest in precious metals should be seen as a component of a larger set of beliefs about the outside world. The image of a world on the verge of tremendous upheaval motivated the membership to prepare for hard times. Feeling besieged by a growing stream of negative publicity, an air of paranoia grew within Camelot. High-ranking members of the church staff circulated instructions to the members to be less trusting of outsiders "whose vibrations are psychic and dangerous" and to decree against "discarnate evildoers" who were attacking the group and its leader.[32]

From Prophet's vantage point, CUT's unflattering image in the media was part of a larger campaign designed to intimidate and humiliate the children of God.[33] While the organization was still in Colorado, Mark Prophet warned his followers against a tendency "to be naive when it comes to assessing the character of enemies" opposing the Lightbearers.[34] Laying out a dualistic vision that would intensify in future years, Mark Prophet's call for vigilance against the forces of Darkness made a lasting impact. Just several months after his death, the ascended former leader delivered through Elizabeth an alarming message that outlined the thinking behind the church's developing conspiratorial mind-set: "There is no question that the world is in a far greater state of crisis than most people realize. The Forces of Darkness are working feverishly night and day to secure their strongholds in preparation for nothing less than the complete takeover of the planetary body and the establishment of a one-world government with none other than Lucifer as its head."[35]

Having married the church's founder at quite a young age, it is likely that Elizabeth Clare Prophet absorbed many of her husband's ideas about the elite's plans for abolishing national sovereignty and instituting a program to achieve world government. Indeed, it was her fear of government-led persecution of the church, along with her ideas about impending social upheaval, which led the inexperienced Messenger to launch CUT on a course of survivalism.[36] Following Mark Prophet's lead, Elizabeth proved to be equally enthralled with the notion that a vast spiritual conspiracy operated as the guiding force in human history. Since the objective in this chapter is to explain the effects of externally induced stress on the movement, discussion of the group's eclectic conspiratorialism will have to wait until later. At this point, it is sufficient to briefly remark on the variations of countercultural secret knowledge observed in CUT during this period and how these ideas helped foster a dualistic organizational outlook that led the group to seek a psychological and geographical separation from the social order.

The Cultic Milieu in CUT's Beliefs

By 1980, the Church Universal and Triumphant was a rapidly growing religious movement. In keeping with organizational policy, the leadership refused to comment on its size. However, media accounts generally estimated the figure to be approximately twenty-five thousand, with five thousand devoted followers at the Communicant level and about twenty thousand others on the church mailing list.[37] As a result of its energetic promotional efforts, CUT spread to new areas of the country and established teaching centers in a number of American cities. While its fast-paced domestic growth was impressive, the group also devoted attention to attracting a worldwide following. Elizabeth Clare Prophet's "stumping tours" for the Ascended Masters yielded dividends overseas in the form of new followers in Africa, South America, Australia, and several European countries.[38]

A center-periphery relationship existed between the church's outlying "bases" and the headquarters at Camelot. CUT's site in Malibu not only served as the group's administrative center and monastic home, but more importantly it represented the ideological core of the movement. Unlike CUT members living away from Camelot, the approximately six hundred adherents living on and near the spiritual headquarters were involved with the group at higher commitment levels.[39] The decision to reside either on or close to the property had a direct relationship with the member's devotion to church beliefs and especially to the "guru-chela" system of spiritual learning that the organization advocated.[40] Whereas the great majority of CUT's followers observed a lower-level commitment to the group's teachings, including many who simply subscribed to church literature, the heart of the movement was located at Camelot whose sacred ground became the base for the group's spiritual elite.

For those members residing at and near Camelot, the organization's spiritual colony provided the support system necessary to carry out life in a group-constructed alternative universe. Camelot offered the devoted believer two psychological aids that granted a measure of comfort in what were seen as troubled times: ideological reinforcement of belief and a sense of community derived from shared views about the world's decline and those responsible for it. Convinced by the Messenger that the forces of Darkness were engaged in a conspiracy to destroy America, members readied themselves for spiritual warfare against a host of enemies believed to be furthering the cause of world evil.[41]

CUT's dualistic, esoteric belief system and the condition of psychological separation that emanated from it conform to the "cultic milieu" concept advanced by Colin Campbell. Describing the socio-psychological environment that characterizes a separatist movement's adherence to unconventional, or rejected, knowledge, the term suggests a distinctive and idiosyncratic social construction of ideas. This means of looking at the world approximates a reverse image of the accepted knowledge and its sources upon which the general society relies. Whereas conventional religion, the state, media, and institutions of higher learning "produce" information and ideas that the society at large receives and accepts, these sources are rejected in the cultic milieu as corrupted and misleading.[42] In such a thoughtworld, the norms and standards for orthodox knowledge are displaced by the conviction that truth lies in more remote and secretive places. Thus conspiracies, the occult, and the pseudo-scientific become elevated to a level of importance corresponding to the role mainstream knowledge assumes in the dominant culture. The cultic milieu represents an "underground" society detached from the prevailing currents of social thought and perpetuated through a network communication system comprised of a subculture of groups and individuals standing apart from the environing order's mainstream beliefs.[43]

The world-denying basis of CUT's belief system was linked to the esoteric religious subculture from which it evolved. Both Theosophy and the I AM movement possessed the cultic milieu features of groups seeking to escape from society's dominant rationalist thought. Establishing the philosophical foundation of romantic utopianism that was passed on to the Church Universal and Triumphant, as well as to a number of other groups in the ancient wisdom family of belief,[44] the Theosophical and I AM cosmologies were steeped in a culture-rejecting mysticism that combined secret knowledge and occult ideas. As intellectual renegades who opposed both the scientism of the Darwinian era and the rational-bourgeois economic spirit of the times, the Theosophists were ideological utopians who formed an esoterically based protest movement.[45] Motivated by a belief in social progress and devoted to improving humanity's condition, the movement's leadership challenged the hegemony of the established churches and railed against the materialistic culture of the West.[46]

Consistent with its antipositivist orientation, Theosophy (particularly under the leadership of Blavatsky) rejected the guiding wisdom of the Victorian period in favor of ancient truths. Madame Blavatsky's early literary work, most notably *Isis Unveiled* (1877), displays the fascination with esoteric initiation and secret societies that enticed Theosophy's followers. The dual promise of occult initiation to an elect body and psychic escape from the disturbingly fluid social and economic changes of the period attracted many adherents.[47] Looking to the arcane and mysterious texts, myths, and religions of the past, including sources attributed to the Gnostics, Rosicrucians, and ancient Egyptians, the Theosophical system drew its inspiration from the forgotten and mystical lore of history. This body of ancient knowledge, however, was deemed by the group's members to possess a cosmic-level truth so powerful as to unlock the answers to the universe.

Theosophy's fascination with secret wisdom shaped a countercultural social movement that led it to organize as an "underground" group possessing the wisdom of the ages. The philosophical composition of its syncretic beliefs, deriving mainly from Hinduism, Spiritualism, and Egyptian lore,[48] made the group's cosmology virtually indecipherable to outsiders. As with any social group observing hidden knowledge, Theosophy's doctrinal impenetrability effectively shielded the movement's ideas from the surrounding culture. Although it must be mentioned that while the goals and objectives of the Theosophical Society stressed peace and brotherhood among humankind,[49] the sociological structure and general ideological environment characterizing the movement reflected its covert style. Surrounding herself with upper-class occult enthusiasts, Blavatsky attracted a following that was engaged in a psychological denial of the Victorian era's rationalism.[50] The group's desire to "escape" from the environing culture is perhaps best seen through the mystical occult fiction that inspired Blavatsky and the Theosophists. As some scholars have noted, the occult novels of the English aristocrat and Rosicrucian Lord Bulwer-Lytton, who wrote several books about secret societies and their alleged powers, may have provided Blavatsky with many of the ideas upon which she based her movement.[51]

While CUT's Theosophical heritage infused the organization with a predilection for the cultic milieu style, its historical linkage with the I AM sect of Guy and Edna Ballard injected a right-wing political component in the church's belief structure. The Ballards' partial co-optation of the quasi-fascist Silver Legion demonstrated the extent to which the two depression-era protest movements shared a similar political orientation. Both the Ballards and Pelley were strident nativists whose fears of America's "communization" and shadowy, elite-led conspiracies were reflected in the cosmologies of their respective organizations.[52] Each movement also combined a mystical belief in the United States as chosen land with a fundamentally dualistic perception of the outside world. Although both the I AM movement and the Silver Legion incorporated apocalyptic themes, it was the latter that elevated the notion of a cataclysmic battle between good and evil to the level of a central millennial conviction.

Whereas the I AM cosmology stressed the possibility for humanity's progressive course to the godhead, with warnings of apocalyptic events used as a reminder of what happens when humankind rejects God,[53] the Silver Legion conceived of a near-term Armageddon when Christ would return to lead the righteous to final victory.[54] It was this expectation of a "cleansing conflict," with the enemy represented by the "Jewish-Sovietist Antichrist," that led the movement to adopt a survivalist mind-set. In preparation for the day of reckoning, Silver Legionnaires stored provisions for the impending war.[55]

The I AM sect and the Silver Legion were driven by a mainstream-culture-rejecting outlook that looked to the past for inspiration and therefore represent examples of esoteric groups occupying a right-wing cultic milieu. Seymour Martin Lipset and Earl Rabb characterized this regressive view of the world as "the Quondom Complex,"[56] involving the glorification of some putatively untarnished past and a concomitant discrediting of the present. Such a form of backward-looking perfectionism pervaded each group. In the I AM cosmology, a period of human perfection once existed upon earth, but this golden age came to an abrupt close some 2.5 million years ago when it was believed the planet's prehistoric civilization pursued material gain at the expense of spirituality. According to the group's beliefs, these once "Perfect, Pure, God-Beings" were destroyed by the "Mighty I AM" so that life could begin anew and gradually evolve to its formerly divine status.[57] Consequently the primary goal of the movement was to restore humanity to perfection and, along with it, usher in the golden age that had existed in ancient times.[58]

In the same way that the I AM movement extolled a mythological past, the Silver Legion also displayed strong backward-looking tendencies. Fundamentally similar in many of their esoteric idiosyncracies, the belief structures of both groups were infused with themes of an occult origin, particularly reincarnation and an abiding faith in the existence of ancient utopian civilizations such as Atlantis and Lemuria.[59] On the whole, however, Pelley's organization corresponded more closely with the general ideological profile of the 1930s nativist groups that sought to return America to a golden age. Its misty conception of "Christian Democracy," a religio-political vision for native-born Protestant leadership of America,[60] was philosophically tied to the image of a single, pure nation untouched by the social and economic problems associated with modernity. This dream of a perfect America, where rugged rural folk worked with their hands in a country emptied of urbanized Jews and communists, was laid on a foundation of heroic narrative glorifying the lives of "divinely inspired" leaders. While the I AM group looked to the Ascended Masters as godlike beings whose spiritual purity provided the example for members to follow, the Silver Legion paid homage to Washington, Lincoln, and a handful of other American heroes as representatives of the "Christ and Country" ideal to which the movement was dedicated.[61]

The I AM sect and the Silver Legion, although primarily religious movements, infused their spirituality with a decidedly right-wing political bent. While extremists of the left have typically envisaged a fanciful future in which the perfectability of humankind might be achieved, those on the right tend to see the past in romanticized terms. Each perspective, it might be added, draws from a psychological wellspring of discontent sharing some basic traits. Foremost among these similarities is an impulse toward monism, or a reluctance to countenance alternative ideas.[62] This ideological rigidity, a feature that defines the extremist outlook of both marginal poles of the political axis, is based upon the certainty of "the cause" and the conviction that its "truth" is beyond compromise. Thus for the believer the complexities of the world are a matter of nonconsideration as the struggle to realize the ultimate vision reduces perspective to a dualistic level. It is from this simplified ideological vantage point, one that Eric Hoffer argued was rooted in frustration with current realities,[63] that the outlook of the culture-rejecting social movement develops.

The Foundations of Esoteric Expression

The Theosophists, the I AM sect, and the Silver Legion provide examples of movements whose heterodox worldviews kept them at a distance from the dominant social order. Each movement adhered to a cosmology that reaffirmed its psychological distinctiveness from the larger culture, and set it apart from a mainstream way of life perceived as hopelessly misguided and impure. The growth of such divinely charted protest groups makes little sense, however, if examined only from the angle of unconventional, antiestablishment ideas. To place these movements and their underlying cosmologies in perspective, we need to briefly consider their evolutionary development.

Emerging in force in Western societies in the mid-nineteenth century, antirational groups proliferated as intellectual currents shifted from their Enlightenment-bred moorings to more primitive urges. It was during this period that the prevailing social optimism defining rationalism and the Age of Reason was displaced by an intellectual revolution of a romantic character. The chronology marking the decline of reason is inexact, but its guiding optimism about the human condition appears to have begun withering by the time of the early-nineteenth-century Industrial Revolution.[64]

The ascendance of a new vision for Western society corresponded with obvious changes in the old world order. From the downfall of the Napoleonic regime onward, an unprecedented fluidity pervaded modern Western existence. On a socio-cultural level, profound changes in the international system, government structure, and industrial technology ushered in a new way of both seeing the world and establishing humanity's place in it. Beginning as a reaction against the Enlightenment's secular humanist and materialistic underpinnings, the romantic period came to fruition as an insurrectionary epoch whipping up desires to overturn the earthbound rationalism of the immediate past.[65] The growing sense that the world no longer conformed to the ordered, time-honored mechanics of eighteenth-century social thought resulted in the efforts of some to return society to better times. However, the romantic vision of the golden age was completely at odds with the formalistic, high culture of the Enlightenment, which focused on early Greek and Roman civilizations as models worthy of emulation. In a radical departure from the Enlightenment's attachment to classicism, the intelligentsia of the romantic movement became transfixed with ancient myths, superstitions, and other archaic forms of belief.[66] This pursuit of "the unreal," which was the motive force behind the movement, signified the total rejection of the main ideas linked with the Age of Reason.

The revival of interest in the occult was a direct offshoot of the romantic attack upon the reigning ideas of advanced industrial culture. Despite its startling bohemianism and world-denying character, occultism was hardly a new phenomenon. Having its roots in religious belief, occultism was part of the Western esoteric tradition whose components included Gnosticism, alchemy, neo-Platonism, and the cabbala.[67] Of these esoteric systems, it is Gnosticism that merits primary concern, not only because these other doctrines were partly influenced by it, but due to the direct impact of the Gnostic worldview on later occult groups. Appearing in the Mediterranean region during the first few centuries A.D., Gnosticism surfaced as a heretical set of ideas observed by groups of early Christians purporting to have *gnosis*, or esoteric knowledge reserved for an elect body of believers.[68] As a speculative blend of Eastern religions, Judaism, and Christianity, Gnosticism was based upon two key tenets. The first, a feature that governed its world outlook, was its dichotomization between the spiritual (good) and the material world (evil). The second, which reaffirmed the notion of group chosenness and had to do with the path to salvation, was the conviction that an inner divine spark, found only among the Gnostics, sought to be reunited with God. This spark of divinity was believed to be locked within the human body, and it was thought that a special, mystical enlightenment (rather than intellectual knowledge) was required to release this energy. Upon the freeing of this manifestation of God within, the believer gained transcendence.[69]

It is not necessary to detail the history of Gnosticism here. For our purposes it is enough to say that its secretive outlook and elitism were passed on to other esoteric groups over time. According to the mythology surrounding the esoteric tradition, its representatives appeared periodically after the disappearance of the early Gnostic sects. Reportedly surfacing in the Western world in various secret societies, most notably in the Rosicrucians, the Freemasons, and the Knights Templar,[70] these inheritors of Gnostic ancient wisdom represented defenders of a suppressed truth.[71] Gnostic beliefs paved the way for later expressions of occultism in Western society. A variety of social protest movements arose over time that incorporated occult themes in their cosmologies and were excited by the Gnostic promise of self-transformation and human transcendence.

The boundary between fact and mythology is difficult to discern in such an obscure field as secretive occult groups. Much of the available literature reflects either the overtly sympathetic or stridently critical posture of those who are obsessed with the arcane, and who desire to reveal the importance of secret societies by rewriting history from an obscurantist angle.[72] Beyond this realm of crank history, however, there is abundant scholarly evidence confirming that occult-based organizations had, at various times, mobilized to become vehicles of social dissent and countercultural protest. The first expression of this alternative vision emerged in the West with Gnosticism, but a host of other underground social movements followed in its wake.

Of the occult, secret movements that derived from hermetic gnosis, two are of particular importance: Rosicrucianism and Freemasonry. Within esoteric circles, each has became synonymous with elect knowledge and mysterious power. Although there are differences between their respective beliefs, both were organized around some common principles. Central to the doctrine of each group was an emphasis upon secrecy. The Rosicrucians and speculative Freemasons were originally founded as brotherhoods of the elect whose access

to an ancient and reserved knowledge was to be protected against the encroachment of the uninitiated.[73] Attracted to similar sources of ancient wisdom, especially alchemy and Christian interpretations of the caballa,
Rosicrucianism and Freemasonry were secretive alliances existing on the occult
fringe of Western culture.

These societies were organized around two main concepts that later students of the occult would attempt to emulate. First, each group observed a kind
of universal humanitarianism that sought to improve the overall condition of
humankind. Second, both the Rosicrucians and Freemasons promoted a body
of knowledge interlaced with esoteric themes and countercultural ideas. That
the Rosicrucians' religious system was based on pantheism and the Freemasons
were a fraternal body is of little significance.[74] Each organization was structured on the principles of fraternity and brotherhood, yet in a manner that was
concealed and insular despite the philanthropic goals both advanced. Functioning as underground movements of privileged initiates, these societies of
the "enlightened" acted as a bridge between early Gnosticism and more modern expressions of the occult movement.[75]

Politics and the Occult

The antireality tradition descending from Gnosticism created an alternative
occult culture for those predisposed to romantic visions of life. For the self-
perceived elect within it, the legendary status accorded to mysterious secret societies fed the imagination. By the nineteenth century, would-be initiates
seeking to escape the limits of the material world mobilized to continue the
revival of the occult. This subculture of the romantic era kept alive the esoteric
spirit in the West through its observance of the ancient hermetic teachings
and eventually formed the core of an avant-garde, antiestablishment social
movement.

Secret societies, both real and imaginary, played a major role in the development of the occult subculture. In addition to the importance attributed to
the Rosicrucians and Freemasons by nineteenth-century occultists, other mysterious groups were credited with carrying forth the primordial wisdom of the
ancients. The most notorious among these was Adam Weishaupt's Bavarian Illuminati. Weishaupt, a German professor of canon law, founded the organization in 1776 as an elite underground fellowship devoted to furthering the

liberal principles of equality and fraternity in the face of monarchism and Catholic (particularly Jesuit) religious intolerance.[76] Although the group dissolved by the mid-1780s, defenders of the establishment order viewed the Illuminati as subversives bent on the destruction of civilized society and intent upon creating a world government based upon Enlightenment ideals.[77]

The Illuminati were typical of the hidden brotherhoods whose historical importance were inflated by utopians drawn to the occult. Such secret orders, and their esoteric doctrines, were an attractive alternative to the monotony of ordinary life. The mythologies surrounding many occult groups provided some in Western society with an outlet for their idealism and pent-up frustration with the mundane aspects of industrial-era culture. This subculture's attachment to the fantastic, thus, may be seen as a preferable option to an anonymous, conventional existence in mass society.[78]

While mythologized versions of secret society history shaped the worldview of occult initiates, there were also underground movements whose exploits were more than imaginary. Western history, from the French Revolution onward into the nineteenth century, was marked by periodic episodes where behind-the-scenes organizations (some of them of an occult character) made a major impact. It is commonly recognized, for example, that the Freemasons played a part in setting the stage for revolutionary activity in eighteenth-century France.[79] Furthermore, during parts of the nineteenth century, esoteric brotherhoods such as Sinn Fein in Ireland and the messianic revolutionary movement of the Italian nationalist Giuseppe Mazzini (1805–72) adopted secretive organizational styles. These protest movements typically challenged the perceived excesses of dominant political institutions and sought to free the oppressed from the established regimes under which they suffered. Often reflecting a forward-looking social vision, the ideologies of these groups derived from a mixture of mystical imagery, republicanism, and nationalism.[80] Symbology, especially that which pointed to the destiny of "the cause," also appeared with some frequency in the rallying cries of the era's protest movements. The esoteric "signs" of the Freemasons offer one such example. Some writers have used the materialization of Masonic symbols, such as the pyramid and the "all-seeing eye" in the Great Seal of the United States, to demonstrate both the mystical leanings of America's founders and their conviction in a special American destiny.[81]

Interestingly, the esoteric and occult components of underground protest groups have never been uniformly progressive in character. Throughout the

nineteenth and into the twentieth century, various reactionary secret movements with an occult orientation also have engaged in struggles against the
prevailing social order. Among the most prominent groups following in this
tradition were the German-bred clandestine orders that owed their inception
to the growth of Theosophy and its emphasis on culture-rejecting hidden wisdom from the past. The Thule Society and several lesser-known secret groups
that emerged in late-nineteenth-century Germany and Austria were inspired
by the fusion of pan-German volkish sentiments with Theosophical thought.
Resulting from this mixture was "Ariosophy," a belief in which occultism and
mystical ideas were used to validate the secrets of the ancients, and as a means
for believers to psychologically disengage from the modern world.[82]

That groups anchored in the esoteric and occult should observe highly differentiated socio-political visions is not surprising. This realm of ideas is rife
with countercultural narratives, imagery, and symbolism that allow for wide-
ranging forms of interpretation. In this sense, the group's cosmology is drawn
from a particularistic and idiosyncratic understanding of reality and the membership's subjective assessment of its own place in history. The apparent distinctions between progressive and preservative (or atavistic) group outlooks
can be traced to the deep reservoir of rejected, heterodox beliefs.[83]

For those historical groups within the ranks of the occult subculture, conspiracism was a natural by-product of the alternative reality that sustained
believers. As we have seen, group-held conceptions of sinister plots and threatening images of some "other" occupy an important place in the occult-inspired
worldview. In the absence of these features of the psychology of occultism,
there exists none of the necessary stimulants required to shape a cohesive
group identity, nor any of the outside forces needed to instill in believers a feeling of chosenness. This belief in elect status can be supported only by conceiving of society in a dualistic fashion. The dichotomization function of occultic
systems performs this task of societal separation between the initiate and
outsider by establishing boundaries marking off the spiritual elite from the
unredeemed.

There are two primary explanations for the occult linkage with conspiracism. The first is that this system of thought (and its social milieu) is predicated on the certainty that the outside world is a contaminated realm co-opted
by the powers of the conspiracy.[84] No less important as an explanation are the
elite overtones inherent in the subculture and the curious form of revealed

truth it generates. The first explanation revolves around issues of purity and the group's conviction that anything associated with the universe of the uninitiated is untrustworthy. This distrust extends to the accepted body of knowledge and opinions in the surrounding society. The second explanation, on the other hand, is derived from the group's self-perception as the lone repository of re-served wisdom. The explanations are actually mutually reinforcing; ultimately, group skepticism with the conventional patterns of social thought fosters the development of an ideological environment that elevates the believer above the uninformed.

The occult organization's natural gravitation toward the conspiratorial is evident in the respective thoughtworlds of the three modern esoteric move-ments discussed earlier. Theosophy, the I AM sect, and the Silver Legion all rep-resent more contemporary manifestations of the occult subculture with the attendant elements found in the long heritage of Gnostic-inspired social move-ments. In this style of social collectivity, it is the group's private reality that both reinforces its divorce from the larger culture and renders its logic impenetrable to outsiders. The general psychological frameworks associated with the early Theosophists, I AM members, and the Silver Legion display these traits.

Although espousing a far more progressive social and political outlook than either I AM or the Silver Legion, early Theosophy exemplified an elite, an-cient-wisdom philosophy that appealed to a small, elect body of occult stu-dents.[85] As is the case with all esoteric systems of thought, the Theosophical cosmology was rooted in the arcane and obscure and, as such, was indecipher-able to outsiders.[86] The Ballards' I AM movement, similarly, represented a modernized extension of the Gnostic-fed alternative reality community. While indebted to Theosophy for its adoption of Ascended Master teachings and much of its occult belief structure, the I AM sect more clearly exemplified the type of exclusive secret order displaying Manichaean tendencies. These traits were apparent in the group's stridently nationalist character, as well as its rigid dualism, and betrayed a psychology consistent with that of the occult subcul-ture in general.[87] Of the three, Pelley's mystical fascist organization embodied most visibly the style of the occult-based social movement immersed in a para-noid conception of society. Perceiving itself besieged by sweeping conspiracies (all of which were attributable to "Antichrist forces"), the Silver Legion existed in an alternative psychological universe governed by a vision of saints battling satans.[88]

Camelot as an Esoteric Community

It remains to look more closely at the private universe CUT constructed during its stay near Malibu to better understand the community's concerns about the future. By the time the church's headquarters was relocated, a high degree of tension marked the relationship between the group and the society around it. What was largely unknown outside the church, however, was that the core membership had developed a style of thought that increasingly directed it to turn inward, away from a surrounding culture considered "dangerous" and "impure," as a means of survival. The ideas that shaped this response to the outside are found in CUT's literature of the period and in the statements of Elizabeth Clare Prophet. Through these sources it becomes clear that the same qualities of thought found in the occult subculture generally were prominent in CUT's belief structure during the stay at Camelot and remained apparent for years afterward.

By the late 1970s, CUT showed signs of tapping into the same obscure netherworld of alternative ideas as some of the better-known secular fringe groups of the period. The difference, however, was that Prophet tied together the diffuse expressions of secularized countercultural belief others held into a religious cosmology. The most obvious example of this was CUT's fixation on the alleged activities of two elite bodies involved in international finance and government policy: the Council on Foreign Relations (CFR) and the Trilateral Commission.

The CFR was formed after World War I as an international institution designed to coordinate Anglo-American policy in the postwar world and epitomized high-level Allied statecraft. Emerging from the pre-World War I semisecret Roundtable Groups in the main British dependencies and the United States, the organization functioned as a body of influential financiers, academics, and attorneys that promoted an Anglo-American cooperative network.[89] The Trilateral Commission, a group of several hundred political, economic, and academic luminaries organized in 1973 by David Rockefeller, was an outgrowth of the CFR, yet it differed from its parent body by including representatives from a number of Western countries.

While these organizations clearly existed, wielded considerable power, and sometimes (particularly in the roundtable groups predating the CFR) functioned beyond the scrutiny of general society, they achieved a mythological status for conspiracists seeking validation for various world-control theories. The late 1970s proved to be an especially fertile time for the growth of such anti-internationalist notions in America. Declining economic conditions played a major role in paving the way for the emergence of these sentiments. Skyrocketing inflation (reaching 20 percent by 1980) frustrated the American public, a feeling compounded by an oil crisis and a humiliating, protracted hostage affair in Iran involving U.S. personnel.[90]

Capitalizing upon these frustrations, extreme rightists gained some support for the exaggerated claims they made about the erosion of American sovereignty and the efforts of menacing world power brokers to impose a one-world government. One such fringe ideologue was Lyndon LaRouche, whose strange, syncretic conspiracy theories had gained a small but ardent audience by the mid-1970s. Originally a Marxist, LaRouche took his following from the extreme left to the far right in 1976 when he declared that his Labor Party would become a superpatriotic organization.[91] At the core of his philosophy was the belief in an unfolding "new Dark Ages" plot, a conspiracy thought to involve British aristocrats and their American counterparts. The insidious plan, according to LaRouche, sought to depopulate the world by wars, birth control, and famines so that fewer people would be left to compete for global resources. Those who were not eliminated in the upcoming Dark Ages would be kept in a state of servitude by international elites through a covert campaign bent on destroying society's capability for reason with drugs, television, and rock music.[92] Unrestrained in his attacks on the CFR and the Trilateral Commission for their attempts at instituting a reign of "economic controlled disintegration," LaRouche repeatedly campaigned for the presidency during the 1970s and 1980s on a platform of raising the status of the general population and challenging the control of the power elite.[93]

CUT had no formal ties to LaRouche, but it does appear that Elizabeth Clare Prophet may have believed aspects of his theory about the new Dark Ages conspiracy. Indeed, at this period some of LaRouche's published work began to be cited in CUT literature. Prophet used virtually identical language in her denouncements of the CFR and the Trilateral Commission as LaRouche used in arguments against the power elite. During a series of speeches she made to CUT audiences in 1980, the issue of "the Rockefeller-led Trilateralists" was repeatedly stressed.[94] Citing the detailed plans these organizations had for gaining world domination, which included weakening America's sovereignty and reducing its population, Prophet attributed to "the international bankers and the Rockefellers in New York" the blame for the decay of human civilization.[95]

Interestingly, the parallels with LaRouche's conspiracies went even further. Much like LaRouche, the church accepted the notion that mind-control "programming" was being used "at the highest levels" to influence the behavior of American citizens and their political leaders.[96] Prophet argued that the global power elite "promoted a culture of death" predicated on social permissiveness and mass consumerism that mirrored LaRouche's perception of the unwinding plot to destroy the nation.[97] Focusing on this elite plot to enslave the general population, LaRouche maintained that the "little people" were forced to retreat into mind-numbing activities while the powerful strengthened their grab for world control.[98]

To some degree, the general thrust of CUT's populism was not too far distant from that of a growing body of Americans in the late 1970s and early 1980s. While the fringe ideas of LaRouche represented an extreme manifestation of antielite beliefs, their underlying message (albeit in a far weaker form) resonated with broad, and more mainstream, sectors of neoconservatives, anticommunists, and conservative Christians.[99] Seen in this context, CUT's hyperbolic populism was a supercharged variant of widespread antiestablishment sentiments. Where CUT parted ways with other groups expressing concern with the concentrated power of the CFR, the Trilateral Commission, and other supranational organizations was over its view of the power elite. To be sure, a constellation of groups on the far right had made these insider groups a fixture of their antigovernment philosophies by the early 1980s.[100] The Church Universal and Triumphant, however, incorporated the standardized CFR and Trilateral conspiracy theories into a much deeper, and more exotic, system of belief than those movements whose concerns were largely political.

Building on the esoteric conspiracism of Mark Prophet, Elizabeth traced the existence of the CFR and the Trilateral Commission, along with other manifestations of earthly evil, to extraterrestrial sources. According to Prophet, who stated her theory at a major church event in Philadelphia in September 1980, the world was currently plagued with legions of "counterfeit beings" who had evolved from the Nephilim, or Fallen Ones.[101] In her speech, Prophet told the audience of their deceitful plans to create a world dictatorship, which she claimed began with the Nephilim's efforts at developing a "slave race" of simulated humans some three hundred thousand years ago. Produced through a process of genetic manipulation, and later bred with humans, these counterfeit beings performed tasks of labor for their masters for a period lasting eons of earthly history and were humanlike in every form except that they lacked a soul. In Prophet's telling of this secret history, not all of the earth's inhabitants had fallen prey to the Nephilim's plans to enslave the human race. Noah and his descendants, Lightbearers (or children of God), survived the Nephilim's sudden decision to kill off their counterfeit creation (the Great Flood, the unintentional result of their manipulations).[102]

Frightened that interbreeding up to the time of Noah had diluted the power of their manufactured beings, the Nephilim orchestrated a campaign of germ warfare and weather manipulation to destroy earth's soulless humanity. As Prophet explained, the Nephilim triggered a sudden change of climate in an all-out effort to exterminate this slave race. The resulting flood destroyed their engineered creation, but Noah survived to father forthcoming generations of Lightbearers. While the flood ended the Nephilim's attempts at achieving an outright world dictatorship with "robotic" humans, the cataclysm did not curtail their plans for advancing evil on the planet. Following the inundation, the Nephilim (who briefly fled the earth in spaceships) returned with a different strategy for winning global hegemony. Convinced that their plans could be better realized through intrigue, the aliens engaged in secret agreements with those humans who were willing to compromise their belief in God for material reward. Thus, according to Prophet's reading of history, the current state of the world was explained through "the dual evolutions" of these two separate races, the Nephilim and the Children of God. As she warned her audience, the Nephilim and their genetic progeny still remain in a position of global power. In a world dominated by their evil, Prophet recommended to CUT members that they remove themselves from Nephilim control by "coming apart and being a separate people."[103]

The topic of Prophet's September 1980 address in Philadelphia was not chosen arbitrarily. By 1980, CUT's concern with evil in high places was obsessive. At the group headquarters at Camelot, the members' fears about the activities of the CFR and the Trilateral Commission were obvious. Just after the 1980 presidential election, the church alerted its nationwide teaching centers and smaller study groups to conduct a twenty-four-hour "vigil of the violet flame" in order that Saint Germain's approved candidates be appointed to President Reagan's new cabinet. So seriously did the church take the threat of these anti-insider organizations that CUT disseminated a list of fifty-nine potential cabinet officers that included information on whether the candidate had ties to these elite groups.[104] The urgency of the message was clear to the faithful; the emergency prayer vigil could very well decide whether or not Reagan's key advisers were to be representatives of the Nephilim.

Prophet's sweeping revisionist portrayal of ancient history not only explained the origins of the global power elite but also introduced an array of themes that would determine the community's future behavior. None of these issues was exactly new; Mark Prophet had laid the groundwork for belief in extraterrestrial races and visions of apocalyptic conflict between the forces of Light and Darkness. Elizabeth fleshed out these ideas more fully in the years following her husband's death. In this collection of heterodox concepts, two stand out, and each assumed an important part of the cultic milieu atmosphere that permeated Camelot.

The first of these group-held convictions had to do with exogenous forces believed to threaten the church's existence. CUT's practice of "othering" enemies, particularly the Nephilim whose origins were extraterrestrial, provided a systematic way of dichotomizing between good and evil and allowed for a means of identifying modern-day agents of darkness. Since the Nephilim represented a parallel civilization of evil to terrestrial (and God-sanctioned) humankind, their use as a symbol for all things CUT opposed became widespread within the movement, which took literally Prophet's claim of the Nephilim's nonearthly character. Of course, the extraterrestrial nature of the enemy was not merely metaphorical. Dating from its inception, the church had an established record of UFO and alien belief, the historic residue of which came most directly from the I AM movement. As early alien "contactees," the Ballards incorporated the "space brothers" concept into that group's religion. In the I AM belief structure, these visitors from other worlds (such as the "Venusian Master" with whom Guy Ballard claimed correspondence)[105] were intent upon helping humanity realize its divine potential. From CUT's perspective, space was decidedly less friendly. It may have been the source of origin for various Ascended Masters, but it also represented the mysterious black void from which the forces of Darkness arrived. Mark Prophet was certainly exposed to the idea of benign space brothers as a member of an I AM splinter group. Yet, interestingly, he emphasized the dangers associated with otherworldly life. When Elizabeth inherited her late husband's religious movement, she continued to universalize the timeless, cosmic battle between good and evil by stressing the demonic role of the space-bred Nephilim.

In order to fortify her theory of extraterrestrial evil, Prophet turned to the ideas generated in popular science literature. The genre, which is distinguished from science fiction by its embrace of pseudo-scholarship, has traditionally advanced notions that reject commonly accepted ideas from both orthodox religion and science.[106] Prophet borrowed from this heterodox assortment of writings to support her alternative history of outer space civilizations and their alleged premodern expeditions to earth. Prophet was influenced by the work of Zechariah Sitchin, an "independent archaeologist" and author of several books on earth's prehistory, and she discussed Sitchin's ideas on the Nephilim race in several of her lectures. Sitchin, whose work has been popular among UFO enthusiasts since the 1970s, claimed that archaeological finds and the translation of ancient Sumerian and Babylonian texts point to alien visits to the planet thousands of years ago. Sitchin maintained that the technologically advanced space travelers enslaved humans and forced them to mine earth's precious minerals and gems. The rule of the alien marauders came to an end, however, when their exploitations provoked an act of retribution (the biblical flood) by an angry God.[107] Although it is difficult to determine precisely the degree to which Sitchin's theories on Nephilim invasions, apocalyptic floods, and Noah's "survivalism" shaped Prophet's understanding of history, there are abundant overlaps in their versions of early life on earth.[108]

The extent to which the UFO subculture had become a prominent tendril of CUT's counterculture expressionism is visible through the group's use of cultic extraterrestrial terminology. In the church's decree booklet, terms such as "reptilian visitors" and "the three men in black" were presented as enemies to the Lightbearers and the sources of planetary discord.[109] The terms are immediately recognizable in the mythology of the UFO community. In this specific orbit of the cultic milieu, reptilians are considered to be one of the several separate races of extraterrestrials that have visited Earth throughout history. The men in black are representatives of repressive forces of the government whose job is to prevent information about the existence of the spacemen from becoming public.[110] CUT's absorption of these pieces of UFO esoterica in decree rituals suggests that the group's gravitation toward government conspiracy theories surrounding the existence of extraterrestrials was well underway during its stay at Camelot.

The other heterodox idea that galvanized the church was the fear that a global disaster of immense proportion was about to take place. Belief in an impending disaster actually complemented the community's extraterrestrial theory of world evil and can be traced to the same psychological wellspring. The ideas performed two tasks, each critical to the social unification of the group. First, both concepts satisfied basic emotional needs. Just as the group's perception of space-based evil derived from the need to reaffirm the absolute distinction between the forces of Light and Darkness, the belief in a forthcoming disaster mandated group cohesion in the face of coming turmoil. Despite their inherently threatening nature, these beliefs gave the group an unusual sense of security by providing the elect with information unavailable to outsiders. By knowing the "real nature" of the enemy, and the shape of things to come, the organization's belief structure gained validation in the eyes of its members.

CUT's wide-ranging use of disaster imagery became a core component of its message through the early 1980s. Economic crisis, communism, societal degeneracy, and nuclear war were all treated, with varying fervor, as potential triggers for a "world emergency" expected to materialize during the decade.[111] The ambiguous character of the envisioned disaster no doubt allowed some flexibility with regard to apocalyptic predictions. By investing too much energy in promoting any single threat, negative repercussions in the form of compromised credibility would be experienced if the scenario failed to play out. For this reason the church left open the question of the future apocalypse when it announced that plans had been made to begin "the building of a new world" in Montana.[112]

The group's departure to Montana took place over a five-year period (1981–86). Fears of a nuclear attack on the United States and the belief that the government would disband the church certainly factored into the decision to relocate. But group concerns about "earth changes" also motivated the organization to leave California. Citing astrological signs that massive earthquakes would strike the region in the 1980s, Prophet was absorbed with the thought that a natural disaster would eliminate her community.[113] This fear hastened the search for a new site that would be safe from the earth-rending geological disturbances that were expected to begin soon.[114] Perceiving the world around it to be in a state of flux, CUT embarked on a retreat to a safer home. The Ascended Master El Morya, speaking through the Messenger in August 1981, revealed the dual purpose of the New Jerusalem. "In one sense, it is a bridge for the golden age. In another, it is a life preserver to all Lightbearers upon earth for the exigency of the hour and even for emergency—should emergency arise. And we pray that it not arise."[115]

While El Morya's message left open-ended the question of future catastrophe, the group's historical fixation with apocalyptic themes shaped an organizational mind-set that was dependent on images of chaos and destruction. Such visions were entirely consistent with CUT's cosmology and became reinvigorated during the time the group was in California. The wide variety of apocalyptic threats the group perceived highlights the degree to which church perceptions of disasters on the world scene defined the members' outlook in the years leading up to its flight to Montana. In addition to the extraterrestrial threat and the growing concern about "internationalists" and their plots, CUT maintained that nuclear war, social permissiveness and abortion, population control, world communism, and sudden environmental disasters all threatened to destroy human civilization. Even as the Messenger presented the Montana relocation as "our dream of the ages"[116] that offered group revitalization from an outside culture thought to be on the brink of destruction, it was the vision of a great coming storm that directed action. Although the organization's golden age millennial dream was firmly attached to the shining promise of life in a new frontier, dark fears about the state of the world determined CUT's new plans.

4

The Road to Armageddon

By the time its move to Montana was under way, CUT was a fully developed apocalyptic movement espousing deep fears about a future catastrophe. Interestingly, though, there were optimistic aspects of the organization's belief structure that militated against the visions of disaster enveloping the membership. In fact, one of these points was the paramount doctrine of the church: the concept of human transcendence to the godhead. While this belief was never lost to the membership, the perception of catastrophe was the immediate cause for the group's escape to the rugged mountains of the Northwest. Concerned for the safety of her following, Prophet stressed that the $7 million purchase of the twelve-thousand-acre site promised Lightbearers "protection from economic collapse, bank failure, civil disorder, war, and cataclysm." [1]

Prophet's stature as the expositor of the group's vision for renewal increased during CUT's years at Camelot. From the time she took over the movement's leadership in 1973, Prophet steered the church in a direction opposite to the currents of mainstream culture to provide the membership with safety from worldly dangers. The first unambiguous traces of CUT's culture clash with the outside world occurred in the same year that she assumed singular authority when senior members purchased an assortment of firearms that were to be used in the event the group was attacked. [2] This act made clear the organization's sense of vulnerability and established a pattern of thought that remained a key fixture of CUT's outlook.

Prophet was the catalytic force behind the paranoia that crept into CUT's thoughtworld. But for the residents of Camelot, many of whom had been anticipating life in a "New Jerusalem" since the church's early days, the Messenger foretold of an earthly utopia in Montana where the faithful could escape disaster and live free of "society's spoilers." [3]

Connections between crisis-prone thinking and visions of group renewal were prevalent in the church from the beginning. Mark Prophet instilled in the membership the conviction that its organized prayers had saved the earth from major cataclysms.[4] These revelations startled the adherents of the New Age religion and had an intoxicating effect. Having been awakened by the Messenger to the importance of their spiritual service to the planet, the faithful became galvanized in their appointed duty to ward off the forces of cosmic evil. But just as the fear of catastrophe motivated the group to defend against its appearance, the dream of ultimate spiritual rebirth likewise inspired the members to perform their divine duty. Looked to by all Lightbearers as the final step on the road to personal divinity, the objective of achieving union with God represented their foremost concern. The path to the godhead required intense spiritual labor and sacrifice that Prophet referred to as "total living unto God and the God flame."[5] Yet this ultimate ideal, a way of life thought to be necessary to bring about a new golden age, was blocked by the contaminated state of earthly affairs. In order to usher in the new dawn of humanity, evil in all its incarnations had to be conquered by those entrusted with the task of combating the growing weight of world karma.[6]

CUT's relocation to Montana paralleled the efforts of other separatist movements who withdrew to isolated regions. The westward flight of the Mormons represents the best-known attempt by an American religious movement at separating from a culture deemed inhospitable to a group's beliefs and way of life. Under the direction of Brigham Young, the Mormons' trek took the group to Utah, where its "Zion in the Wilderness" was established in the 1840s. The act of group retreat, however, has also resulted in more bizarre episodes. The Rev. Jim Jones, intent on fleeing a decaying, capitalistic Babylon in the United States, took his followers to remote Guyana where he founded a secluded, socialistic promised land.[7] Similarly, Elizabeth Clare Prophet looked to the open spaces of "Big Sky Country" as a place where her movement could achieve group renewal. The move itself demanded much work by the church staff. Efforts at making the ranch habitable for nearly six hundred residents were expedited by the sense of mission that hung over the project. Assuming the role of a modern-day Moses leading her flock away from "the death culture" she feared,[8] Prophet informed reporters that the church was divinely led to Montana.[9]

Evidence shows that while CUT was in transit from Malibu to Montana, its fears of Nephilim-led plots against the Lightbearers intensified. Throughout the early to mid-1980s, the group considered the Soviet Union and world communism to be the major earthly representatives of the Nephilim's ongoing conspiracy. In order to instill in the membership a sense of America's vulnerability to the Soviet threat, Prophet invited a high-ranking KGB defector, Tomas Schuman, to address the Camelot community in 1984. Schuman, who had taught Soviet policy at various Canadian universities after his defection, lectured on the intricacies of ideological subversion Moscow used. He warned CUT members that Americans were ill-prepared to survive a nuclear attack and stressed the need for a rejuvenated American civil defense system. Schuman's lecture, which labeled as treasonous the U.S. disarmament community's attempt to promote nuclear weapons reductions, resonated with CUT's hawkish anticommunism.[10] The group's concerns about the Soviet Union also surfaced in other ways. Highly specific decrees calling for the overturning of the Soviet enemy and the neutralization of key Politburo members appeared in the church's 1984 prayer book.[11]

Strategic Retreat and Combat

It was from the group's new home bordering Yellowstone National Park that CUT's most devoted adherents waged their strategic war against world evil. But the withdrawal to the mountains also represented something more than a pure retreat from a society believed to be on the cusp of disaster. Although the relocation was driven by Prophet's desire to remove her group from harm's way, the membership did not necessarily perceive the move as having been dictated only by fear. Cheri Walsh, a former senior member of the church's staff, put this matter into perspective in a July 1994 interview when she reflected upon the reasons for CUT's change of locations. Looking back to the time of the move to Paradise Valley, Walsh indicated that the Ascended Masters appealed to Lightbearers to "flee from the karma on the east and west coasts of America." Comparing the move to a "prudent insurance policy," Walsh pointed out that expectations of cataclysmic events were running at a high level in the organization by the mid-1980s but that the ranch symbolized much more than simply a place to weather a future apocalypse. She observed that the Royal Teton Ranch was a place where Lightbearers could work to mitigate the flow of negative earthly karma and, thus, return the world (through directed spiritual energies) to a safer condition. In the eyes of CUT's permanent staff, the Royal Teton Ranch offered an isolated site from which the community's focused powers could be directed against the forces working to destroy humanity. This effort to cleanse the world of impending dangers and to warn against their approach was taken as "a serious responsibility" by the ranch's residents.[12]

According to Walsh, in 1969 Mark and Elizabeth Clare Prophet first declared that a "Dark Cycle" of returning karma had begun on Earth. The church's coleaders claimed that this period of accelerating human discord had a thirty-three-year duration and would end in 2002. It was widely felt within the church that the cycle would mark an intensification of events on the human "physical plane of existence." The Prophets' declaration was not initially an object of organizational fixation. After the group moved from California to Montana, however, Walsh observed that much more attention was devoted to "tracking karma" so that the group might better prepare itself for unsettling future occurrences.[13]

In late 1985, Elizabeth Clare Prophet delivered a message from Saint Germain that stressed both the holy nature of the new community and the worldly threats facing CUT.[14] The statement, which was made at the church's fall conference at the Royal Teton Ranch, illuminated Prophet's conception of the site's spiritual mission and her growing fears of repressive forces bent on achieving world domination.

> The company of priests and priestesses of the sacred life who tend the flame of the altar of the Inner Retreat are indeed tending the flame of the Royal Teton Ranch Retreat and our abode in the Grand Tetons. They are tending the flames of the governments of the nations and the mandala of God-government in the golden age. They are tending the fires of Freedom against those who have already carved up the world to their designs in their concept of a one-world government to thwart and turn back and oppose the God-government of the Ascended Masters and the Lightbearers in the Earth.[15]

The message from Saint Germain was noteworthy for several reasons. First, it pointed to the sanctified quality of the Montana ranch. Its status as holy ground distinguished the tract and its residents from environs contaminated by earthly evil and controlled by forces that sought the destruction of the church. Second, the statement emphasized the mission of the settlement and resonated with a call for the community to remain watchful and prepared against the intrusions of powerful, godless foes with ambitions to create a global superstate. Lastly, there was an unmistakable suggestion that the group was accomplishing a critical task at its remote Montana home. By standing firm against surrounding enemies, the community was preserving a way of life consistent with the dictates of God.

While these points underscored the group's self-conception as a world-saving body of the elect, there is another aspect of Saint Germain's statement that merits attention. The inclusion of political themes in the divine message called attention to CUT's development as an otherworldly sect whose counter-cultural beliefs and apocalypticism placed it on a society-rejecting trajectory. Such groups, according to sociologist John Hall, are utopian in nature, perceive the outside world as evil, and harbor a belief that the elect will ultimately triumph over their enemies.[16]

The group's perception of a cosmic quickening of earthly history continued to be tinted with the same political themes that had informed CUT's worldview from its infancy. At its roots, this political outlook was nativistic. Convinced that its ideological vision of a divinely ordained America was imperiled by threats both at home and abroad, the group readied itself for spiritual warfare against foes believed to be impeding the nation's progression to a golden age civilization. CUT's battle to preserve the Great White Brotherhood's vision of America as the New Atlantis, where a high level of spiritual consciousness would promote moral regeneration,[17] was waged along a spiritual front. Although some groups espousing nativistic sentiments have mobilized around concrete objectives, such as geographical boundaries and tracts of land,[18] the church's nativist fears were manifested more abstractly. Much like the American social movements of the past that followed in this tradition, the organization saw the United States as a threatened paradise.[19]

Combined with CUT's nativist proclivities was another philosophical feature that emerged forcefully after the move to Montana. In CUT literature, themes involving crisis and combat began to appear more frequently as the community took shape. In March 1986, Prophet delivered a message from the Archangel Michael that told of "the battles that must be fought and won in every area of America" in the face of the "Canaanites" who were said to have taken over the country. The Messenger reported that the promise of the church's teachings was the only hope against the invasion.[20] Similar statements of mixed desperation and hope were made when CUT was in California. It was, in fact, the growth of a crisis atmosphere within the Camelot settlement that had fostered the urge to divorce from the outside culture. While still located at Camelot, Elizabeth Clare Prophet looked to ancient history to explain the decaying condition of America. Comparing American society to that of Rome in its final days, Prophet drew attention to the culture's moral failings to awaken her following to the declining state of the nation.[21] Equally sobering was her gloomy forecast for the international banking system and the power elite interests that operated it. She cautioned the membership that reincarnated fallen angels ran the world's economic empires, and she worried that this "behind the scenes" body of evildoers was about to meet God's Judgment.[22]

The Catastrophic Impulse

The concept of humankind's transformation to a higher state of existence has generally dominated popular thinking about the New Age movement. There is, however, an often overlooked aspect to the concept of the millennium that has also shaped the beliefs of some New Age groups: the perception of apocalypse and suggestion of the arrival of a future cleansing period that is believed will bring about sudden catastrophic changes on earth. According to Charles Strozier, this New Age vision of the millennium is enmeshed with predictions of global cataclysms.[23] The unfolding of the catastrophe, whether it takes the form of floods, earthquakes, famines, or other disasters, is widely thought to symbolize a cosmic event, one that eradicates the past and sets the stage for the realization of the New Age. This transition is believed to carry with it a transformation to perfection for humanity.[24]

The variation of New Age belief entertaining predictions of disaster has generally attracted fewer adherents than the more optimistic type for which the movement has historically been known. The New Age community is usually identified by its association with several beliefs—including the rejection of what is believed to be a repressive Christian ideological framework, belief in reincarnation and karma, and use of holistic healing and meditation—and it is typically thought of as a philosophically flexible social movement with a peaceful perspective on the future.[25] In its mainstream form, the New Age millennial view is progressive and involves the expectation that a collective earthly salvation will come about through human participation in a divine plan.[26] This view of humankind's "quantum shift" to a higher state of spiritual consciousness symbolizes the rejection of the earthly past and eagerly awaits the events thought to bring about the new millennium.

While CUT had always adhered to conceptions of human transformation that emphasized the path to human divinity and the realization of an earthly golden age, its expectation of cataclysm—rather than a gentle metamorphosis—was what sparked activism in the organization. As the group grew over the years, the disaster imagery became more pervasive and foreboding. Although the members were informed by the Messenger that "the Lords of Karma" would only use earthly catastrophe as "a final resort to usher in the golden age,"[27] the church's writings relied more often on apocalyptic visions of the future. From Mark Prophet's renegade bands of space aliens to Elizabeth's turn toward survivalism and power elite conspiracies, the catastrophic focus became more thoroughly integrated with CUT's worldview as time passed.

Organizational literature dating from the time of the church's stay in Colorado reveals that the arrival of sudden earthly change could take place in one of two forms. Displaying a tension between visions of progress and catastrophe, the group's view of the millennium seemed uncertain and ambiguous.[28] One possibility for the advent of the golden age was fundamentally progressive and stressed God's role in bringing about a "cataclysm of light" that would result in the salvation of humanity.[29] The alternative scenario was far less hopeful. This possibility involved the descent of human civilization on a course leading to its ultimate destruction. Although prayers, decrees, and other spiritual exercises were used to avert worldly catastrophe, the specter of an apocalyptic event preoccupied the members of the church. Motivated by a desire to escape the disaster, a survivalist philosophy was adopted in order to preserve the group from danger. Fittingly, the biblical story of Noah was invoked to stress the need for group preparedness and warn the membership to "escape to the mountains, lest thou be consumed."[30]

The forces of Darkness, the evil alliance believed to be responsible for the world's eroding condition, would be destroyed in the denouement of history. But, as an elect assuming the obligation to pass on the church's teachings to future generations of Lightbearers, the group planned to survive and, thus, readied itself for the dangerous times ahead. CUT's preparations for disaster were undertaken at both spiritual and tactical levels. In order to mitigate the intensity of the karma thought to be provoking an imminent catastrophe on the global stage, the organization devoted much of its energy to praying against the arrival of its appearance.[31]

The prayers took various forms and reflected the wide array of images that CUT used to convey the threat of disaster. In addition to perceptions of the apocalypse triggered by nuclear war, geological and climatological changes, or foreign invasions of America, some of the prayer exercises pointed to catastrophic developments of a more unusual character. Suggesting a penchant for conspiracy and "fringe" science, startling disaster motifs with a basis in convictions about arcane knowledge appeared in prayers during CUT's years in California. These included references to esoteric scientific technologies and the ill intentions of various national governments, including the United States, and tended to portray the arrival of the disaster period as unfolding incrementally. Catastrophes of this type appeared possible since they represented the predictable outcome of the power elite's plans to gradually create an atheistic world dictatorship. In this vein, the group substituted the insidious machinations of a world power elite for total war or environmental catastrophe and charged these Fallen Ones with the use of advanced, secretive technology against the church community. Among the repressive tools believed to be used to destroy the elect were "mind-reforming" psychotronic devices designed to alter the thoughts of the group's members, as well as other "energy-directed" machines capable of "manipulating mental, emotional, and physical states."[32] While less immediately apocalyptic than the church's other catastrophic visions, this perception of a gradual Armageddon was equally bleak.

On a tactical level, CUT prepared its members for earthly disaster by training them to withstand the deprivations they would experience in the future. When Elizabeth became the church's sole Messenger, a survivalist program was put into place. It was organized to teach the membership how to weather the rigors of life in the trying times that loomed ahead and included a "psychological readiness" component, as well as instruction in wilderness living.[33] The group's preparation for the worst, however, did not mean that all hope for the future had disappeared. If the anticipated catastrophe were to take place, CUT had already gone about making the necessary plans to survive the event intact to emerge in the postapocalyptic world as the builders of the New Age.

The Path to Armageddon in Perspective

Viewing the organization's experiences in Colorado and California as a guide, it becomes apparent that the church was headed for a rendezvous with the apocalypse when it departed for Montana. In retrospect, the community's lingering fears about enemy besiegement and Prophet's remarks concerning the coming of a dark future made the Montana phase of CUT's history predictable. In any case, the outbreak of millennial activity on the Royal Teton Ranch was directly linked to sentiments that were expressed at Camelot and even earlier. When the church was based near Malibu, dualistic rhetoric was increased to hone the desire to exist apart from a world that appeared to be on the verge of disaster.

Obvious indications pointed to the group's preoccupation with global calamity. Years prior to the resettlement in Montana, the myth of Atlantis was often discussed in organizational literature to show the fate of civilizations that deviated from the path of God. Following in the tradition of Helena Petrovna Blavatsky and Edgar Cayce, who both used Atlantis as a metaphor for earthly catastrophe, Mark and Elizabeth Clare Prophet adapted the story to demonstrate the nearness of the approaching event. In the church's account of Atlantean history, that society's men of science caused the destruction of the continent by introducing to the culture evil technological "abominations." [34] Among the inventions thought to have been produced on Atlantis were genetically mutated "robots" and other "monstrous creatures" designed to serve as workers for the decadent society. [35] In CUT's reading of the Atlantis saga, God intervened by destroying the civilization and its half-human creatures in order to stem the course of wickedness and hubris the culture had pursued. The meaning behind the church's use of the legend was clear; Atlantis represented the modern condition of world society. Just as the population of the Lost Continent severed its ties with God in pursuit of self-serving enlightenment, humankind was believed to be playing out the same scenario in the late twentieth century. [36]

The group's attachment to a convulsive understanding of history was also borne out by the increasingly frequent references to a heroic figure's reported prophetic vision of calamitous times. Beginning in the mid-1980s, growing attention was focused on the importance of George Washington's prophecy for America. Washington's legendary forecast, which has untraceable origins, allegedly came from a dream he had that told of "three great perils" that the United States was to encounter. [37] According to the legend, the general was given a glimpse of three tumultuous events that would occur in the republic's future if its people were not diligent in "living for God, his land, and Union." [38] Prophet told her following that the first two calamities (the American Revolution and the Civil War) had already come to pass. However, she maintained that the third catastrophe of which Washington spoke was to arrive soon and would be a war fought upon American soil. The Messenger left open the possibility of forestalling the disaster but warned that CUT members must immediately make ready for the advance of "a cloud of destruction." [39]

In a 1986 Thanksgiving dictation from Saint Germain, Prophet exhorted her Montana ranch community to begin preparing underground shelters as a means to survive a nuclear war. The sobering report from the Ascended Master pointed to the likelihood of a surprise Soviet missile strike and provided the impetus for CUT's newest survival plan. In accordance with Saint Germain's instructions, the community was to begin the construction of underground shelters in anticipation of "the almost inevitable scenario of nuclear war."[40] While this was the first time that a group retreat into the earth had been openly addressed, Prophet had spoken of the idea in the past. In September 1980, she told an audience of church members that adepts and their students had used a strategy of subterranean survival in ancient times to weather catastrophes on the planet's surface. Crediting these early "Lightbearers" with "keeping the torch of our spiritual culture," Prophet maintained that bands of the elect descended into underground habitats and sustained themselves until the danger had passed.[41] Perhaps anticipating the group's eventual resort to a similar strategy, the Messenger told her listeners of an Ascended Master who led a group of devotees to an underground world in the American Northwest prior to a disaster in Earth's prehistory. Prophet, who claimed to have personally seen the underground site, observed that this subterranean location paralleled the geography of the earth's surface—complete with water, flora, and fauna.[42]

Her discussion of life underground was significant for two reasons. First, suggestions of subterranean habitation have roots in some realms of esoteric thought. Such arcane, unusual concepts germinate in the environment of the cultic milieu, in which the church was becoming fully absorbed in the years leading up to the creation of its utopian society in Montana. And second, more concretely, these early statements on underground survival seemed to prefigure in an uncanny way the group's eventual course of action.

Prophet's mention of group retreat into the earth in her September 1980 speech echoed a theme with an established foundation in fantasy literature. The introduction of the underground world concept in esoteric circles can be traced to Lord Bulwer-Lytton's utopian novel *The Coming Race* (1871). This story followed in the occult fiction genre for which the Victorian author was known and recounts the strange experience of an American narrator who accidentally discovers a thriving race of subterranean humanoids while exploring a cave. Having retreated from the surface to escape an ancient planetary disaster, these denizens of the underworld reveal to the narrator their advanced technological capabilities, which will be employed against human beings when the cave-dwelling race ascends to the earth's surface. After escaping from his malevolent hosts, the explorer tells his bizarre tale to warn humankind about the sinister plot to destroy human civilization and take over the planet.[43]

Bulwer-Lytton's occult fantasy, in fact, had gained the attention of Mark Prophet, who referred to the story in his book *The Soulless Ones.*[44] Displaying his own penchant for esoteric knowledge, Mark Prophet's mention of *The Coming Race* suggests the extent to which arcane lore pervaded the organization in its early years. While he used the story as a metaphor to point to his movement's ongoing struggle with evil, conspiratorial forces in the world,[45] it is interesting to note that he relied upon a source widely believed to have influenced the ideas of Blavatsky, as well as others in the Western occult tradition.[46]

Elizabeth Clare Prophet's claim that she personally visited a vast underground world at an unspecified location in the American Northwest also focuses attention to her interest in the same variety of esoteric thought that had appealed to her husband. Her account of the experience, as revealed in her address to group members, also bore similarities to Guy Ballard's alleged travels to the Yellowstone region with the Ascended Master Saint Germain. In *Unveiled Mysteries* (1939), Ballard tells of the fantastic subterranean dwelling places of enlightened beings who govern the spiritual flow of humanity. Among these sites, according to Ballard, was a hidden place in Yellowstone Park where buried cities, mines, and secret chambers of the Ascended Masters have remained undiscovered by the human race.[47] Ballard's story may well have been adapted from Blavatsky's earlier accounts of the subterranean sanctuaries of ancient civilizations,[48] but it also introduced a theme that in all likelihood appealed to Prophet's interest in survivalism. Just as Ballard envisioned the subsurface world under the Yellowstone region to be a disaster-proof environment resistant to periodic cataclysms, Prophet likewise believed that safety for her flock could best be found underground in the Montana Rockies.

While Prophet's feeling that the world was headed for a nuclear confrontation became more intense after CUT's move to Montana, her attachment to doctrinal dualism also increased. In July 1986, some four months prior to Saint Germain's warning of nuclear war, the Messenger gave a final lecture at Camelot that conveyed to the staff her belief in the group's elect status. Comparing those in the church with the early Gnostics, Prophet maintained that her group was undergoing persecution at the hands of "a conspiracy of orthodoxy."[49] Her attack on mainline religions was based on the Messenger's conviction that these bodies order followers to observe a spiritual path rooted in tyrannical dogma. She informed her audience that orthodox religions do not

teach the truth and argued that the established churches had historically perse-
cuted those who sought to pursue the true path of Christ.[50]

Prophet's comparison of CUT to an early Gnostic sect elucidates her perception that the forces of the outside world were aligned in a plot to suppress
the group's teachings. Christianity's repression of Gnostic belief in the first few
centuries of its history, she argued, was undertaken in order to perpetuate the
dominance of its orthodox faith. Locating her group in the tradition of the secret societies that observed Gnosticism, Prophet envisioned the new ranch
community as a spiritual bastion holding to its belief of the divine within
against the modern tyranny of "the dictatorship of the World Council of
Churches."[51] Although the Messenger concentrated on the theme of religious
persecution in her lecture, her sentiments can also be read in a wider context. In
the days preceding CUT's apocalyptic mobilization, the group began to see itself standing alone in a world full of dangerous opponents. The nearly omnipotent power of these enemies warranted the adoption of a retreatist strategy
aimed at insulating the church from the threats seen to be looming on the
horizon.

No conclusive evidence exists to show that CUT was considering the construction of an underground group shelter prior to Saint Germain's 1986
Thanksgiving message. It is, nonetheless, quite possible that the idea was at
least considered years before the resettlement to Montana and that time was
needed to acquire the necessary space and funding for the project. Given the
group's growing fear of nuclear war in the 1980s,[52] this possibility is not far-
fetched. It is important to recognize, however, that nuclear angst was not the
only pressure on CUT in the time preceding the "shelter cycle," which was the
name the Messenger gave to the period when the ranch community was to
focus on its survival program. The proximate cause behind the group's survivalist program in Montana was its fear of a surprise nuclear attack on the
United States, but other worries also motivated the membership to ready itself
for the return of karma brought on by humankind's misdeeds.

Geographical Space and Ideological Homogeneity

The Colorado phase of the group's history infused the membership with an
ethic of survivalism while the organization's stay in California implanted a desire for sanctuary. These general impulses were accompanied by the group's
skeptical attitudes about the surrounding society and its sense of precarious

safety. Among these convictions was CUT's belief in a global power-elite conspiracy bent on eliminating state sovereignty and the sense that world society
had reached a cataclysmic breaking point. The former notion had antecedents
in the movement's early history and the personal views of Mark Prophet, while
the latter became amplified during Elizabeth Clare Prophet's tenure as Messenger. Each idea, however, was grounded in CUT's theology.

The third wave of millennial activism in the church also was steeped in beliefs that were hatched in the organization's past. Yet the Montana phase of
apocalyptic activism was also marked by new developments that slightly altered the way that the catastrophic impulse was communicated throughout the
membership. The means by which the group's sense of impending disaster was
magnified in Montana had to do with the environmental, or spatial, changes in
the structure of the new ranch settlement. Camelot provided a general model
for the insular form of communal existence that CUT would adopt in Montana. Established as a self-sufficient monastic community, Camelot offered
CUT's most devoted adherents both an insulated and highly organized social
network and an environment ideally suited for shutting out a surrounding culture held in contempt. But, as distant as the organization stood ideologically
from the environing society in Malibu, its close geographical proximity to
those living a corrupted life in a declining world provided the group with a
constant reminder of its besiegement.[53]

By December 1986 CUT had completely vacated its spiritual headquarters
in California. Since 1981, when the organization began acquiring property
near Yellowstone National Park, plans had been formulated to begin building
the New Jerusalem at this more remote location. In distinction to the geographically restricted 218-acre Camelot site, the spacious tract in Paradise Valley, Montana, offered virtually boundless opportunities for growth. Prior to
CUT's formal move, a "work camp" of about two hundred members was established at the ranch to prepare the site for more arrivals. Part of these preparations involved the drawing up of a thirty-three-building development plan, the
size that was thought to be needed to accommodate the thousands of devotees
expected to live on the property.[54] The change of environment, however, made
an impact upon the community that extended beyond the structural planning
of its new communal home. In what was almost certainly Prophet's deliberate
strategy, the group's departure from the more populous Malibu region resulted
in the further evolution of the church as a separatist community. This is not to

imply that either Camelot or the ranch site were confinement centers for the movement's followers. On the contrary, the decision to reside at either spiritual center was left completely to CUT members.[55]

The physical expansiveness of the ranch and the geographical buffer it provided between the core members and outsiders gave the group a high level of social insulation that surpassed that of Camelot, where many residents retained some connections with the non-CUT world by working outside jobs to supplement meager staff incomes. Staff members sometimes continued this practice on the Royal Teton Ranch. But because relatively few ranch residents could secure either the transportation or time off from church duties to work another job, fewer people attempted it. Staff members were never expressly forbidden to keep up with worldly news by reading newspapers, watching television, or listening to the radio. Interestingly, during the time when the organization's shelter facilities were being constructed, Prophet actually urged her following to stay abreast of international developments. But for staff on the Royal Teton Ranch, the rigorous work schedule allowed little opportunity to stay current with what was taking place beyond the boundaries of the church. Of her own experience living on the Royal Teton Ranch, Cheri Walsh said that Prophet asked the staff to keep informed about the declining state of the world's condition, but that the Messenger's request was an impossible task given the heavy workloads of those living on the ranch. Residents of CUT's Glastonbury community, conversely, had greater access to outside sources of information largely due to the decreased obligations they had to the church as individual lessees of plots on the organization's 4,500-acre subdivision tract.[56]

The combination of the geographical realities of rural Montana and the group's status as a body of the elect fostered the creation of a new social system within the organization. Having left California to preserve group autonomy, Prophet made it easier for her church to raise defenses against the forces that threatened its security. But in addition to leaving behind the dangers associated with living in California, the change in locale marked the advent of a new development in the way that the group received information. At Camelot, the group's countercultural attitudes were, at least to some degree, tempered by the orthodoxies of the social environment enveloping CUT. Because of its involvement (albeit unwanted) with the social control function of the larger community, the group increasingly found itself restricted by the prevailing ideology of the cultural mainstream. On occasion, the environing community's restrictions on the church prevented the realization of organizational goals, such as site expansion, and led to widespread skepticism of Prophet and her followers.[57]

Although the church soon encountered community relations problems in Montana, the new property offered a measure of group insularity unavailable in southern California. With the presence of social control reduced in rural Park County (population 14,000), and having the advantage of vast property holdings to physically separate themselves from outsiders, CUT was far less bound by the regulating effects of the larger culture.[58] By extension, the group's newfound autonomy enabled the crystallization of shared organizational beliefs to take place. At the ranch, culture-defying beliefs were protected from the encroachment of mainstream ideology by the spatial boundaries of CUT's land. With such geographical "barriers" in place, the pressures of conformity that had previously moderated the views of the organization were minimized. The relative absence of these social control forces on the group in Montana facilitated the further entrenchment of a countercultural outlook. As a consequence of the group's increased detachment from the larger society, CUT's alternative worldview became solidified.

After the relocation, the ranch community functioned more effectively as a self-contained social network. Following a pattern commonly found in utopian communities with a charismatic leadership structure, a close-knit communications framework developed promoting ideological homogeneity.[59] In the more isolated environment of southwestern Montana, the group turned increasingly inward, away from the general society, and became locked into its own information system. The combination of rural retreat and a membership entirely devoted to the church's teachings created an organizational enclave that naturally fostered uniformity of thought. When CUT had been accused of "brainwashing" before, particularly by the media during the group's stay in California,[60] these sensationalistic reports tended to conflate the crude coercion of thought reform with the membership's high level of devotion to CUT's teachings. Rather than brainwashing, which experts view as a manipulative psycho-technological process of questionable efficiency,[61] the organization's ideological unity was attributable to its virtually closed information system. To a greater degree than at Camelot, the church's Montana headquarters possessed all the qualities needed to sustain a belief system at odds with the social, political, and religious visions of the mainstream culture.

Prophet's exalted role as Messenger enabled her to define the way that the

membership interpreted reality. Prior to the organization's Montana relocation, the Messenger had occasionally reported to her followers the occurrence
of great acts of cosmic significance about which the Ascended Masters had informed her. One such case took place in 1974 when the group was still located
in Colorado Springs. In a dictation from the Archangel Uriel, Prophet announced that a short period of time would be made available for the Fallen
Ones to renounce their evil ways. The following year, Prophet told the church
community that ten thousand Fallen Ones had left the ranks of Lucifer and
joined the forces of God.[62] Such dramatic statements reflected the way that
world history was rewritten from the group's theological vantage point. Appearing with growing regularity after the establishment of the ranch headquarters, Prophet's messages to her community were the foundation upon which
CUT's group-specific reality was based. The Messenger's access to the movement's spiritual deities was an irrefutable fact for the membership. Thus, when
her remarks took an apocalyptic turn, the faithful received them as divine
revelation.

Old Enemies Revisited and New Fears

After Prophet's delivery of Saint Germain's 1986 Thanksgiving message, the
ranch community focused its energy on surviving a surprise nuclear attack by
the Soviet Union. But the perceived likelihood of a nuclear first strike represented only one apocalyptic possibility in the group's crisis-minded outlook.
Although the nuclear attack scenario loomed large in the eyes of the membership, the three-year period between Saint Germain's warning and the group's
all-out mobilization for nuclear war was marked by the introduction of other
disaster themes, some of which had had a lengthy presence in the church's philosophy. Anticommunist sentiments and fears about sinister plotting of a
global elite class were two early concerns that were resuscitated at CUT's colony
in Montana. These threats had a far-right political tone, but the membership
understood them to be linked to the larger context of the group's teachings.

The fusion of far-right ideology with expressions of alternative spirituality
was, of course, nothing new for CUT. However, the several years leading up to
the group's shelter cycle stand out for the way that right-wing rhetoric quickly
intensified and blended with the organization's religious doctrine. Mark
Prophet began the synthesis when he introduced the concept of "God-
government" to the group in its early days as the Summit Lighthouse.[63] This in-

volved the gradual evolution of the sordid "human governmental hierarchy" to a higher, divine status as a utopian form of rule overseen by the Great White Brotherhood of Ascended Masters. In order to be operationalized, CUT members believed that "highly placed people" must assume leadership positions in American society so that the Brotherhood's influence might crush leftist foes and bring about "the perfect, divine plan for the earth."[64]

Once situated on the ranch, the community of believers received a steady flow of the religio-political ideas that had, for over two decades, informed the membership's outlook on the world. When in Montana, Elizabeth Clare Prophet's obsession with socialism, which she saw as an insidious anti-American philosophy, gained expression as a key component of CUT's worldview. Church literature cautioned against the growth of totalitarianism on the planet in the form of socialist government. In a February 1988 issue of *Pearls of Wisdom* entitled "Jesus on Socialism," the philosophy's dangers were stressed. Prophet recounted the Ascended Master Jesus Christ's views on the vexing problems that socialism's government policies held for humankind's spiritual advancement. All socialist policies were said to be part of the global elite's plot to control all aspects of human activity.[65] In response to this threat, she emphasized the need to embrace a philosophy of individualism and conveyed Jesus' concern about humanity's dependence on "economic redistribution." The reason that socialism in all its forms had to be rejected, according to the dictated statement, was due to the interruption in "Karmic Law" the leftist doctrine caused. Since CUT teachings instructed that the mitigation of one's karma came through individual effort, socialist planning was viewed as an artificial obstruction denying humanity the capacity to purge itself of accumulated "karmic weight."[66]

With socialism seen as an impediment to humankind's spiritual evolution, it was logical that the organization turn its attention to the most visible and extreme representation of the philosophy. The Soviet Union had been the group's chief ideological opponent from the beginning, largely due to Mark Prophet's hawkish ideological stand as a cold warrior. While unconfirmed journalistic reports have indicated that the organization expected a war with the Soviet Union as early as 1973,[67] it appears as if CUT's preoccupation with a Soviet nuclear strike scenario began during CUT's stay in California. By the time the church was departing Camelot, the prospect of a Soviet missile attack on the United States had inspired a high level of survival readiness within the group.[68]

CUT's gravitation toward nuclear survivalism was drawn from its religious vision and, to some extent, from ideas in American popular culture. The organization's teachings stressed that reincarnation permitted humanity to evolve to a point, through numerous reembodiments, whereby a soul's karma could be expurgated, resulting in ascension to the godhead. In order that this pathway of soul evolution might continue, it was necessary that the history of the human race continue. Without the physical presence of humankind on earth, the process of moving to a higher state of being would come to a close.[69] The destruction and loss of life nuclear conflict would bring about imperiled the path to divinity that CUT recognized as the foundation of its teachings. Beyond the intrinsic basis of the church's nuclear fears, the group's thinking on the matter was shaped by a society that was once again absorbed with the issue of total war. Subsiding to a great extent during America's involvement in Vietnam, popular culture's nuclear anxieties of the 1950s and early 1960s were resurrected in the late 1970s and through the years of the Reagan administration after the distractions of Vietnam and widespread social unrest receded.[70]

America's renewed interest in the nuclear threat was prompted by a series of developments on the world stage. India's detonation of an atomic bomb in 1974 was the initial incident that revived concerns about nuclear war, but other events followed. The Soviet invasion of Afghanistan in 1979 (which caused the United States to withdraw from the SALT II treaty), along with NATO's proposed deployment of limited-range, nuclear-equipped missiles in Western Europe, also triggered growing awareness of the possibility of a nuclear conflict.[71] Although CUT had always strived to maintain its ideological separation from the larger culture, the resurgence of nuclear worries in America resonated with the atmosphere of crisis thought already prevalent in the organization. Society's thinking on the nuclear issue, in this sense, helped intensify CUT's dominant image of the apocalypse.

When in Montana, the group became increasingly convinced that the Soviet Union was planning a surprise nuclear attack on the United States. Perceiving in the Strategic Defense Initiative (SDI) a means to protect the country, CUT strongly supported the Reagan administration's high-tech missile defense program. In order to educate the membership about SDI and the seriousness of the Soviet nuclear threat, the church asked two defense policy experts, Gen. Daniel Graham and Dr. Dmitry Mikheyev, to address a ranch audience at the 1987 summer conference. Graham, a former deputy director of the CIA and founder of High Frontier (a pro-SDI lobby), and Mikheyev, a physicist with expertise in Soviet military planning, offered a grave assessment of America's future in the absence of a space-based missile defense system.[72] CUT's advocacy of SDI was driven, however, by its own concerns about an imminent nuclear exchange and not due to any particular support for the Reagan administration. In a lengthy issue of *Pearls of Wisdom* devoted entirely to the topic of strategic defense, Prophet pointed out that "an International Capitalist/Communist Conspiracy of the power elite," which included Reagan, was responsible for the unsafe condition of the world.[73] Prophet believed these conspirators had evolved from the Fallen Ones and that Western elites in high-level finance and statecraft had secretly fostered the technological and economic development of the Soviet Union. Thought to have been originally hatched during the 1917 Russian Revolution, this strategy was reported by Prophet to have been designed by international capitalists who sought the realization of a one-world-government, New World Order.[74]

The subcurrents of conspiratorial thought relating to elite-led plots to control the world gained force in CUT after its move to Montana, but the roots of this thinking extended well into the group's past. Following a practice Mark Prophet established, outside speakers were paid to come to the organization's headquarters and inform church audiences about subjects deemed to be of special importance. One of the first such visits to the church in this capacity was made in 1973 by Archibald Roberts, a retired Army colonel who had written several books about the decline of American sovereignty and the international elite's plan to construct a one-world corporate state.[75] Roberts's theories were appealing to conspiracists who believed that a coterie of powerful capitalists secretly sought to overthrow the U.S. Constitution and establish a stateless, global society. Mark Prophet, who was reportedly impressed with Roberts's "research,"[76] extended an invitation to the writer to speak on the subject of the United Nations' threat to American power at the group's Colorado Springs headquarters.[77]

From the time that Elizabeth Clare Prophet assumed leadership of the church until the move to Montana, CUT continued to adhere to the belief in a power-elite conspiracy aimed at achieving global dominion. Both the level of intensification and the sophistication of this idea were enhanced after the group left Camelot. Seeking expert confirmation of her own international capitalist/communist theory, Prophet hosted conspiracy researcher Antony Sutton as a guest speaker at a special "Summit University Forum" held during the 1987 annual summer conference. Sutton, a one-time researcher at Stanford's Hoover Institute, had written prolifically on topics including Soviet technological espionage, world corporate elites, and the mysterious secret societies he believed were controlling global politics and international commerce.[78] In his talk, Sutton corroborated the general framework of the power-elite conspiracy, which had circulated in a roughly similar form since the Populist era of the 1890s,[79] but he offered an analysis of the elites' "secret plan" that presented the membership with a new version of history and a frightening glimpse of the future.

In Sutton's view, capitalist power brokers seeking to create a global super-state had secretly funded the Bolsheviks, as well as other revolutionary forces throughout the twentieth century. Sutton supported his claim by looking to the ultimate motivations of Western society's (and particularly America's) business establishment. Believing the strategy of "Rockefeller, Morgan, and the Wall Street interests" to have been driven by the desire to achieve a "one-world order synthesis," Sutton argued that Western elites employed a plan of "managed conflict" to bring about international change favorable to this group of establishment insiders. Sutton's theory was steeped in conspiratorial Hegelianism. Since the synthesis of an elite-led, corporatist world society was the objective, a strategy of conflict between opposing forces was first necessary to produce a new outcome.[80] According to Sutton, the power elite collaborated with the Marxists, and later the Nazis, in order to promote a dialectical shift in world order. Western elites, whom he believed had based their strategy on Hegelian logic, strategized that promoting the clash of ideological foes would help bring about the eventual realization of "the State as God" to which common people would be completely subservient.[81]

Sutton's account of the West's internationalist establishment differed from CUT's theologically driven perception of the power elite over matters relating to the origin of this group of capitalist power brokers. But there were enough parallels concerning the alleged motivations and strategy of the elites that more commonalities than differences were apparent. Clearly, Sutton looked mainly to the economic character of the establishment's plans, while Mark and Elizabeth Clare Prophet saw societal elites connected directly to ultimate evil. But both conceptions pointed to the arrival of an elite-led, one-world government. Sutton's theory also approximated that of the church in other areas. Appealing to the group's penchant for intrigue and secret, alternative explanations for historical events, Sutton's attribution of nearly total global power to a few establishment secret societies, particularly Yale's Skull and Bones Club, fascinated

Prophet and the membership.[82] Sutton maintained that "Bonesmen," many of
whom became the ruling elite's politicians, businessmen, and financiers, controlled the shape of world society and intended to do away with state sovereignty in their bid for global domination.[83]

Sutton, like the Prophets, believed that the power elites financed war and
revolution for their own gain. However, he thought that the internationalists
may have made a fatal mistake by having provided the Soviets with advanced
technology and scientific information. In his analysis, Western elites misunderstood the military applications of their assistance. This blunder, he argued, resulted in the Soviet Union's development of nuclear capability and its advanced
research into high-technology weapons. Among these were "weather modifica-
tion systems and psychotronic warfare devices."[84] Sutton claimed the Soviets
probably used one or both to destroy the space shuttle Challenger in spring
1986. The mention of such obscure and futuristic scientific technology was not
new for CUT's membership. As early as 1980, Prophet had written in some detail about totalitarian forces' use of mass behavior control as a tool to construct
the model "new man" required in the future era of one-world government.[85]
But Sutton's ideas about the specific use of such technology went further. As he
viewed it, the West was headed for "a showdown" with the Soviet Union between 2000 and 2010. The proposed scenario for this near-term clash included
the use of behavioral control warfare against U.S. leaders to make them more
compliant to a Soviet demand for America's total surrender.[86]

Sutton and Prophet were of like mind on many issues, but none more so
than in their distrust of the American political class. For each, the right/left political dichotomy had become little more than a ruse the establishment used to
conceal from the American people the power elite's international character and
its ultimate goals.[87] For Prophet, the conspiracy ran deep. Long before the
group's move to Paradise Valley, she informed the membership that the
Nephilim, through their ownership of "the banking houses," controlled all aspects of world politics.[88]

The belief in an antidemocratic conspiracy of power-hungry internationalists is hardly a novel concept. In its most comprehensive right-wing form, the
idea can be traced to the British writer Nesta Webster who advanced the semi-
nal version of the far right's New World Order thesis in her 1924 book *Secret Societies and Subversive Movements*. Webster, whose elaborate theory has
undergone mutation in rightist circles since its original formulation, claimed
that various Jewish-controlled secret societies throughout history worked to

destroy Western civilization. These clandestine associations, according to Webster, adhered to esoteric beliefs that were enmeshed with an ambitious and revolutionary political philosophy.[89] While the seeds of this seditious doctrine were thought to have originated in groups deriving from the ancient occult tradition (particularly the early Gnostics), Webster felt that its modern roots extended from the internationalist philosophy of Illuminism. Believing that the Illuminati's goals of world revolution and the creation of a "dead and heartless" socialist civilization were passed on to later initiates, Webster called for the mass mobilization of a "great national movement" to combat the internationalists' scheme for global dominance.[90] Underlying Webster's presentation of the elite-led plan for a New World Order was the threat of socialist government, which the conspirators would impose on a worldwide basis. At a primitive level, Webster's theory tapped into the conspiracism pervading the mind-set of the far right, most elements of which adhered to some variation of the "internationalist threat" doctrine.[91]

CUT's eclectic belief system, of course, was not genetically linked to the secular antisocialism of the far right. Nonetheless, aspects of these theories had trickled into the group's cosmology. One member living at the Royal Teton Ranch credited Mark Prophet with understanding the nature of "the socialist strategy" and organizing his church "to do something about it." This member, who had been with the movement since the mid-1960s, believed the global power elite was advancing schemes that would rob individuals of their personal freedoms and, eventually, create a "global tyranny of socialism." In this subject's view, "this cadre operates in secrecy." He considered the power elite in world society to be "absolutely evil" and began as early as the 1950s to read everything he could about them.[92]

AIDS and the Alien Foe

CUT's concerns about a Soviet nuclear strike continued to build after the group arrived in Montana, but other impressions of a future disaster also filtered into the organization's worldview. Antony Sutton's appearance at the ranch reflected the community's sharpening suspicions of the power elite's plans for world government and reinforced fears that a nuclear war was soon to occur. These convictions had been a central part of the organization's outlook since the 1970s. However, as apocalyptic expectations grew, the conspiratorialism emanating from the group began to resonate in novel ways. Deviating somewhat from the right-wing-inspired views that had circulated in the movement, new images of societal chaos began to germinate.

At the July 1988 summer conference, Elizabeth Clare Prophet presided over a two-day panel discussion with authorities in the fields of AIDS research and extraterrestrial investigations. Prophet's decision to concentrate upon these particular topics signified a visible shift in the formerly right-wing political character of CUT's conspiratorial beliefs. Whereas the Soviet Union and the international power elite were the standard concerns of post-World War II groups on the American far right,[93] beliefs about extraterrestrials have nonspecific political moorings and the AIDS epidemic attracted the attention of conspiracists on the left.

The AIDS virus, which the medical community had discovered in 1981, was perceived by Prophet as a "genetic threat" to the continued spiritual evolution of the Lightbearers. As early as March 1986, Prophet had conveyed to the members the views of the Ascended Masters on the dangers the AIDS epidemic posed. In a March 1986 statement attributed to the Archangel Michael, the disease's far-reaching, negative consequences for "the true genes of the Lightbearers" were stressed. Blaming the spread of the plague on agents of darkness who knowingly passed on the virus, the Archangel's message was a warning. If the forces of righteousness upon the earth did not put a stop to the disease by curtailing the activities of known AIDS carriers, the gene pool of God's progeny would be damaged to such an extent that the evolution toward "a golden age race" would be rendered impossible.[94]

By interweaving group theological teachings with fears about a growing medical crisis, the church came to see AIDS as part of the apocalyptic scenario that was playing out on the world stage. Strangely, though, this particular symbol of the apocalypse did not emerge from the same reservoir of right-wing ideas that had previously determined the organization's position on sociopolitical matters. The increasing awareness of the worldwide AIDS epidemic was largely due to the efforts of the homosexual community (the highest risk population) and the political left.[95] It was from these ranks that various conspiracy theories emerged concerning the origins of the virus. Historically, the church had equated the left with decadence, moral failing, and anti-Americanism. Thus it was surprising that the left's most feverish conspiratorial explanations for the epidemic were well received at the Royal Teton Ranch.

At the church's 1988 summer conference, the dark truths behind the AIDS conspiracy were addressed by Prophet and members of an expert panel who were invited to the ranch to discuss their theories. The panel participants, two medical doctors and a journalist, shared the belief that AIDS was man-made and that "the scientific establishment" had a vested interest in the further spread of the disease. According to one of the physicians, Dr. Alan Cantwell, the origins of AIDS lay in the government-funded medical community's secret experiments in biological warfare on portions of the world population. Cantwell, a dermatologist who turned to fringe medicine and political activism late in his career,[96] maintained that homosexuals were deliberately targeted for this testing because of their status as a "hated minority." Concurring with Cantwell, Dr. Robert Strecker (a gastroenterologist) claimed that the epidemic originated in U.S. medical labs and that the scientific establishment had actively pursued the creation of the virus as early as 1971.[97]

While the physicians on the panel concentrated mainly on a clinical discussion of the disease, Jon Rapoport, an investigative reporter specializing in political issues, turned attention to the government-policy-related consequences of AIDS. In Rapoport's view, the virus was developed with the support of foreign governments to help promote an atmosphere of global panic, which in turn would justify the use of policies designed to place society under the rule of a world elite. For Rapoport, who believed that the public's fear of AIDS would lead it to relinquish civil liberties, deliberate government fear mongering about the spread of the virus expedited the arrival of a global fascist state in which individual freedoms were curtailed.[98] Prophet, like the attending audience, clearly agreed with the speakers' assertions about government collusion with science in the manufacture of AIDS and, in particular, with Rapoport's theory that the disease was a tool internationalists used to gain world power.[99] That the left-leaning Rapoport saw the impending threat as a fascist world order, while the church envisaged a socialist form of international rule, was of little importance to Prophet's movement by this point. The certainty of a forthcoming cataclysm had so thoroughly permeated CUT at this stage of the organization's development that even a conspiracy theory of the left merited serious attention. CUT's unusual flirtation with left-wing antigovernment beliefs pointed to the start of a strange conspiratorial "fusionism"[100] that began to surface in CUT's collective psychology.

All variations of socialism had traditionally been scorned by the organization, although it was the looming prospect of an elite-led global superstate that deviated most from CUT's populist philosophy.[101] As the statements of the guest speakers demonstrated, suspicions about the arrival of one-world government were not always couched in traditionally rightist terms. The belief in a sweeping New World Order conspiracy served as a common ground between the extreme poles of right and left and fused together the otherwise disparate views separating the two ideological camps. In fact, this connection was logical given the antielitist tendencies inherent in each fringe bloc. The far left's antiestablishment proclivities shared with the far right similar beliefs regarding the corruption of government and communicated the sense that ordinary people had become marginalized by the prevailing elite-dominated international system.

With anxieties about a near-term crisis already brewing in the church, news of the growing AIDS epidemic helped support the membership's conviction of a global disaster. Furthermore, the perception that the disease was part of the power elite's bid for a world takeover reaffirmed for the group its notion that a total conspiracy involving government, corporations, and the scientific community had been undertaken against the powerless in society. In this way, AIDS fit neatly as an apocalyptic metaphor into CUT's pessimistic view of the future.

The AIDS plague was not the only symptom of crisis that the ranch community recognized in the months prior to the construction of its multiacre underground shelter site near Mol Herron Creek. Featured along with the AIDS symposium at the 1988 summer conference was another panel that dealt with a topic more familiar to the membership. At the request of the church, experts in the field of UFO research arrived at the Royal Teton Ranch to enlighten conference attendees about alien visitors and the alleged attempts of the U.S. government to conceal their existence from the public. The guests included some of the leading authorities in this unusual field of study. Participating in the forum were Dr. Stanton Friedman, a nuclear physicist and well-known UFOlogist, Linda Moulton-Howe, a UFO researcher and television producer, Dr. Bruce Maccabee, a nuclear engineer and chairman of the Fund for UFO Research, and Budd Hopkins, an author on the UFO abduction phenomenon.[102] The expert forum, which was titled "The UFO Connection: Alien Spacecraft and Government Secrecy," was a dramatic event. Appealing to the group's enduring interest in science fiction themes, the guests' observations concerning space alien visits to Earth tapped into a current of CUT's cosmology that had roots in the beliefs of its forebears.

Social movements in the Theosophical tradition, particularly the I AM group, have often exhibited a strong level of interest in extraterrestrial motifs owing largely to their belief in the existence of cosmic beings thought to control the evolution of the universe.[103] As a new religious movement descending from this lineage, CUT's interest in the subject followed in the wake of its predecessors. However, the church did not embrace the cheery portrayal of alien beings as "space brothers," which not only characterized the outlook of its Theosophical ancestors but also represented the prevailing views of American UFO writers throughout the 1950s and 1960s.[104] Mark Prophet's warning about evil extraterrestrials in *The Soulless Ones* was the organization's first, and most comprehensive, statement on the subject, but it was followed in later years by specific mention of alien-related themes in group literature and decrees.[105]

Attuned to church teachings about extraterrestrials that emphasized the dangers they posed to the planet, the membership was well primed for the outside authorities' ideas about the UFO phenomenon. The panelists delved into different aspects of UFO research, but what was most significant was the thinly veiled antigovernment sentiment in the discussion. Stanton Friedman, who called the American government's attempt to keep the matter secret "a cosmic Watergate," maintained that the public had been kept "in the dark" about UFOs since 1947, when the U.S. Army was alleged to have recovered and then hidden a spaceship and several aliens near Roswell, New Mexico.

In Friedman's estimation, the government kept knowledge about alien life secret for two reasons. First, it was likely that the sudden release of such information could spark widespread panic in the general population. According to Friedman, top-level members of the U.S. intelligence community were concerned about this scenario and the social turmoil that such a revelation would engender. Second, the government was thought to be studying the alien technology it acquired in order to capitalize upon its military potential. Believing that the government wanted to keep its findings a secret from other countries, particularly the Soviet Union, Friedman conjectured that the safest policy was simply to deny the existence of extraterrestrials.[106]

Friedman's theories actually represented a "mainstream" position in the UFO subculture. Dating from the late 1940s, when stories about UFOs first began to attract public attention, those believing in "flying disks" tended to suspect government involvement in the phenomenon.[107] By the 1980s, though, believers had become far more convinced of the government's role in UFO activity. A growing body of UFO literature disputed official government accounts of the Roswell incident and other alleged encounters with spacecraft thought to be of alien origin.[108]

For UFO researcher Linda Moulton-Howe, who electrified the church audience with her bizarre tale of extraterrestrials conducting genetic experiments on humans, the government was involved in a more sinister strategy than that Friedman reported. According to Moulton-Howe, who had produced Home Box Office (HBO) television documentaries on UFOs in the early 1980s, the government had been negotiating with one "race" of aliens (the so-called grays) in order to acquire their technology.[109] Claiming that she had been shown confidential documents outlining the negotiation, Moulton-Howe indicated that the government offered the space visitors access to certain underground bases in the United States. At these hidden facilities, the extraterrestrials were to be permitted to engage in genetic research that involved the "harvesting" of both animals and humans. It was believed that this work was necessary since the aliens with whom the government was secretly negotiating were on the verge of biological extinction and needed DNA structurally similar to their own for experimental purposes.[110]

If the panelists made one point clear, it was that the government was lying to the public about UFOs. The theories of the other panelists fell somewhere in between Friedman's relatively mild explanation of a cover-up and Moulton-Howe's extreme account of subterranean aliens. Not surprisingly, perhaps, Prophet's position on the alien issue aligned most closely with that of Moulton-Howe. Pointing out that her church had never accepted the popular myth that extraterrestrials were benevolent beings, Prophet told the panelists that humanity needed to defend itself against their negative spiritual energy.[111] Like Moulton-Howe, Prophet speculated that the government had provided extraterrestrials with underground bases on American soil, one of which she said was located near Dulce, New Mexico. Based on an unnamed report she claimed to have seen, Prophet indicated that the space visitors' experiments were aimed at creating hybrid life forms and that the government was facilitating the project. Such collusion between the government and the aliens, she suggested, indicated the lengths to which American leaders had sold out to the forces of evil.[112]

The Monument to Armageddon

CUT's 1988 summer conference was, in many respects, the conduit for disaster-focused ideas that were building up to climactic levels on the ranch and at Glastonbury. The featured panels on AIDS and UFOs helped hone the catastrophic millennial beliefs that, by this time, had reached a zenith within the group. Yet despite the considerable array of potential dangers the church fore-saw in the future, the most immediate threat remained the scenario of nuclear war. Prophet firmly believed that Moscow had tricked the West into believing that the communist enemy wished to end the Cold War and reform its failing economic system. Even as Gorbachev's transformation of the Marxist state re-sulted in unprecedented changes both within the country and in its foreign re-lations, the church maintained that the Soviet policy of *glasnost* was a propaganda sham.[113] For Prophet, who would later address in her 1991 book *The Astrology of the Four Horsemen* the reasons she expected a Soviet nuclear strike, the signs pointing to the coming cataclysm were irrefutable. Her convic-tions, she claimed, were largely based on Saint Germain's past warnings of an atomic Armageddon, but also on the word of experts who were said to be fa-miliar with Soviet nuclear strategy.[114]

By late November 1988, following an extensive design and planning pe-riod, the community was well underway on its construction of the Mol Herron shelter. Referred to as "Mark's Ark" by the staff in tribute to the late Mark Prophet, the H-shaped underground shelter was designed to provide security for up to 750 ranch residents both during the anticipated nuclear war and for several years afterward. The steel-reinforced facility, which cost in excess of $3 million to build, was divided into sections that included a dormitory, a com-munal kitchen, a shower and laundry area, and an emergency medical station. Less spacious parts of the shelter were reserved for food and weapons storage, a community school, fuel-operated generators, and a chapel.[115]

Work on CUT's underground "town" started in secret. Only months later would local Montanans find out about the project being built at a mountain-side meadow on a remote section of the ranch staff members called "the Heart." Since it was situated about five miles away from Highway 89, the road running adjacent to a lengthy strip of the ranch, the shelter was shielded from the view of outsiders. A similar construction effort began at the same time at CUT's nearby Glastonbury property, the subdivision located approximately fifteen miles north of the Royal Teton Ranch near the tiny hamlet of Emigrant. Here, four hundred church members choosing to live off the ranch pooled their re-sources to build smaller fallout shelters that ranged from relatively crude fam-ily-sized structures to a one-hundred-person facility modeled on the design of the ranch's shelter. In an effort to save fellow believers from the disaster, many of the approximately forty-five shelters constructed in Glastonbury had spaces reserved for those residing some distance away.[116]

The group's Mol Herron shelter was completed in early March 1990 after more than a year of intense labor. Although the building of the facility escaped public attention for some time, a startling piece of news in summer 1989 had alerted the local population to CUT's survival preparations. In the most damaging blow yet to the church's relations with its neighbors, two CUT members attracted national media coverage when they tried to purchase arms illegally as part of the defensive strategy to protect their religious community in the days following the nuclear strike. On July 7, 1989, the organization's "security chief," Vernon Hamilton, was arrested in Spokane, Washington, for trying to buy various types of semiautomatic weapons under a false name. Federal agents seized over $100,000 in weaponry in the raid on Hamilton, along with 120,000 rounds of ammunition and $26,000 in cash and gold, and they discovered plans in his possession to equip two hundred members of CUT with arms.[117] According to the seized documents, which a local newspaper (the *Livingston Enterprise*) obtained through a Freedom of Information Act request, Hamilton wanted to acquire the weapons in order to establish a perimeter defense for the area surrounding the ranch's shelter.[118]

Hamilton's efforts to obtain the weaponry set loose a wave of panic in the Yellowstone region. The equipment he sought to buy, including Barrett .50 caliber sniper rifles, AR-15 assault weapons, and an old armored personnel carrier, suggested to many area residents that CUT was preparing for an all-out war with outsiders. In an attempt to calm CUT's neighbors in Park County, Prophet met with locals in late July to address the controversial issue. Declaring that the weapons initiative was undertaken privately by a small group within the church, Prophet attempted to separate the organization from the allegedly unauthorized activities of private individuals. While she denied knowledge of the scheme and claimed that the church was not involved with the affair, uncomfortable questions arose in the media concerning the leader's role in the attempted arms purchase. The complicity of Prophet's fourth husband (Edward Francis, CUT's acting vice president) in the illegal operation convinced many locals that the plan to secretly amass an arsenal had the church leader's blessing.[119] Francis, who quickly admitted to his involvement in the plan after Hamilton's arrest, pleaded guilty to federal weapons charges in Spokane and received a short prison sentence for his part in organizing the operation.

Prophet's denial of any knowledge about her husband's plan to outfit the shelter's occupants with arms was viewed with skepticism by those pointing out that weapons and security concerns had been traditional themes in the

Aerial view of the Mol Herron shelter under construction at
the Royal Teton Ranch in 1989.
Courtesy of the *Billings Gazette.*

group's history. Evidence surfaced that CUT had considered storing guns for defensive purposes as far back as 1973. Confirming that some of the organization's leadership planned to amass a weapons stockpile, a confidential memorandum appearing in the local press indicated that a formerly high-ranking CUT member, Martin Lassiter, felt that the church needed to prepare itself "militarily" for future conflicts.[120] The *Livingston Enterprise* reported that Lassiter warned church leaders in 1973 that it might be necessary for the group to acquire an arsenal sufficient to dispel an armed attack by either "roving bands driven by hunger and fear" or by invading armies.[121] Coming from an individual once invested with a leadership position in the church, Lassiter's memorandum showed that "final conflict" scenarios had been a long-standing subject of discussion within the organization. Other reports from sources knowledgeable about CUT indicated that the group wanted a supply of weapons to defend its stockpiled food against outsiders in the post-nuclear-war era.[122]

In the weeks following the first revelations about the gun-buying plan, *Newsweek, Time, U.S. News and World Report, Macleans,* and a number of other national and international media sources offered profiles on "the Church with an arsenal."[123] These media reports tended to cast CUT as a "mind-control" group whose members had been stripped of their capacity to think independently. Thus, with the church already labeled as a "gun cult" in the initial media frenzy over the attempted arms purchase, CUT was portrayed in a way that confused its millennial fears with pathological behavior.

Evidence indicates that the church had considered at least two specific dates for the Soviet attack. The first of these is thought to have been October 2, 1989. Just prior to this day, according to a former CUT member, hundreds of the faithful living outside Montana streamed into Paradise Valley to get to the organization's property before the disaster took place.[124] While the October 2 prediction cannot be confirmed, news reports on the group's activities prior to this date suggest that the day had, at minimum, factored into CUT's apocalyptic timetable. According to a July 24, 1989, story in the *San Francisco Chronicle,* Prophet cited October 2 as the start of a period when nuclear war was likely to occur.[125] The church set a later date when October 2 passed uneventfully. This second prediction for the disaster fell on March 15, 1990. Although CUT did not acknowledge for several years that this day held particular importance for the group,[126] more recent pronouncements by organization leaders show that it was understood throughout the church that March 15 marked the start of the nuclear strike.[127] Some CUT critics claim that the group's declaration of a prayer vigil in the months leading up to March 15 was a ploy to divert public attention away from the millennial fear that had enveloped the movement. According to this argument, Prophet and her advisers devised using the prayer vigil story after the March 15 prediction did not come to pass in order to save face and to convince the media that CUT was not expecting a nuclear catastrophe.[128]

The church had, in fact, ordered the members on the ranch and at Glastonbury to report to the shelters for overnight stays on at least several evenings leading up to March 15. One participant in these preliminary mobilizations in the days before March 15 explained that she and others felt there was some possibility that the nuclear attack might arrive a day or two earlier than predicted. However, it was said throughout the church that the "karmic increase" taking place would reach its greatest peak on March 15.[129] Staff member Brenda Wilson recalled that the ranch community was in "a high stress mode" by the time the date for disaster approached. Wilson said staff worked in teams to prepare the Mol Herron shelter and its inhabitants for the nuclear war. One of these tasks involved transporting and processing the many tons of food needed to keep ranch residents alive after the destruction of world society. Remembering her own role in this operation, she described taking inventory of canned foodstuffs in stacks over twenty feet high that, along with hundreds of tons of wheat, were stocked in the shelter. Wilson said that CUT staff had to acquire their own supply of clothing and personal items to last for a period up to seven years, although it was understood that the group would not be underground for the entire time. Since space in the shelter was limited, as were the bank accounts of staff members, the ranch residents were forced to make hard decisions about what personal supplies they could take with them when they descended. Coins were considered to be especially important; survivors could use hard currency for barter after the nuclear holocaust.[130]

Wilson described the CUT ranch as a "ghost town" the winter before the expected event. Every other activity on the ranch had ceased by this point as virtually all the staff were assigned to some aspect of the shelter project. When she was reassigned to another work team at the shelter site, Wilson labored long hours in frigid conditions under spotlights brought in by project supervisors who tried to expedite the completion and provisioning of the structure. She recalled that as the March 15 date neared, armed guards in radiation suits were stationed at points around the shelter.[131]

When March 15 arrived, CUT members at Glastonbury and on the ranch

Occupant of a shelter in Glastonbury.
Courtesy of the *Billings Gazette.*

followed their instructions and reported to the shelters by early evening. After the date passed, organization officials referred to the exercise as a "surprise practice run," [132] but most of the group firmly believed that the long-expected Soviet missile strike was about to happen. A staff member who went through the experience in the crowded Mol Herron shelter related that "everyone who went into the shelter that night was scared to death," and told of fellow occupants engaging in all-night prayer sessions in the cavernous, dimly lit facility. [133] Such reports about the March 15 "drill" suggest that a panic-stricken mood had set in at the ranch. When the missiles did not arrive, this observer indicated that people emerged emotionally exhausted from the Mol Herron shelter. [134]

Prophet's ranch community applied all its energy to ensuring that the Mol Herron shelter was completed by March 15. [135] Local authorities also watched with interest as the project approached completion. When news of the March 15 prediction became public, officials from the Environmental Health Department stepped in. Inspectors had discovered during a visit to the massive structure a few weeks before CUT's mid-March mobilization that the shelter had no waste treatment system. After the group's emergence from the facility on

Aerial view of shelter construction project under way at Glastonbury in 1989.
Courtesy of the *Billings Gazette.*

March 16, church officials were informed that they had violated county codes and that legal action would follow if another underground exercise took place.[136]

The press continued to follow CUT during this stage of their history and reported that a steady flow of group members flocked to the ranch and Glastonbury during the late winter of 1990. The influx of CUT's membership into Paradise Valley was the focus of national media attention. Press accounts of the mobilization pointed to the new arrivals' fears of worsening earthly conditions but particularly emphasized CUT's concerns about an imminent nuclear war.[137] Media coverage tended to stress the desperate nature of the group's preparations for disaster. In growing numbers, stories circulated in early 1990 about CUT members closing out bank accounts, selling off belongings, and acquiring as much clothing and emergency medical supplies as they could afford.[138]

Bob Raney, a state senator from Park County, confirmed that the early months in 1990 were a time of panic for those belonging to the church. For Raney, who observed the sudden appearance of several thousand CUT new-

Aerial view of main headquarters on the
Royal Teton Ranch near the Yellowstone River.
Courtesy of the *Billings Gazette.*

Administrative building located on the Royal Teton Ranch.
Courtesy of the *Billings Gazette.*

comers in Paradise Valley, the scene was chaotic and potentially dangerous. Concerned that the "frantic behavior" he saw building within the movement might result in "a volatile situation," Raney appealed directly to Montana governor Stan Stephans "to do something" about the escalating apocalyptic fears on the Royal Teton Ranch.[139] Raney's greatest worry was that local law enforcement would not have the necessary manpower to intervene if constituents from his district undertook a posse-style operation against the church and forced their way onto the group's property. Indicating that the residents of Park County were confused and fearful about CUT's survivalist activities, Raney believed at the time that an armed conflict could have erupted between group members and outsiders. Raney was disappointed that the governor rejected his call to dispatch an emergency force of state police and National Guard troops to ease the mounting tensions on both sides. Reflecting upon the unsettling period, Raney pushed for "some form of public discourse to cool things down."[140] In his view, however, it was CUT that should have initiated this effort. According to Raney, the secretive nature of the church's plans, along with the July 1989 disclosure about the illegal gun-buying effort, contributed to the local population's uneasiness about the group.[141]

In the wake of the March 15 shelter incident, bizarre stories about CUT's "doomsday prediction" circulated throughout Paradise Valley. Anxious to cover an interesting episode, major media sources often relied upon locally generated rumors about the church as the foundation of their reports. The most persistent of the rumors had it that CUT members had energetically prayed for the nuclear destruction of the world and looked forward to an extended stay underground after the apocalypse. Variations of this story appeared in press accounts throughout the spring in 1990.[142] But while the membership had prepared itself for Armageddon, there is no evidence that the organization was engaged in its promotion. In contrast to the rumors that cast the group and its leader as atomic sociopaths, the movement sincerely wished to avert the crisis it had seen looming over humanity long before CUT's move to Montana. Throughout its history, CUT had urged its membership to give forceful decrees for the purpose of forestalling what would otherwise be a great "karmic reckoning" resulting in widespread death and destruction.[143]

In the end, the group's efforts to save the world from catastrophe were no match against the forces of Darkness. The relocation to Montana was to have offered the church a strategic position from which the elect could focus their spiritual energies to usher in a new golden age.[144] But following the move, CUT's perception of the world grew increasingly dim. As feelings about world corruption, conspiracies, and social chaos steadily infiltrated the group's outlook, the response was to prepare for the worst. The membership believed that the global environment had bottomed out by the end of the 1980s under the weight of accumulated karma. In accordance to divine precept, the faithful followed the admonition of Saint Germain and steeled themselves for the oncoming event. At this point, in the face of rapidly declining worldly conditions, CUT set out to protect its own.

5

The Apocalyptic Nonevent

Disillusioned CUT members fled Paradise Valley in droves after the nuclear disaster failed to happen. By some accounts, half of the three to four thousand CUT adherents who had come to Montana from 1986 until the time of the emergency call suddenly left the area once expectations for a massive Soviet strike dissipated. These included a sizeable portion of Prophet's ranch staff.[1] Many who left did so confused and angry. Most of the newcomers who came to Montana in late 1989 and early 1990 had left jobs, family, and friends to prepare for survival in the High Rockies. The costs associated with such plans were considerable for the largely middle-class membership in the organization. Having rented space or otherwise made shelter arrangements with other CUT followers, those not residing at the Royal Teton Ranch poured their money and energy into the underground safe havens.[2]

Believers who paid to reserve a place for themselves in the private fallout shelters in Glastonbury (at costs up to $7,500) quickly attempted to sell off their berths to interested buyers at bargain prices.[3] In many cases, those who had migrated to the area to be near the shelters had invested thousands or even tens of thousands of dollars in their construction. The money for reserved spots in the cluster of shelters on CUT's subdivision property was required in advance to finance the assembly of the underground structures and, thus, was often a financial burden. When the Soviet missile strike did not occur, CUT members who had come to the region preceding the envisaged cataclysm found it necessary to locate employment to support themselves and, in some cases, to pay off the debts they had incurred to get to Montana. Problems emerged for CUT's newcomers, though, when they tried to find jobs. Rural Park County offered few work opportunities for the late-arriving members and their dependents who had made the trek to Paradise Valley from a number of distant states and several foreign countries.[4]

Aside from financial considerations, other pressures also weighed on the membership after the nonapocalypse. The stress associated with psychologically preparing for the disaster caused at least part of the group to reconsider ties with the church. While the organization cited its members' economic problems as the explanation for the sudden exodus, some of those looking for safety in Paradise Valley returned to their homes because of a loss of confidence in the Messenger.[5]

The tense months of waiting for the missile attack imposed enormous stress on members of the CUT community, but for those who left secure jobs and close personal attachments to make it to Montana, the strains were especially great. Unlike CUT's devoted followers who served on the Royal Teton Ranch, the newcomers tended to have a greater investment in the outside world than the group's most committed core followers. For these members, whose connection to the organization was at a less totalistic level, the Messenger's sudden call for the flight to Montana uprooted them from the normal routines of life.[6]

Even those who did not report to Paradise Valley to weather the expected catastrophe felt compelled to respond to the Messenger's warnings. In some areas, CUT members assembled their own underground shelters and stocked them with supplies in preparation for the attack. One such endeavor was undertaken by group members residing near Cranbrook, British Columbia, an isolated town of fifteen thousand, approximately 250 miles southwest of Calgary. Built to provide a contingent of Prophet's Canadian followers with security during and after the nuclear war, the shelter was situated on a privately owned ranch. The subterranean safe haven was built furtively at a secret site in order to protect against marauders in the period of anarchy expected to follow the nuclear strike.[7]

Believers who lacked the financial resources to make the trip to Paradise Valley exercised other options. Responding to the church's admonitions about a coming nuclear attack on the United States, some members acquired a supply of survival food and emergency equipment for their homes. Among the items considered indispensable was survival literature that would provide members with reference resources needed to deal with life-threatening contingencies after the nuclear war.[8]

Aboveground entrance to shelter located near Cranbrook, British Columbia.
Courtesy of the *Calgary Herald*.

Unfulfilled Expectations and Cognitive Dissonance

CUT's mobilization for the apocalypse triggered the ridicule of the local community when the calamity failed to occur. In the aftermath of the group's survivalist efforts, local residents derided "the doomsdayers" and their spiritual leader. Some inhabitants of the region reported that Prophet's disaster predictions had been heard before and that the church's apocalyptic warnings were received as bizarre jokes. By mid-1990, several months after the group's preparations for the catastrophe had subsided, "end of the world" parties were routinely held in Paradise Valley by Park County residents ready to mock Prophet and her followers.[9] Despite the surrounding community's harsh response, CUT was not seriously damaged by either negative public attention or by a loss of credibility in the eyes of some of its adherents. For the majority of the membership, the experience did not cause them to give up their beliefs. That most of the group's members retained their faith following a sudden disconfirmation of the predicted disaster requires special consideration.

An examination of CUT's worldview in the years leading up to the shelter period reveals that nuclear war was considered as more than a mere possibility. From 1986 onward, the nuclear threat had become incorporated into the church's doctrine. Believing that the devolution of humankind's karma had placed society on the brink of disaster, the organization made decisions about how to prepare for the cataclysm and its aftermath that disclosed its total investment in the realization of the event. The community's conviction that the disaster would occur sparked desperate measures. On the ranch, select staff members armed the Mol Herron shelter with 50 AR-15 assault rifles (along with 110 other guns) to protect the group from dangerous outsiders after the missile attack.[10] But the clearest evidence that the church was responding to a perceived apocalyptic certainty can be seen in the actions of those members who flocked to Paradise Valley at the Messenger's behest in late 1989 and early 1990. In particular, the sustained labor required to prepare the Mol Herron shelter made clear the community's panicked belief in the Messenger's prophecy. Indeed, as one CUT senior staff member said several years after the episode, "We worked long, hard sixteen-hour days to get it ready in time. It was mind-numbing work, but we knew it had to be completed."[11]

Denying that she had ever firmly predicted a nuclear holocaust, Prophet told the media after the incident that she felt there was only a "good potential" for such a disaster. In an attempt to justify the group's shelter construction program to the press, Prophet minimized its importance and referred to the structures as being "just an insurance policy."[12] Yet the heightened degree of fear-driven activity in the previous months, both on the ranch and at Glastonbury, undermined Prophet's public effort at downplaying the incident.

The relative resilience of the membership's beliefs in the wake of a major disconfirmation forces us to consider why there were not more defections from the group. In their classic study of unfulfilled prophetic belief, *When Prophecy Fails* (1956), Leon Festinger, Henry Riecken, and Stanley Schacter examined the effects of cognitive dissonance on a flying saucer cult that made failed millennial predictions for catastrophe. The group under study was led by Marian Keech, a middle-aged student of esoteric philosophy who claimed to have had spiritual contact with an extraterrestrial being. According to Keech, the alien life-form told her that a vast flood would submerge much of the North American continent on December 21, 1954. When the predicted event did not happen, Keech and her small circle of believers never relinquished their conviction in the correctness of the prophecy. Instead they rationalized why the catastrophe had failed to come about and continued to devote their energies to spreading the group's doctrine.[13]

The Festinger study used the Keech group as a case analysis to highlight some interesting aspects of the failed predictions response. Viewing cognitive dissonance as unrelated or ill-fitting components of a belief structure that causes discomfort to the adherent, Festinger, Riecken, and Schacter ascertained that constructs will arise to blunt its damaging effects. In order to mitigate the dissonance associated with unrealized expectations, the believer may exercise a range of options. The first is to discard the ideology from which the failed prediction emanated and return to a more normalized routine. As the Festinger study noted, however, it is unrealistic to assume that the group's disavowal of its belief system will always follow the disconfirmation. This extreme reaction to unrealized expectations involves the total rejection of a guiding philosophy to which members tend to adhere with an extraordinary degree of commitment.[14] Short of relinquishing the belief to eliminate dissonance, an option exists for the group to simply deny that the prediction was not realized. But this strategy also presents problems for the dissonance-mitigating efforts of the group. The act of ignoring an established fact presupposes the group's absolute detachment from reality, which exceeds the cognitive parameters within which psychologically healthy individuals function.[15]

Nonetheless, there may be ways of decreasing the dissonance associated with failed predictions that do not necessitate either the group's rejection of its belief structure or require that clear realities be ignored. Based upon their findings with the Keech group, the researchers observed that rationalizations aimed at explaining why the event did not occur can serve to reduce dissonance. These explanations, which may assume elaborate forms, need to be undertaken with the support of fellow believers in order that the group might recover from the strains it experienced following the nonevent. But despite the attempt to explain away the failed prophecy, rationalizations alone may not be enough to ward off the dissonant experience. As was the case with the Keech group, those having already seen the prophetic failure (no matter how it is rationalized) are forced to come to grips with the unpleasant fact that their preparations were unnecessary.[16] According to the Festinger study, rationalizations for the disconfirmation can effectively eliminate group dissonance only when coupled with increased efforts at proselytizing. By spreading its beliefs to the larger society, the group engages in a strategy of self-confirmation. Through the act of convincing outsiders of the correctness of its beliefs, an act that involves recruiting new converts, the group gains reassurances about the "truth" of its belief system and, thus, reduces the dissonance to manageable levels.[17]

The Festinger study rests upon the assumption that unconventional beliefs are inherently fragile. It may be, however, that groups having gone through the experience of failed predictions are less susceptible to damaging consequences than social scientists have believed. Such would seem to be the case with CUT after its preparation for an imminent nuclear war. In the aftermath of the unrealized catastrophe, the church embarked upon a two-track response to the unanticipated return of life as usual. At a public level, the organization claimed that the early months of 1990 represented only a "possible time" for a nuclear attack.[18] While hardly able to deny its desperate preparations for the expected disaster, CUT's claim that its survivalist exercises were taken as a precautionary measure gave the impression that the group never believed that the apocalypse was a certainty.[19] Interestingly, though, CUT dealt with the nonevent in a different manner within its own ranks.

In an important address given on the ranch on November 28, 1991, Prophet discussed the significance of the group's preparations for nuclear war in the previous year and cautioned the members that the prophecy for disaster remained in effect through the year 2002.[20] Prophet's lecture incorporated an analysis of the twentieth-century prophecies of the Virgin Mary, who in Catholic apocalypticism has been attributed with delivering warnings of disaster if humankind did not repent of evil.[21] The best-known of the prophecies in Catholic apocalyptic lore are the messages believed to have been communicated by the Virgin to three children at Fatima, Portugal, in 1917. The Virgin was said to have given the children a three-part prophecy foretelling of a grim future. Two of the three "secrets of Fatima" had long since been revealed by the witnesses to the Marian apparition and involved a warning for humanity to cease its offenses against God, followed by the prophesied outbreak of World War II and the Virgin's directive for the consecration of Russia. But at the time of Prophet's address, the final message from the Virgin remained a mystery since the Catholic Church refused to release it to the public.[22]

Using the then still-mysterious third secret of Fatima as a justification for her community's survivalist initiative, CUT's Messenger warned that the undisclosed prophecy stated that "Satan will infiltrate government and the churches" and that those aligned with the forces of Darkness will provoke a future catastrophe.[23] She stressed that the church would continue to accept this foreboding image of the future and told the members that their shelter construction efforts must be expanded. In her justification of the group's civil defense project, Prophet made it clear that the organization had relocated "to the wilderness of Montana" to prepare for the apocalypse and to survive in order to pass on its teachings to posterity. Most importantly, however, the Messenger informed her ranch staff audience that its prayers and preparedness during the last year had been the reason for the prevention of nuclear war.[24]

Prophet's November 1991 address was only one of several occasions when CUT's leader indicated that the group's emergency mobilization helped avert the disaster. A September 1993 *Pearls of Wisdom* said that the group's very act of preparing the shelters had forestalled a calamity. To further substantiate this claim, Prophet detailed the account of a tense international incident that took place at approximately the same time that CUT was readying itself for nuclear war. The Messenger pointed out that the Bush administration dispatched high-ranking officials to help resolve a potentially volatile territorial squabble between India and Pakistan in spring 1990.[25] The incident did not gain attention until after it was resolved, but Prophet, who credited the Ascended Masters with foreknowledge of the affair, used the episode as a validation of CUT's shelter-building program.[26] Although Prophet said she had no prior knowledge of the potential nuclear confrontation, she knew from the Ascended Master El Morya's prophecy that the world "was at the brink of nuclear war" at this time.[27]

These examples of the church's private reactions to the failed prediction clearly display the rationalization response Festinger discussed. By informing the membership that their diligence had forestalled the disaster, the dissonance that otherwise would have accompanied the nonmaterialization of the catastrophe was mitigated. Furthermore, Prophet's attempts to establish that the group's mobilization period had been a particularly dangerous time substantiates Festinger's observation that the apocalyptic group will seek to find reassurances in the correctness of its beliefs after the unrealized prediction. However, there appeared to be no attempt on CUT's part following the disconfirmation to actively proselytize or even to justify the correctness of its beliefs to society. Unlike the actions of the Keech group, CUT did not immediately attempt to persuade others outside its ranks that its course of action was necessary and justified. In fact, as is demonstrated by church literature produced after the disconfirmed prophecy as well as by Prophet's interviews with the press, the group's attempts at outreach were limited to arguing that the media had mischaracterized the organization's preparations for disaster as a firm prediction.[28] As will be discussed in the following chapter, CUT would later attempt to "go public" with its teachings, but in these cases (which occurred in 1993 and 1996 respectively) the purposes for public outreach had little to do with alleviating any cognitive dissonance attached to the disconfirmation.

Contrary to Festinger's findings, it would seem that the church's rationalizations about the failed prediction were sufficient to counteract a sudden and dramatic loss of faith for most group members. CUT's avoidance of aggressive proselytizing following the disconfirmation suggests that its beliefs were resilient enough to largely maintain the commitment of the membership without requiring the further step of active ideology promotion by the believing community. The church's reactions to unfulfilled prophecy may have implications for understanding other collectivities that adhere to unconventional beliefs. While it is commonly assumed that dissonance-reducing strategies (especially proselytizing) are necessary to alleviate the effects of disconfirmed events, clear evidence of the unrealized prediction may not be uniformly acknowledged by members in all apocalyptic groups.[29] Depending upon the level of conviction adherents express, the reaction to a failed event may be characterized by the resort to varying strategies, not all of which necessitate an effort at "public enlightenment." Through rehabilitating its belief system with rationalizations made within the organization, the church demonstrated that its worldview could withstand the pressures of disconfirmation without employing other strategies. The durable nature of such convictions might also alert scholars against setting artificial standards for gauging the "predictable" response to falsified ideas within a countercultural movement.[30]

Apocalypticism and Violence

While the local population in Paradise Valley nervously observed CUT's rushed preparations for the apocalypse, the organization was preoccupied with its own timetable for the disaster. But despite the potentially explosive mixture of catastrophic visions and guns, at no time did church members on the ranch or at Glastonbury assemble as an armed contingent looking to do battle with outsiders. Prophet's adherents understood that the cataclysm would bring about a period in which defensive combat against enemies would be likely; however, this course of action was seen purely as a matter of group survival in the difficult times that would follow the nuclear war.[31]

CUT's nonviolent actions throughout the mobilization reflect what is actually a typical response among new religious movements functioning under millennial stress. The relatively few cases where violence has been present in incidents of millennial excitement stand as the rare exception, not the rule. As the record of their actions indicates, millennialists of all varieties, including highly encapsulated ones, have overwhelmingly tended to observe peaceable practices even during times of heightened agitation. Inaccurate stereotypes perpetuated by media and anticultists have, unfortunately, cast millennial movements as inherently violence-prone and threatening to the public order.[32] In order to distinguish between CUT's nonviolent brush with the apocalypse and cases where violence erupted, it is important to consider factors relevant to the group psychology of millennial movements. Most notably, group-specific constructions of "enemy" imagery have contributed in some cases to fostering environmental conditions conducive to violence.

In the examples of Jonestown and the Aum Shinrikyo Supreme Truth sect, the groups came to envision themselves as chosen communities of the elect under siege by enemies conspiring to destroy them. In these paradigmatic cases of millennial communities whose apocalyptic visions and conspiratorialism led first to their separation from the outside world, and ultimately to violence against perceived enemies, each held society-rejecting images of the environing world that had violent implications for the group's existence. It bears repeating, of course, that we are discussing infrequent examples of collectivities that (under "ideal" conditions) created an alternative social system to the larger culture.

In the minority subset of violence-prone apocalyptic movements, there are several traits that tend to characterize both the group's social structure and the process whereby it interprets the world outside the community's boundaries. Such traits include a charismatic/authoritarian leadership framework in the group, the community's effort to establish a rigid ideological boundary separating insider from outsider, an attempt to break off communications between the group and the larger culture, and a generalized atmosphere of extreme skepticism or fear that pervades the group's outlook on outsiders and results in the community's defensive posture.[33]

Both Aum Shinrikyo and Jonestown possessed these general traits. In fact, each represents the most highly distilled manifestation of the separatist group as a norm-rejecting collectivity adhering to a way of life in opposition to the general society. However, the circumstances surrounding each group's path to violence were different. This distinction is important insofar as it provides a reminder that millennial ideologies take on highly varied forms depending upon the group's specific characteristics. Such factors include, most importantly, the structure of the group's leadership and the degree to which it embraces a rigidly dualistic outlook envisaging outsiders as enemies.[34]

The Jonestown incident, in particular, offers some critical insights into the enemy-construction process common among volatile apocalyptic movements. By the time Jim Jones and his followers in the Peoples Temple resettled from California to Guyana in 1974, the group had already entertained visions of imminent turmoil in America. Believing that the country was on the verge of economic collapse and that the government was about to embark upon a campaign to exterminate blacks and other minorities, Jones and his adherents fled to Guyana in order to escape the problems that were thought to be awaiting the American Babylon.[35] After the resettlement, Jones continued to preach his Final Days doctrine, which had taken on an increasingly conspiratorial tenor following the construction of the isolated jungle community. While initially intent upon building a model socialist promised land, Jones and his followers came to see themselves as participants in a struggle against an evil American government believed to be plotting against them.[36]

The Jonestown community's apocalyptic expectations and pervasive conspiracism helped forge a dualistic worldview that ideologically separated the enlightened group from its foes. Balanced against the community's self-perception as a righteous elect was the ever-present and psychologically necessary specter of the outside world poised to destroy it. If a triggering mechanism was necessary to unleash the potentially violent forces undergirding the group's belief structure, it came in the form of U.S. Representative Leo Ryan's fact-finding mission to Jonestown. Accompanied by news reporters and the relatives of some of the members who lived at the settlement, Ryan's arrival at Jonestown in November 1978 was interpreted by the community's leadership as evidence of the plot to bring about the demise of the communal experiment. Having perceived a growing campaign of cultural opposition to the Peoples Temple spearheaded by the American media and anticult groups, the community saw the Ryan expedition as a demonstration of the outside world's hostile intentions. It was this interpretation of the congressman's visit, fueled by some members' defections, that led to Jones's decision to ambush Ryan's entourage upon its departure from Jonestown and to order his following's "revolutionary suicide" in defiant expectation of outsiders' further attempts to destroy the group.[37]

The Jonestown episode emphasizes the way that a volatile apocalyptic movement observing a clear distinction between insider and outsider may interpret threats to group life. It is within the shaped universe of group perception where the behavior of outsiders may be understood to be threatening. Sociologist of religion Thomas Robbins has drawn attention to the scholarly analysis of apocalyptic movements from the projected vantage point of the "besieged" group and refers to this practice as "the interpretive approach."[38] It is important to consider, however, that complete reliance upon this interpretive framework to explain the enemy-production process may lead to faulty inferences about a movement's adoption of violence. Robbins argues that this form of analysis leads us to conclude that the group's hostile actions are the result of outside forces, such as the state and law enforcement agencies, whose actions serve as the triggering mechanism for violent activism.[39] The interpretive approach looks at the visible interaction between the outside world (as represented, for example, by state authorities) and the group as a means of illustrating the reciprocal nature of the conflict between millenarian movements and their perceived foes.[40]

The Japanese apocalyptic sect Aum Shinrikyo suggests the strong possibility that the group-outside world dynamic the interpretive approach stresses is not universally valid. Whereas the Jonestown community's resort to mass suicide was precipitated by the arrival of Ryan's team, the apocalyptic violence Aum Shinrikyo embarked upon seemingly occurred without an outside catalyst. Despite a lack of external provocation, the sect became convinced that a catastrophic World War III was on the horizon and began preparing for battle against the evil forces believed to have spread throughout the world.[41] According to Shoko Asahara, the movement's authoritarian leader, the main worldly agents of these dark, cosmic powers were the Japanese and American governments. Asahara claimed that each, along with alleged coconspirators,[42] sought to seize world control and, in the process, abolish Aum along with all other religions. These notions were sustained in the ten-thousand-member eclectic Buddhist organization despite the absence of clear threats to the group.[43]

By the early 1990s, Asahara's vision of an approaching Armageddon dominated Aum's thinking. While prevention of the prophesied calamity through spiritual learning was stressed early in the group's history (1987–90), Asahara's outlook became increasingly fixated on the apocalypse and its aftermath. In the monastic Aum communes in Japan, which housed the sect's most devoted members, orders were given to prepare for imminent war. Already separated from mainstream society, the twelve hundred Aum renunciates living in these encapsulated communal sites were trained to survive what was preached would be the end of civilization.[44] As Asahara saw it, however, the destructive ravages of World War III would not demolish the ranks of the chosen. Exhorting those in the Aum compounds to ready themselves for the end of corrupted human existence, Asahara directed that his followers establish a parallel government to that of the Japanese state. This new Aum "state," which was comprised of numerous departments and agencies, was designed to provide the group with an organizational means both to survive apart from the surrounding secular world and to establish a framework for Aum's orderly continuation after the total war.[45]

With Aum's creation of a separate society parallel that of the state, the group's most deeply committed members lived in complete isolation from outsiders. Residents of the compounds had a growing sense that the unenlightened forces of evil in the world were readying for an attack on the organization's elect. Alleging that the United States (in tandem with the Japanese government) was responsible for Aum's persecution, Asahara ordered that the group pursue a plan of all-out militarization to prepare for what he envisioned would be a world-engulfing nuclear war that would turn Japan into a wasteland.[46]

In accordance with Asahara's prophetic vision of a colossal war before the end of the century, Aum followers adopted a war footing to preserve the group through the expected cataclysm. By 1993, as a result of the growing conviction of its adherents that Aum was the target of world conspiracy, the group's philosophy toward the outside world turned overtly hostile.[47] At Asahara's urging, members of the sect made intensive efforts to acquire a high-tech arsenal, including weapons of mass destruction. Aum representatives spent millions of dollars to develop munitions factories and to further the organization's research on the production of nuclear, chemical, and biological weapons. While interested earlier in merely surviving the coming disaster, Asahara grew more preoccupied with instigating the event.[48] Believing the conflict to be imminent, the sect purchased a forty-eight-thousand-acre ranch in Australia for its members to wait out the war. Following the nuclear apocalypse, followers were to use the site as a base from which to create a golden age civilization from the ashes of humanity's destruction by repopulating the earth with Aum adherents.[49]

Aum's attempt at precipitating World War III finally came on March 20, 1995, when a contingent of Asahara's disciples released containers of sarin, a crude chemical nerve gas, along the main line of the Tokyo subway system. The attack, which killed twelve commuters and sickened five thousand, was intended to inspire public panic and, within the sect's membership, reaffirm the validity of Asahara's End Time prophecies. In his "prediction" of just such an attack by American military forces before the incident, Asahara publicly declared that Japanese citizens would be gassed in the near-term, final conflict.[50]

While both Jonestown and Aum ultimately adopted violent tactics against outsiders, the two cases differ with regard to the way each arrived at this decision. In the Jonestown example, the community responded to visible actions by outsiders believed to be threatening the group. With Aum, however, the decision to resort to violence was stimulated purely by group-held images of its persecution.

Apocalypticism and Nonviolence on the Ranch

The use of the interpretive approach to explain the church's activity in Montana falls short of providing a convincing rationale for the group's apocalyptic excitement. From the time of its relocation to Montana until the conclusion of its hurried preparations for nuclear conflict in spring 1990, there were few plausible threats facing Prophet's ranch community. While CUT was presented with some unexpected problems during this time, at no point (as happened at Jonestown) did outsiders intervene in the group's activities in a way that provoked a sudden panic among the membership. The primary interactions were the relatively minor dispute between the church and the National Park Service over lands purchased as part of the Royal Teton Ranch and the summer 1989 arrest of CUT officials for their role in purchasing weapons. These incidents were sources of trouble for CUT, but neither assumed the function of a triggering event that sparked the group's millennial enthusiasm. The community's land dispute with the Park Service took shape shortly after its acquisition of the

Royal Teton Ranch. Although environmental interest groups and the Park Service targeted CUT's expansive property holdings as an impediment to Yellowstone National Park's future growth, the issue was resolved without federal officials acting on their threat to acquire the ranch property.[51] Likewise, the arrest of Vernon Hamilton and Edward Francis by federal police in Spokane, Washington, was not widely seen in the church as a catalyst for apocalyptic activity. The summer 1989 arrest of the two church officials took place almost a year after the group's shelter construction project had begun. The fact that the organization's nuclear war preparation program was well under way by the time of this embarrassing criminal violation illuminates the foundations of the group's millennial outlook. Rather than being mobilized to action by external threats, the CUT colony in Montana evolved into an agitated millennial community via intrinsic properties within the group's belief framework.

The absence of a triggering event for the community's millennial outburst bears more similarities with the Aum Shinrikyo affair than with Jonestown. Both Aum and CUT largely avoided hostile encounters with political authorities, yet apocalyptic anticipation within each movement steadily increased. In each case, the confrontation between the group and outsiders that marked the Jonestown episode was missing.[52] The ranch community's similarities with Aum are strictly limited, however, to the ways that intrinsic forces extending from CUT's teachings and general worldview resulted in the movement's frenetic apocalyptic behavior. Unlike Aum, which ultimately sought to incite a cataclysmic war as a precursor to its golden age dream, CUT members withdrew passively from the world in expectation of a nuclear conflict. Nonetheless, as CUT's plans for its defense in the post-nuclear-war era reveal, the ranch community was prepared for the worst-case scenario of armed combat with outsiders.[53]

CUT relocated to Montana to protect Prophet's flock from the social unrest, natural disasters, and the nuclear war that the Messenger pictured in the future. Despite gaining a measure of perceived safety from these threats following the move, the community became more fully absorbed than before in its apocalyptic fears. However, at no point during CUT's excitation phase in Montana did it make the philosophical transition from passive to aggressive millennialism. Even as conspiracies and ideological dualism came to dominate the core membership's thinking during 1989–90, the church never deviated from its historical emphasis on nonviolence. This is not to imply, though, that organized resistance to violence was forbidden. Early in her stewardship of the organization, Prophet had given a dictation in which nonresistance to violent, "one-world order threats" was discredited.[54] Dating from the time the group was located in Colorado Springs, there were clear indications that the membership was preparing itself for the possibility of armed hostilities with perceived foes.[55] While defending itself against armed attack in uncertain future times was considered a necessity, this contingency was viewed as an emergency option and did not displace the nonviolent survivalist plans employed during the shelter cycle.

Conspiratorial threats to the church's existence became a fixation for Prophet and her Montana following during the apocalyptic mobilization, but the group lacked the total worldly detachment and complete antinomianism needed to reconfigure its spiritual struggle with evil into an overtly violent form. CUT had achieved its desired state of geographical and psychological emancipation from society when it established the New Jerusalem in Montana, but its teachings prevented believers from behaving in a hostile manner toward outsiders. As it was stated within the organization, members "had a responsibility to mitigate the earthly karma" that was thought to be endangering human civilization.[56] This task necessitated the church's strategic retreat from coastal California, where it was believed that negative karma was fast accelerating,[57] to the mountains of the Northwest. From its new home, Prophet's flock waged spiritual warfare with the knowledge that the fate of humankind was at hand.

The group's attempt to forestall the arrival of earthly catastrophe never ceased during the mobilization for nuclear war. It was only in the final phase of the organization's apocalyptic cycle in early spring 1990 that Prophet's elect fully resigned themselves to the group-constructed reality of imminent disaster. But even then, when the community's faith in its ability to avert the cataclysm had eroded, the faithful simply withdrew from the declining world.

The specific manner in which disaster was received by Prophet's followers helps explain CUT's nonviolent path to Armageddon. Aum Shinrikyo and Jonestown progressed from being renunciate-style societies to becoming combative, separatist enclaves. In contrast, Prophet's church navigated through its apocalyptic phase without experiencing the psychodynamic shift that led to violent activism. Group teachings and the responsibilities they carried for believers prevented CUT from becoming an apocalyptic "warring sect."[58] But, moreover, the particular way that the community responded to its prior experience with disaster-focused thinking points to the group's paramount desire to escape an endangered world. This urge, which was devoid of violent suggestions, was rooted in the group's expectation of a future disaster, an event from which Prophet sought to protect her flock.[59]

6

Post-Prophetic Failure and Decline

The church's active mobilization for nuclear war concluded on the morning of March 16, 1990. With the world still intact, the ranch dwellers and the CUT members at Glastonbury emerged from their underground safe havens and got on with their lives. Despite the bewilderment and surprise many of the members experienced following the nonevent,[1] Prophet's community in Paradise Valley weathered the threatened apocalyptic storm without serious incident. While most of the newcomers who had flocked to the region quickly departed, the majority of the ranch's permanent staff, as well as those living at the Glastonbury property, stayed on.[2] CUT lost about one-third of its total membership in the immediate aftermath of the shelter period,[3] but, for the most devoted, the nonappearance of the expected disaster was not enough to cause them to break ties with CUT nor to shake their faith in the Messenger.

In 1989, during the time that CUT's survivalist program was fully engaged, the Internal Revenue Service (IRS) turned its attention to the organization's finances. Materials obtained via the Freedom of Information Act show that this was not the only time that the government had taken an interest in Prophet's church. FBI documents dating from the time when CUT was in California show that the bureau was interested in the church's funding, most of which was said to come directly from members "donating their money, skills, and labor in the name of church expansion."[4] The IRS investigation, however, came about with the help of an informant in the church who had been with the movement in Montana. Alerted by the informer that members were operating profit-generating enterprises in violation of the group's tax-exempt status, the agency began to closely scrutinize the church's commercial ventures. The informant alleged, among other things, that Prophet and other high-ranking officials concealed financial assets to avoid taxation.[5] CUT's construction of the multi-million-dollar Mol Herron shelter and the 1989 arrest of two members on federal weapons charges certainly caught the attention of the IRS, but additional information surfaced that caused the tax agency to become skeptical. Detailed examination of numerous church-owned or church-connected companies, including a lucrative publishing business and several enterprises involved with modular home construction and chiropractic care, suggested to the agency that "excess commerciability" was evident in the tax-exempt organization.[6]

The IRS intervention was not the only source of legal trouble that faced CUT as it concluded its shelter phase. After scrutinizing the group's weapons acquisition plans, Justice Department attorneys argued that CUT's leadership had displayed a twenty-year pattern of arms buying that was concealed from both the general membership and the public. The Justice Department maintained that the organization's leadership had been involved since 1973 in an elaborate money-laundering plan designed to permit an inner circle of staff members to purchase guns for CUT's defense. According to government lawyers, a select group of staff members undertook the scheme with the full authorization of Elizabeth Clare Prophet. The Justice Department viewed the failed July 1989 attempt to supply CUT with arms as a continuation of the group's overzealous pursuit of security and recommended that the IRS revoke the church's tax exemption.[7]

After completing its three-year audit in 1992, the IRS revoked CUT's tax-exempt status and sought $2.5 million in back taxes and penalties. The investigation cited illegal firearms procurement and several business irregularities, including sheltering taxable subsidiaries.[8] Immediately following the government's decision, CUT filed a lawsuit to regain its tax-exempt standing as a religious organization. CUT's lawyers claimed that the organization was a victim of religious persecution, arguing that the IRS and the Justice Department had overreacted to critics' reports of its "doomsday" preparations and, as a result, unfairly singled out the group as a target in a government campaign against nontraditional religious organizations.[9]

The tax-exemption issue was settled in July 1994 when the government agreed to restore the church's official designation as a religious organization. The dispute's resolution came a little over a year after the Clinton administration's tragic mishandling of the Branch Davidian incident in Waco. According to church critics, many of whom resided in the Paradise Valley region, the settlement with the IRS demonstrated the government's trepidation about being viewed as an opponent of nontraditional religious movements. These sources argued that the mistakes made by federal law enforcement agencies at Waco directly contributed to the government's willingness to settle with CUT out of court.[10] However, the IRS decision to restore the tax exemption came with a number of stipulations. In addition to requiring the church to pay income taxes on its business enterprises, the agency mandated that all communally owned weapons were to be sold and that a period of tax revocation (1988–90) be observed as a penalty on the organization.[11]

During the time when CUT struggled to regain its tax exemption, its officials arranged for an academic study of the Royal Teton Ranch community. This initiative, which was the first of two efforts mentioned in chapter 5 when CUT "went public" after the spring 1990 shelter episode, was aimed at improving the group's tarnished reputation. The immediate reason for the church's interest in participating in such an endeavor was to demonstrate that it did not fit the dangerous cult stereotype in which it had been cast by the media.[12] With some concern after the Waco affair that federal authorities might next target the ranch, Prophet and other officials in the organization turned to outsiders in the scholarly community to help the group dissociate itself from the mainstream culture's cult image that dominated news reporting after Waco.[13] It was most likely unknown to CUT officials at the time that federal police agencies were not especially concerned with the organization's activities. Documents from the FBI show that Prophet's church received virtually no attention from the bureau after Vernon Hamilton's arrest on gun charges in Spokane in July 1989.[14]

The bloody confrontation at Waco affected the way in which new religious movements were dealt with in the media. Waco quickly rejuvenated the fervor of the 1980s anticult crusades and, in the process, David Koresh's name became the symbol in popular culture for the authoritarianism and violence-prone characteristics perceived in new religions. As a result of the media's charge that unsettling similarities existed between the Branch Davidians and Prophet's church, CUT found itself caught in a cult-scare media frenzy. Television stories and national newsmagazines tended to ignore basic doctrinal differences between the groups and, instead, focused exclusively on the gun issue. Adding paramilitary overtones to brainwashing claims in light of Waco, reporters routinely portrayed the church as "armed to the teeth" and ready "to declare war" on outsiders.[15]

The academic study of CUT was performed by a team of scholars affiliated with the Association of World Academics for Religious Education (AWARE) and involved experts from various fields, including sociology, psychology, anthropology, and religion. Following a weeklong field study at the Royal Teton Ranch, the participants contributed reports on their findings to a special issue of *Syzygy: The Journal of Alternative Religion and Culture.*[16] The published AWARE study, which the church financially supported, highlighted the positive aspects of the group's communal life, such as the psychologically healthy atmosphere that researchers found in the community.[17] But, as two participants on the AWARE research team later maintained, the study was carried out in such a way that serious questions about the organization were entirely ignored.[18] According to these critics, the project, while well intentioned, was thoroughly marked by biased investigation and avoided addressing issues with which CUT officials were uncomfortable. Among the significant gaps in the study were the almost total absence of discussion about the group's survivalism and the omission of reports from former members of the organization.[19]

CUT's out-of-court settlement with the IRS and the stamp of approval the 1993 AWARE study provided marked the arrival of a short-lived period of better times for the organization. Having repaired some amount of the fractured public image it suffered since the start of its apocalyptic period, the church emerged from its travails with an optimistic vision for future growth. Elizabeth Clare Prophet displayed exuberance over the positive IRS decision when I met her for an interview at her home on the Royal Teton Ranch on July 3, 1994. Reflecting on the terms of the agreement with the IRS, Prophet told me that those "persecuting" her and the church "had been clearly defeated" in their attempts to destroy the organization. She attributed the victory over "representatives of the power elite" to a demonstration of "the will of God," and indicated that the IRS decision signaled a divinely inspired resurrection of the church's reputation. In her view, the restoration of tax exemption heralded the arrival of a new era of acceptance and a validation of the church and its teachings. In defense of her belief that the organization was now viewed in a more favorable light, Prophet cited the findings of the AWARE study as evidence of CUT's "graduation" from a sect to an accepted religion.[20]

By mid-1994, CUT appeared to be displaying faint signs of a revival. Although the organization had lost a fair portion of its membership after the apocalyptic failure of 1990, this shortfall was at least partly offset by the group's success in expanding its international recruitment. Already claiming to have adherents in some forty countries, CUT further expanded its multiracial, multiethnic composition in 1994 by initiating activity in South Korea and Russia.

In order to accommodate anticipated growth in the membership, plans were also made to enlarge available residential spaces on the Royal Teton Ranch. In 1995, blueprints were drawn for a new, expanded base for the church's head-quarters. Designed to be situated on an undeveloped seventy-five-acre site on the ranch, the planned model headquarters reflected the organization's opti-mism about increasing its size in the future. Authorization soon came for the project after the state approved the group's environmental impact statement. The development plan for the site included the proposed construction of new housing facilities for five hundred additional members, dining halls, a commu-nity center, and new classroom facilities.[21]

Claiming that her antagonists (including the IRS and local Montanans liv-ing near the ranch) had given up on their efforts to bring down the church, the Messenger was pleased about the "new acceptability" she saw for her organiza-tion.[22] Prophet's belief that her group had finally defeated those who sought CUT's elimination was soon tested, however, by a number of major events that shook the church community. The first of these involved a shoot-out between local law enforcement officers and CUT member Mitchell Mandell, a thirty-four-year-old property owner at the church's Glastonbury subdivision. Man-dell, who rented his property and mobile home to another CUT member, attempted to evict the tenant from the site on December 21, 1993. Upon receiv-ing word that Mandell had assaulted the tenant, officers from the Park County Sheriff's Department and the Montana Highway Patrol were dispatched to Glastonbury to investigate. After arriving on the scene, the officers were con-fronted by Mandell, who refused to leave his property. During the one-hour standoff that ensued, Mandell reportedly engaged in ritualistic acts to "com-bat" the police, including shouting church decrees and waving a ceremonial sword members used to disable evil spirits.[23] Following a period of attempted negotiation, Mandell became increasingly hostile and eventually opened fire on the officers with a semiautomatic pistol. The police, who had by this time surrounded the property, returned fire and killed Mandell.[24]

CUT representatives responded to the Mandell shooting by emphasizing the connections the deceased reportedly had with antigovernment tax-protest groups. At the annual winter conference held on the Royal Teton Ranch shortly after the shoot-out, special attention was given to the unfortunate incident. CUT used the winter meeting as an occasion to make clear that it held no sympathy for the "fanatical, tax-protest causes" in which Mandell was alleged to be involved.[25] In order to display its opposition to antigovernment beliefs, the church mandated that members attending the 1994 winter conference sign a pledge indicating that they were not affiliated with groups espousing such doctrines.[26] The symbolic statement against "patriot" activity came only months before the favorable IRS decision and was intended as a demonstration of the church's law-abiding character. In a show of concern about the group's mistaken association with the radical tax-protest groups, which by the 1990s had become a well-known feature of the political landscape in the Northwest, CUT officials forcefully stated at the winter conference that the membership was to avoid "fanatical causes."[27]

The shooting of Mitchell Mandell took on added importance for CUT in late 1995 when a wrongful death lawsuit was filed against Elizabeth Clare Prophet and the police who responded to the incident. The suit was filed by Mandell's mother, Marlene Motzko, who alleged that the officers used excessive force against her son and that the church was negligent in not intervening and mediating in the affair.[28] After lengthy legal proceedings, CUT eventually reached a private, out-of-court financial settlement with Motzko over her son's death, but the well-publicized lawsuit did nothing to improve the organization's public image.[29]

Other troubles also began to plague the group after the shooting incident at Glastonbury. Beginning in 1995, indications appeared that CUT was faced with a growing morale problem. Although rumors about discontentment among the staff at the Royal Teton Ranch had circulated since the time of Prophet's failed apocalyptic prediction,[30] the first concrete evidence of the problem surfaced when CUT literature sent to group members pointed to the peaking frustrations of those living on the Park County, Montana, commune. In an unusual pamphlet that the church disseminated, references were made to the community's dissatisfaction with the rigors associated with the highly structured, semimonastic life on the spiritual colony. Somewhat surprisingly, the publication also suggested that the Messenger, while having the complete "sponsorship of God," may have occasionally made human errors of judgment in placing certain church members in management positions.[31] The general tone of the pamphlet was nonetheless parental. Exhorting the membership to be patient while the morale problem was addressed, the message emphasized that devoted Lightbearers needed to better understand that hard work and discipline were required to walk CUT's spiritual path.[32]

Reports of low morale within the ranch community made local headlines in the Paradise Valley region from 1995 through 1996. By this time it was alleged that many staff members had grown weary with the structured, hierarchical lifestyle on the Royal Teton Ranch. Furthermore, it was reported that Prophet's rigid management of the organization had met with stiff opposition by some CUT members.[33] As internal strife increased within the group, numerous defections took place. Most damaging to CUT, however, was the steady flow of resignations from its board of directors by high-ranking ministers and other key officeholders. Although the turnover rate had always been high for Prophet's immediate subordinates on the board,[34] the number of departures in 1995 and 1996 attracted local media attention.[35] Some former members of the church sought to spread news of the morale crisis on the Royal Teton Ranch. One defector group based in Livingston, Montana, established a monthly anti-CUT periodical funded by donations from former members highlighting the group's ongoing difficulties. Another group of apostates joined ranks in Bozeman, Montana, in a support network to deal with the emotional problems members encountered after severing ties with the group.[36]

As news circulated about the disillusionment of the membership, church officials announced publicly that there would be a sweeping overhaul of the organization's management structure. Downplaying the effects of sinking morale and defections, spokesmen attributed the sudden organizational change to Prophet's desire to concentrate solely on her role as the church's Messenger and spiritual leader.[37] As part of the restructuring plan, Prophet resigned as president of the church, a post she had held since 1973. The position was assumed by Gilbert Cleirbaut, a Belgian-born Canadian management consultant once employed by Union Carbide, who was selected to handle business operations. The organizational change was necessary, according to outside observers, because CUT had been suffering from serious management and financial troubles.[38] Reports suggested that Prophet's adoption of a rigid, bureaucratic management style on the Royal Teton Ranch had damaged morale, stifled staff efficiency, and hindered prospects for the church's growth. In accordance with the new organizational framework, Cleirbaut was to establish a more democratic structure for CUT operations in which management decisions were not simply generated at the top.[39]

Unable to generate sufficient revenues to house and feed the staff, maintain the ranch property, and publish literature, CUT looked for ways to reduce its expenditures. With its public financial report showing revenues at $8.2 million for 1996, and expenses listed at $8.9 million, the church was faced with a budget shortfall that had to be remedied to restore its financial health.[40] By summer 1996, CUT had embarked on a "downsizing plan" to reduce the staff population on the Royal Teton Ranch. Financially incapable of continuing to provide ranch residents with free room and board (along with a very modest stipend),[41] the leadership eliminated most of the staff jobs and scaled back the total membership residing on the ranch from seven hundred, its approximate size in 1990, to three hundred.[42] Although CUT officials stated that the reduction was made to maintain organizational efficiency, the real cause for the community's declared "reenergizing process" was due to an overall decline of the church's financial resources.[43] The organization's faltering economic condition was brought about by the numerous defections since 1990 and led it to cut costs wherever possible. Indeed, CUT's financial woes had become so burdensome that, in addition to initiating its downsizing plan, further steps were taken to allay the cash-flow problems.

In a surprise move designed to shore up its financial position, the organization began to permit people not affiliated with CUT to buy property at Glastonbury, the nearby church-owned residential property. Established in 1982 as an extension of the group's communal ranch headquarters, the Glastonbury settlement was considered to be part of the church's community of elect. However, since the settlement had been traditionally comprised of members who found employment in the surrounding area, the increased degree of interaction between its residents and nonbelievers gave the Glastonbury colony a decidedly less monastic character than the Royal Teton Ranch.[44] The approximately four hundred residents of the settlement were required to lease their property from CUT and were barred from either owning their land or bequeathing it to family members.[45] After the downsizing plan was begun, CUT signaled a change in its oversight of the colony when Prophet announced that Glastonbury would now be opened to outsiders wishing to purchase land on the site. While Prophet described the decision as a directive from the Ascended Masters to make the settlement "more inclusive," the timing of the new policy added fuel to speculations that the organization was in financial turmoil.[46]

The series of setbacks CUT experienced during the mid-1990s was amplified in early 1996 by the news that Prophet and her husband, Edward Francis, were going to divorce. Francis, who had been with the church since the early 1970s, had served CUT in a number of important capacities, including posts as the group's business manager and vice president. The dissolution of their fifteen-year marriage came as a shock to the membership, since the union was believed to have been arranged by the Ascended Masters.[47] Carrying with it a divine seal of approval, the Prophet-Francis marriage was viewed by the membership in symbolic terms as an integral part of CUT's institutional foundation.[48] Church officials attempted to minimize the significance of the divorce by stressing that the breakup would neither impede the goals of the organization nor interrupt the restructuring process already under way.[49] Two years before the divorce, at the age of fifty-five, Prophet gave birth to a son, Seth, the couple's only child. CUT's leader had already raised four other children, all born during her marriage to Mark Prophet, and had seven grandchildren.[50]

Marketing to a New Age Audience

Despite the considerable problems CUT encountered since the 1990 shelter episode, the organization only made two efforts to promote itself to nonbelievers. The first of these was the group's sponsorship of the 1993 AWARE study. In summer 1996, CUT embarked on a second attempt at public outreach when it began a major recruiting initiative in Latin America. Unlike its first experience at going public, CUT's second foray into image enhancement was more directly connected with membership recruitment.[51] Along with an entourage of twelve staff members, Prophet went on a thirty-three-day tour of six major South American cities to spread the group's Ascended Master teachings. The Messenger's involvement in an international recruitment campaign was not an unprecedented development. Since the time of her marriage to Mark Prophet, CUT's spiritual leader had lectured in twenty-eight different countries.[52] However, this speaking tour outside the United States began during desperate times for the church. Wounded by defections and sinking morale among the staff on the Royal Teton Ranch, the organization's officials arranged the summer 1996 South America tour as a means to reinvigorate the church. On the tour, Prophet was well received by audiences often numbering up to several thousand who were eager to hear her talks on subjects ranging from reincarnation and the dangers of "negative karma" to discussions of South America's social and political problems.[53] Calculating that the group's eclectic theological message and Ascended Master teachings would meet with acceptance by New Age devotees,[54] leaders in the church recognized the importance of targeting the speaking engagements to audiences of potential members.

CUT's foray into South America signified a new development in the group's public image strategy. While the 1993 AWARE study facilitated the organization's efforts at "mainstreaming" itself in the public eye, the South American tour highlighted CUT's New Age orientation as a marketing strategy designed to garner new adherents. Recognizing that a potential seedbed of recruits existed in several non-church-affiliated New Age groups in the region, Prophet emphasized her message of human transcendence and the arrival of the Aquarian Age to approving audiences familiar with these general New Age concepts.[55] Although the Messenger also distinguished her church's theology from popularized New Age thought, mainly by delivering some solemn dictations at public gatherings stressing regional political troubles and the potential for future world catastrophe,[56] her talks usually tapped into standard New Age themes. Among these, the subject of reincarnation was emphasized. Indeed, Prophet used the excursion as an opportunity to promote her recent book, *Reincarnation: The Missing Link in Christianity,* and spent much time discussing the concept of past lives, which was showcased as an important part of the tour.[57]

Following the South American venture, CUT stepped up its promotional efforts. With Prophet taking the uncharacteristic role of the organization's lead media spokesperson, the church worked to integrate itself into the popular New Age movement. Since the time of the relocation to Montana, Prophet had adopted a very low-profile posture toward the media, but at rare times she deemed it necessary to converse with outsiders. Such an occasion arose prior to and immediately after the failed appearance of nuclear war in early 1990 when the heightened level of CUT activity in Paradise Valley forced Prophet to make public statements in the group's defense.[58] Her reluctance to make public pronouncements changed suddenly, however, when the church began to experience other problems. In a dramatic public relations move that involved the Messenger's adoption of a more accessible persona, the organization pursued a media strategy that cast the leader in a less sectarian light as a spiritual visionary, New Age writer, and learned guru. As part of a marketing approach focused upon disseminating CUT's teachings to a wider audience, the newly gregarious Prophet began hosting a taped radio program from the Royal Teton Ranch called *Heart to Heart* that catered to New Age listeners. The taped show was broadcast from a powerful AM station (WALE) in Providence, Rhode Island, and addressed topics such as personal spiritual growth, near-death experiences, and the role of angels on earth.[59]

Prophet's reconstructed public image as a New Age spokesperson was made clear when she appeared as a guest on *The Art Bell Show,* a syndicated late-night talk radio program embracing UFO belief, psychic phenomena, and assorted theories about a coming New Age global transformation. The occasion for Prophet's April 17, 1997, appearance on the show was to reflect on a disturbing event that had taken place in Rancho Santa Fe, California, only weeks before. In late March, thirty-nine members of Heaven's Gate, an apocalyptic UFO sect residing in a rented mansion in the community, took their own lives in anticipation of achieving otherworldly renewal as highly evolved extraterrestrial beings.[60] The group's millennial agitation was spurred by the winter 1997 arrival of an astronomical occurrence of unusual magnitude—the appearance of the spectacular Hale-Bopp Comet. Reacting to rumors spread by some UFO believers that the brilliant comet shielded "a companion object" thought to be a spaceship,[61] members of Heaven's Gate seized upon these speculations as a validation of their End of the Age philosophy. In accordance with the group's belief that it would board the hidden spacecraft, followers ended their earthly lives in order to pass into what they believed was the "Next Level" above human existence.[62]

Bell's radio interview of Prophet was noteworthy for two reasons. First, it clearly signified the church's attempt to ingratiate itself with those elements of the larger fringe spiritual culture that comprised Bell's listenership. Stating that she now planned to speak with the media more often, Prophet's guest appearance marked her "coming out" event.[63] While she spoke directly to "the misguided people" of Heaven's Gate who wrongly "took the law of God into their own hands," discussion on the show was mainly directed at promoting her books and addressing subjects that were of interest to a New Age audience.[64] Second, the interview was significant because strands of Prophet's conspiracy-prone outlook and dark view of the future surfaced in her dialogue with Bell, whose own record as a purveyor of cataclysmic New Age visions was well established.[65] Prophet interspersed her reflections on such mainstream alternative spiritual topics as mitigating karma and discerning human auras with other issues that, she claimed, held dangerous implications for humanity. Prophet pointed to the same agents of earthly evil that had dominated CUT's thinking during the shelter period in Montana, including the powerful nonhuman beings familiar to church members who were said to be responsible for bringing about a state of global discord. Citing Zechariah Sitchin's theory that ancient visits to earth by aliens had brought on the world's problems, Prophet stated that these original visitors to the planet continued to multiply and gravitate to

positions of prestige and power. The malevolent deeds of these alien conspirators, she argued, would continue to take place until the arrival of the new
Aquarian Age.[66]

Rocky Relations with the New Age

Despite CUT's overt attempts to integrate with the New Age community, the
success of this linkage was fated to be problematic. Prophet's remarks on the
Art Bell radio program underscored the chief problem the church faced in its
outreach campaign: the theologically justified conspiracies that had traditionally accompanied CUT's outlook were not universally accepted aspects of contemporary New Age thinking. Although such concepts may have had a natural
appeal for some in the New Age fold, particularly to those anticipating catastrophic events before the forthcoming golden age, foreboding and disaster-
focused ideas remained associated with a minority following. Prophet's own
feelings about the individualistic pursuit of spirituality commonly associated
with the modern-day New Age movement point to her disapproval of its
largely unstructured and amorphous beliefs. When I interviewed her, Prophet
was candid about her distaste for the New Age label her church had received in
the popular culture.[67] In contrast to the strategy CUT began using in 1996 to
tap into the New Age religion market, Prophet pointed out her own dislike of
its "self-indulgent" aspects. She castigated the movement for its "adoption of
shallow phenomena" and argued that the defining yardstick for New Age
thought was the license to believe virtually anything.[68] As she saw it, professed
New Agers misunderstood the real meaning of the concept. Prophet observed
that "these people are terribly self-absorbed and their movement allows them
to indulge themselves with whatever they want." CUT's leader went to great
lengths to distinguish between "self-indulgent" New Age believers and the origins of what she saw as the real New Age concept, which Prophet declared was
based on the original philosophy of the Summit Lighthouse. In her view, "The
Summit Lighthouse was talking about the New Age back in the 1950s, and it
had nothing to do with this nonsense." She made clear that the contemporary
New Age movement had lost its true bearings when its adherents lost sight of
the real meaning of the Age of Aquarius that, for Prophet, meant "obedience to
the Holy Spirit" and "not being idolatrous."[69]

   Prophet's own negative impressions of the contemporary New Age movement were reflected in the statements several interview subjects made at CUT's

1994 summer conference. When asked whether the organization might be fairly associated with the New Age movement, respondents overwhelmingly rejected the connection. Gene Voessler, a high-ranking minister in the church, offered a view that represented the sentiments of many interviewees. For Voessler, "the New Age description doesn't really fit." Pointing out that the church rejected the label, he said that it was society that "stuck us in this category, because if they can't figure out where to put you they'll put you where they think you belong." Voessler, however, viewed the New Age label with equanimity. "It's just one of those things," he said. "We've been labeled 'doomsday cult' and 'end of the world people,' too."[70]

Other interview subjects were even more forthright in their denunciation of New Ageism. Several interviewees indicated that CUT was actually attempting to divorce from this "nonreligious" movement and that the New Age description was "pulling down the church."[71]

But despite the apparent differences between the church's theology and the freewheeling spiritual expressionism usually associated with New Ageism, clear aspects of the philosophy have long been a fixture of CUT's existence. Prior to the leadership's calculated efforts at blending in with the current New Age scene,[72] some traces of this thinking could already be found. Detectable elements of a cross-fertilization between popular New Ageism and church doctrine were visible at the 1994 summer conference.

As part of the organization's restructuring process, the number of staff working at the Royal Teton Ranch had been reduced to the point where it was no longer possible for the summer conferences to be held at the Montana headquarters. Without the requisite workforce to prepare for the event, the church began holding its major yearly gathering at hotels in large metropolitan areas.[73] Until 1995, when CUT leaders decided to temporarily end the practice, the annual summer meeting at the Royal Teton Ranch consistently attracted between two thousand and three thousand worldwide members. In the early to mid-1990s, alternative spirituality motifs such as "Soul Evolution" and "The Environment of the Soul" had been used as general themes for the summer gatherings. These conclaves offered widely varied educational and entertainment options for those attending, including sessions on astrology, guided tours of Yellowstone National Park, and weeklong classes in yoga and tai chi.[74]

CUT's absorption of some common New Age currents had been reflected in the inclusion of human potential and self-exploration topics in past conference course offerings for attendees. Periodically, the church also hosted well-known personalities, especially psychologists and authors, affiliated with the dominant and more optimistically oriented wing of the New Age movement.[75] Yet the attention given to "understanding the inner child" and "unlocking the potential of the brain"[76] always represented a fairly narrow part of CUT's belief structure. The more catastrophic aspects of the church's beliefs, by comparison, have been a more powerful presence in its group outlook. As was clear at the 1994 summer meeting, group perceptions of earthly calamity were obvious and suggested that CUT's vision of the future resonated with caution and uncertainty.

These attitudes about impending earthly disaster were apparent in the weeklong course on fallout shelter construction taught in 1994 by a Glastonbury resident who designed and built several of the structures at the time when the group was readying itself for nuclear war. I attended these class sessions with about twenty male and female CUT members who ranged in age from the early twenties to over sixty. The daily two-and-a-half hour sessions were conducted by the instructor in an informal, relaxed style, but the deadly seriousness of the topic was lost on none of the students, all of whom seemed to take copious notes and ask questions demonstrating something more than a layperson's familiarity with the arcana of survival techniques, shelter construction, and the effects of a nuclear blast. The main message of the short course appeared to be to disseminate "how to" information to students for planning, building, and maintaining small underground shelters. However, some sessions were devoted to topics such as psychological preparation for disaster and critical analysis of U.S. civil defense readiness.[77]

Students seemed most interested in the instructor's recommendations for the structural design of the emergency facilities and in what type of equipment (such as generators and radiation-detecting dossimeters) they should acquire. The instructor also advised students on "shelter management" in the face of a catastrophe. Noting that occupants might become psychologically unbalanced after a prolonged stay underground, which was said could last up to several years, he urged the survivalist-minded audience to exercise caution in admitting "unstable" people to one's shelter and to resist the natural urge to accept more occupants in the facilities than they could accommodate. In addition to this information, detailed attention was given to the regions and specific sites in the country thought to be likely targets in a nuclear war. Regionally, these targets were said to include the nearby city of Bozeman, Montana (pop. 23,000), which is home to a small civilian airport, as well as a cluster of inter-

continental ballistic missile silos near Harlowtown, Montana, situated approximately eighty miles north of the Royal Teton Ranch. Considerable time was
spent in the course discussing the disparities between Russia's Soviet-era civil
defense program and that of the United States. The instructor cited figures
pointing to the former Soviet state's funding of a massive civil defense program
beginning in the 1950s[78] to demonstrate the unpreparedness of "common
American people" to a nuclear war Russian leaders perceived as "winnable." He
maintained that while "the elite" in America (including "politicians and members of the board of the Federal Reserve") have been provided space in secret
underground shelters, the great majority of American citizens could not defend themselves from a nuclear attack.[79]

Interest in disaster themes also appeared in other activities at the 1994
summer conference. On one afternoon, CUT spokesman Gene Voessler gave a
two-hour presentation on the prophecies made by the sixteenth-century seer
Michel Nostradamus, whose vague, poetical predictions of future events occultists and some New Agers regard as accurate.[80] The dramatic talk, which was
accompanied by videos and slides, emphasized Nostradamus's prediction of
total global war in the last decade of the twentieth century. The event was one
of the main attractions during the week and drew a crowd of over three hundred church members.[81]

Besiegement, Dualism, and New Enemies

Throughout the church's history, the Prophets' convictions about their movement's elect status were impressed upon the membership. In order for the
co-Messengers' sentiments to take root, it was necessary for the two leaders to
give their following the sense that outsiders posed a challenge both to the sanc-
tity of CUT's theological teachings and to the group's way of life. Mark
Prophet's early warnings to his flock about the dangers he saw in communist-
inspired "communal atheism" and extraterrestrial visitors were adopted by his
wife (in a slightly varied form) as a means to promote group cohesiveness and
to further dissociate the movement from a threat-filled world. Her conception
of an international power elite descending from the biblical fallen angels became an often-used representation of the enemy during the Montana phase of
the group's experience. Four years after the mobilization for nuclear war,
Prophet indicated that "this element of global society emanated from another
race and represented true evil."[82] In her estimation, these "highly placed inter-

nationalists" had accumulated such a vast quantity of negative karma in their past embodiments that "they have no use for God."[83]

While in Montana, Prophet relied upon many of the same archetypal fears that her late husband introduced into the group's thinking, although she refined and updated them so that they remained plausible sources of concern in the eyes of her community. This process of upgrading group fears to adapt to new times and threats was visible in CUT's inclusion of more current global security issues in its survival program and was reflected in Prophet's frequent references to technological gains made by the former Soviet Union in its nuclear fighting capabilities.[84] However, her efforts at modernizing the organization's traditional specters extended further than to thinking on matters of nuclear war. In the group's experiences between 1988 and 1990, for example, conspiratorial threats about the AIDS virus and alleged government involvement with malevolent alien plots against humankind also represented attempts to infuse contemporary fringe beliefs with CUT's world outlook.[85]

Prophet indicated that she had long made it a requirement for the members of CUT's permanent staff to read Sun Tzu's The Art of War in order to develop an understanding for the "entirely different psychological mind-set of cunning outsiders."[86] Believing that the Chinese general's ancient tract on warfare and strategy offered her community lessons on deception, Prophet considered it to be a valuable guide providing insights into the enemy mind.[87] Written about 500 B.C.E., The Art of War is best known for its discussion of calculated tactics and strategies of warfare by indirect methods based upon trickery, gamesmanship, and psychological skill. The treatise's central dictum, "all warfare is based on deception," reflects its uncompromising harshness and emphasis on politics and human nature as cornerstones of war-fighting operations.[88] However, Prophet admired the tract for more than its use as a primer on enemy thinking; in her opinion, The Art of War represented an inherently Oriental perspective on human affairs and conflict. She included CUT's old political nemesis, the now defunct Soviet Union (along with China and North Korea), as states harboring "an oriental philosophy" and argued that a different mode of thought defines this outlook.[89] In her view of international politics, Prophet associated this understanding of the Oriental worldview with communism: "The Russians can tell any lie and we'll believe it. The West doesn't understand propaganda—nor do they really understand the philosophy under which the Soviets operate. I'm not sure, maybe it was Gorbachev, anyway, this person recently said, 'We are an Oriental people.' We know that Orientals don't think in the same way that Westerners think. Deceit is part of the normal political process to them." [90]

CUT's use of enemy contrast identities, of course, was long a part of its history. Whether these group-constructed foes were ostensibly political, such as the Soviet Union, or otherworldly, as was the extraterrestrial threat, they shared a common trait. Each symbolized a form of total evil at odds with the church and its members. Such attitudes necessitated the establishment of rigid boundaries between outsider and insider, a position at variance with mainstream New Age conceptions of universal brotherhood. Until the mid-1990s, CUT literature occasionally continued to bear strong traces of the organization's reliance upon "othering" selected foes, a practice the church used since its founding. [91]

Even while CUT was publicly announcing its adoption of a new internal structure, [92] evidence sometimes appeared that suggested that dualistic thinking remained a powerful undercurrent in the organization. While in public CUT tended to stress optimistic views about the future, the group's members continued to receive startling reports from Prophet's ascended advisors about the world's corrupted and dangerous condition. At times in 1996 and 1997, the Ascended Masters speaking through the Messenger addressed serious issues concerning the existence of "enemy forces" preparing to strike against the church's Lightbearers. In an issue of *Pearls of Wisdom* published during Prophet's South American lecture tour, the Messenger warned the members about the threat of karma not native to the people of the Americas. [93] According to Prophet's dictation, those who possessed this foreign karma were "the peoples of the Near and Far East" who inherited it from extraterrestrial visitors. [94] In an even more unusual example of enemy projection, Prophet delivered a message to CUT members at a small gathering on the Royal Teton Ranch in early 1997 stating that aliens had positioned themselves on the dark side of the moon in preparation for an assault on the earth. [95] The Messenger congratulated the members for their heroic efforts at forestalling this plot, an act said to have been facilitated by the ranch community's organized prayer services, but she relayed to the group the Ascended Masters' warning that continued diligence was required to defeat the plans of these nefarious visitors from space. [96]

By far, the greatest visible change made in CUT's public relations campaign involved de-emphasizing its traditional anticommunism and pervasive conspiracy beliefs. Until quite recently, the group highlighted these themes at Summit University Forums held both at Camelot and the Royal Teton Ranch. The scope of the forums revealed clear indications of CUT's embrace of secret "truths" and hidden knowledge. Some of these events have been promoted in church literature under themes having to do with alleged government UFO cover-ups, AIDS conspiracies, and communist threats to the United States.[97] Since the antiestablishment, "fringe" quality of these panel forums could be used by critics to demonstrate the group's political character, CUT has used caution in its promotion of these activities.[98] In order to deflect charges that the church subscribes to controversial conspiracy theories, and to protect its tax-exempt status as a religious body, purveyors of these theories are no longer sought out to speak at group functions. Noting that the selection of speakers at the forums has been a function of gauging "what might interest and educate members," Edward Francis, CUT's former vice president, indicated that the primary focus for the organization has never been purely political, conspiratorial, or about national defense.[99] Francis suggested that the church's religious beliefs have been misunderstood and observed that the media tends to portray CUT as a far-right group. In supporting his point, Francis said that national defense and belief in America's destiny were parts of the church's religious foundation. He maintained that these attitudes "were not part of any political activism goal in the organization."[100]

Mark Prophet's close attachment to the I AM movement's splinter factions in the 1950s passed on to him the Ballards' distrust of government and a conviction that the United States was being subverted by a diabolical power elite. He used politics as an educative device in the church by relying upon foes on the left to unify his followers. For Mark Prophet, the sordid political world provided a viable "other" against which his movement was mobilized. Its constant source of threat gave him the opportunity to illustrate the dark side of humanity and its failed attempt at substituting a religion of secularism in place of God.[101]

Mark Prophet's populist and antistatist attitudes placed him at odds with "establishment" politics and, clearly, his patriotism found expression in the Summit Lighthouse's rebuke of leftist enemies. But according to Francis, CUT loosened its adherence to Mark Prophet's political outlook some time ago and has changed much about its view of the secular world: "I think we have evolved along the way. Twenty or twenty-five years ago I would have said that we had a very conservative and patriotic viewpoint. I wouldn't totally rule that out today, but back in those days it was more a right-wing thing, and that's much less so today for a number of reasons. On the one hand there's a broader range of membership now than there was twenty-five years ago. And it's certainly not a requirement that a member have a particular political view." [102]

Francis' views about the changes in CUT are generally accepted by scholars having some familiarity with the organization's history, some of whom have also noted that the membership is not as monolithic as has often been reported. [103] Indeed, since the failed apocalyptic prediction in 1990, the rightist, superpatriotic aspects of CUT's belief structure have eroded, largely due to the conclusion of the Cold War. A sudden and unexpected dissolution of the Soviet Union deprived CUT of its historic political enemy, leaving the group to search for new foes symbolizing more imminent threats. While post-Soviet international security concerns such as terrorism, the proliferation of weapons of mass destruction, and the actions of rogue states have partially filled this void, [104] the implosion of the Soviet enemy eliminated the arch-nemesis upon which the group's patriotic spirituality was dependent. CUT's efforts to ingratiate itself with a nonpolitical (and decidedly antimilitarist) New Age audience also explains the growth of different attitudes within the church and will almost certainly expedite the toning down of its superpatriotism and right-wing tendencies. Finding itself in competition with other new religious movements, especially those whose cosmologies are grounded in the same Ascended Master tradition, [105] it is likely that the church will continue to creatively promote its message to spiritual seekers.

Beginning in 1998, a wave of developments took place within the organization that indicated that a process of radical change had begun. The first of these involved putting up for sale portions of the Royal Teton Ranch. In March 1998, CUT officials announced that a $13 million agreement was pending that would transfer about half of the twelve-thousand-acre Royal Teton Ranch property to the U.S. Forest Service. The proposed deal would make this section of the tract a public property protected from development. Denying rumors that the land sell-off foreshadowed the group's eventual departure from Montana, CUT representatives said that parts of the ranch had been sold before. Gilbert Cleirbaut, the church's new president, indicated that the organization was committed to retaining its spiritual home on the Royal Teton Ranch, although he told local media that the costs associated with keeping the property were burdensome. [106]

While the land sale was being contemplated, reports circulated in the Montana press that CUT's administration was further reducing the number of full-time staff living on the Royal Teton Ranch. In accordance with the new management's policy of trimming operational expenses, the already scaled-down community was further reduced to 144 members in summer 1998. Concerned about the group's declining financial position, church officials stated that the ranch's employee force would eventually be still smaller.[107] The reduction would help channel organization money to programs designed to promote growth in other countries.[108]

However, by far the most startling news came in an official CUT news release to the media on January 1, 1999. Prophet would be stepping down as the group's spiritual leader in a few months' time. Although it had been reported a year earlier that she had been diagnosed with "a degenerative neurological disease,"[109] CUT officials had not clarified the nature of her condition. The shroud of mystery surrounding Prophet's health was removed when she told the members attending the annual New Year's conference in Miami that she had been diagnosed with Alzheimer's disease. In the announcement, Prophet said that she would continue to seek medical help for her condition and that, at sixty years of age, she felt it was time to moderate her schedule.[110] Even before the Messenger's declaration, church representatives spoke openly of her declining health and suggested that her future role in the organization was uncertain.

It was generally unknown throughout CUT's ranks that Prophet had experienced epileptic seizures from the time she was a child. But it is apparent that the organization's officers were aware of her past health problems and were also cognizant of the decline in her mental abilities brought about by Alzheimer's disease. Several months prior to the diagnosis, Gilbert Cleirbaut addressed the need for CUT's membership to prepare for a future leadership structure without Prophet. In the months immediately before Prophet's own public declaration of her intentions, Cleirbaut made it clear that the group was engaged in charting a new course. He told the media that "fanaticism" and "living in fear" were chapters in the church's past, and that CUT's central mission in the future would be simply to spread the teachings of Elizabeth Clare Prophet and the Ascended Masters.[111] The church's pronouncements about Prophet's retirement were framed in a positive light and credited her with having been a religious visionary who "enriched the lives of thousands, if not millions," but the eulogistic overtures were obvious.[112] However, in spite of Prophet's malady and recent retirement, CUT's spokespersons have reassured the membership that she is still the sole appointed Messenger for the Ascended Masters.

By summer 1999, still more changes unfolded. Cleirbaut unexpectedly resigned his position as CUT's top executive in July, and shortly thereafter, a "presidential triumvirate" of three long-standing members was elected by the church's board of directors to occupy the vacated post. The officeholders, Kenneth Frazier, Kate Gordon, and Neroli Duffy, continued to pursue the downsizing strategy Cleirbaut launched and soon announced plans to release more of the full-time staff employees at the Royal Teton Ranch. Under this newest operating plan, CUT retained between sixty and seventy-five staff workers on the ranch, which administrators divested of its agricultural, civil engineering, and construction divisions.[113] Although the layoffs reduced its operating expenses, CUT continued to run a budget deficit of about $1 million in 1999. The organization's financial problems were ameliorated, though, when the previous year's proposed land sale to the United States Forest Service was signed. The deal, which was signed in a ceremony attended by U.S. Secretary of the Interior Bruce Babbitt on the Royal Teton Ranch on August 31, 1999, ironically earned CUT accolades from two sources with whom its past relations have been strained: environmental groups and the federal government.[114] In return for the $13 million the church received, the government acquired about eight thousand acres of ranch property adjacent to Yellowstone National Park. Conservationists applauded CUT's desire to sell the tract to the Forest Service (which ensured that the ground would remain free from future development) and expressed relief that the park's roaming bison could safely migrate to the newly acquired government land during the winter when the animals seek lower elevations.[115]

As part of the land deal, the U.S. Forest Service obtained the geothermal rights on CUT's property. The acquisition of these rights to underground supplies of hot water on the Royal Teton Ranch was important to the government since, if penetrated, the natural subsurface flow feeding the geysers and hot springs of Yellowstone National Park could be disrupted. The church, on the other hand, benefitted from a land swap written into the deal that provided it with more acreage near the main shelter facility it continues to maintain. CUT officials disclosed that the $13 million the organization received would be used to establish new teaching centers in the United States and abroad and to build a retirement fund for the ailing Elizabeth Clare Prophet.[116]

The Church and Its Future

Just as the Church Universal and Triumphant came to life as the offspring of Guy and Edna Ballard's I AM movement, it appears that CUT will follow its leaders' course of decline. The I AM movement did not entirely fade away as a result of either the Ballards' deaths or the legal problems that beset the group from the mid-1940s until the early 1950s. While membership dropped precipitously and splinter factions formed claiming to be its legitimate successors,[117] the I AM movement continued to exist but assumed a new organizational identity as a decentralized and relatively small religious society. The final step in this process came after the death of Edna Ballard in 1971, which left the group without its source of charismatic leadership.[118] Although never again able to attract the sizeable following it had during the depression, when it may have had close to one hundred thousand members, the I AM movement sill remains a visible presence among the minor constellation of new religious movements teaching Ascended Master doctrine.[119]

Like the Ballards' organization, CUT adhered to a charismatic authority structure. As prophetic figures with exclusive access to the Ascended Masters, the Messengers' leadership style was determined by the group doctrine they themselves shaped. The rigidly hierarchical organizational framework that developed was based on the accepted identity of Mark and Elizabeth Clare Prophet as the semidivine conduits between the membership and the church's deities, a recognition with natural implications for the group's behavior. With Elizabeth Clare Prophet's role now marginalized, the organization has attempted to transform itself in less authoritarian directions. This has involved the decentralization of decision making and the creation of a bureaucratic management structure in the church, steps that Max Weber associated with a charismatic religious movement's route to institutionalization.[120]

Following Weber's theory, the "formal rationality" model of authority caters to the approval of social systems and, to satisfy those comprising these networks, invests authority in legally constituted offices. Thus, in the maturation of the contemporary Western social system Weber observed, rational-legal authority displaces charisma (and charismatics) as the basis upon which social order functions. As applied to new religious movements with a charismatic leadership structure, the transition to a legal-rational framework is often difficult. Although the more successful of these movements adopt some form of bureaucratization, some scholars have noted the tendency for charismatic leaders to oppose the process since it results in the "routinization" of their charisma.[121]

With its Messenger ill, and with no stated plans to recognize another, CUT occupies strange, transitory ground as a new religious movement in the midst of an identity crisis. For forty years, group doctrine made the Messengers virtually indistinguishable from the pantheon of Ascended Masters for whom they spoke. In the eyes of believers, Mark and Elizabeth Clare Prophet represented the link between the movement's spiritual seekers and the godhead to which they aspired. But by early 1999, CUT officials were already informing the membership that "the torch has been passed" and that the church needed to end its "codependency" on Elizabeth Clare Prophet.[122] Whether or not CUT can transform into a successful post-Prophet religious organization remains, at best, clouded by uncertainties. But the prospects for a revival of its charismatic leadership tradition are slim since the family line of succession among Prophet's progeny has been interrupted. Currently, none of her four adult children are part of the church.[123]

The crisis that is presently playing out in the church stemmed directly from the nonevent of March 15, 1990. Morale problems and declining financial health soon followed, but were exacerbated by the de facto elimination of CUT's chief ideological foe, the Soviet Union, when the Cold War concluded. The "loss" of its Soviet enemy quickly deprived the superpatriotic group of its anticommunist ideological foundation, which was the main catalyst for the organization's embrace of survivalism. Left without the opponent with which it conducted spiritual warfare for over three decades, CUT faltered and a period of organizational confusion set in. Church representatives have openly spoken of the need to scale back the group's "survival mentality" to better market its theology.[124] But it is difficult to ascertain what might fill this void in its teachings.

One of my interview subjects, Paula, a plainspoken woman in her late forties, made clear to me the extent to which CUT's religious doctrine has been intertwined with survivalism. Paula agreed to give me a tour of the communal shelter she helps maintain near her Glastonbury home. She explained that the twelve- to twenty-person facility, complete with lighting, a water supply, several spacious rooms, and a radiation decontamination chamber, was constructed ten feet below an open pasture in 1989 after Prophet told church members to expect the nuclear attack. Like some of the other shelters at Glastonbury, from the outside only the appearance of a heavy wooden door propped against the ground gives away the existence of the man-made cavern. Paula told me that the church's preparations for disaster had been misunderstood. "We're not here just waiting for the world to end," she said after our walk-through of the sizeable shelter, "but Saint Germain gave us the admonition to be ready for nuclear war and the carnage that followed, so we saw the building of the shelters as our obligation." Over four years after the mobilization, Paula still firmly believed that unstable world conditions mandated that the membership have access to the emergency structures. As she put it, "disaster isn't necessarily inevitable, but it may be likely, and the Ascended Masters have spoken about this." [125]

Recognizing that its future depends upon attracting new members, group leaders have focused on overseas recruitment. This strategy was behind Prophet's 1996 Latin American tour, but since then CUT officials have emphasized Russia and Europe as regions where the organization will build new teaching centers and spread its doctrine. [126] In order to bolster recruitment and enhance organizational visibility, CUT will be forced to seek further integration with the larger New Age movement, a plan it is already vigorously pursuing. As reported in the church's news bulletin, the group has accelerated its promotion of Prophet's books at New Age venues. This it has done with some success. Prophet's most recent title, *Saint Germain's Prophecy for the New Millennium,* was touted to have become "a New Age best-seller," with some twenty-five thousand copies sold by late 1999. The coauthored work, whose contributors included onetime CUT officeholder Murray Steinman and Patricia Spadaro, the organization's press editor, was promoted at the International New Age Frankfurt Book Fair and will be published in Spanish and Portugese, as well as several other languages. [127]

Any future plans CUT had to further dilute its theologically driven survivalism will encounter doctrinal constraints laid down in the organization decades ago. In 1969, while still in Colorado Springs, the group's leaders turned their attention to the negative karma believed to have accumulated through the past 25,800 years of human history. The church's position has been that these negative energies are created by human misdeeds and "return" to earth over a cyclical time pattern. According to CUT doctrine, waves of negative karma descended on the planet in 1990 at the end of that cycle, and the next "delivery cycle" (which was believed would be more "physical" than the previous) built to its peak in the year 2002. [128] While CUT maintains that the karmic onslaught can be turned back, the group continues to heed the cautionary advice of the Ascended Masters that a future cataclysm is still quite possible.[129]

CUT no longer views the prospect of a forthcoming, massive nuclear war as the high-level threat it was considered to be during the Cold War, but "potential worldwide instability" is still thought to be capable of producing a disaster that requires the readiness of the membership. Additionally, like much of American society, the group expressed worries in the late 1990s about the potential effects of the "Year 2000" problem and listed it among the threats that could negatively impact the future of the church.[130] Because CUT's doctrine has pointed to an uncertain future, the organization keeps ready its main shelter on the Royal Teton Ranch in the event that it is needed. Likewise, the shelters at Glastonbury remain in service although some of these structures are now reported to be in a dilapidated state of repair.[131]

The colossal change process will leave the church a radically altered and smaller organization, with some two hundred worldwide teaching centers and study groups forming the new core of the movement. In this new organizational model, localized networks of members will be the hub of CUT's reconfigured spiritual community. Such a plan is logical in light of the church's recent de-emphasis of the ranch as the locus of organizational authority.[132] Despite the considerable costs of operating the church, which were estimated to approach $11 million in fiscal year 1998,[133] the $13 million land deal with the federal government should allow CUT to retain the scaled-down Royal Teton Ranch and to finance its publishing business. Although membership contributions (in the form of tithes) are said to be at record low levels, a development that contributed to CUT's decision to sell large parts of its property,[134] spokesmen still point to the tract's status as "holy ground" and suggest that parting with the ranch would damage the organization's image in the eyes of its members.[135]

As the church's attempted metamorphosis takes shape, new splinter organizations will almost certainly appear in order to preserve factional impressions of the "true" doctrine. Such an occurrence has already taken place with a former high-ranking member establishing the Temple of the Presence, a small CUT offshoot located in Chelsea, Vermont.[136] Its charismatic founder, Monroe Shearer, originally organized the Ascended Master group in Redlands, California, in 1996 at a time when the Church Universal and Triumphant's morale problems became public knowledge. Shearer and his wife, Carolyn, who act as the group's co-Messengers for the Ascended Masters, claim they are not in competition with CUT for members. However, the leaders of the fledgling sect have made a practice of coming to the Bozeman, Montana, area to promote the new religious activity, which may at present have a few hundred adherents.[137] News of Prophet's declining health may well cause other church members to exploit the disarray in the group's leadership and form new charismatic movements in the Ascended Master tradition.

One area in which new splinter-group growth is possible is survivalism. If the church should continue on a course designed to "mainstream" its theology by eradicating the more conspiratorial and disaster-focused aspects of its belief system, it is conceivable that a faction of catastrophic believers would emerge as an alternative movement. The causes for such an action are understandable; any effort by CUT to compromise its historic teachings on disaster and group survival would be resented by those perceiving themselves to be the upholders of the group's divine wisdom. Even if the church succeeds in muting the catastrophic component of its teachings, it is unrealistic to assume that the entire membership will embrace the readjusted theology. Indications of this resistance have surfaced in the form of survivalist literature produced independently by members. Recent survival manuals and books marketed and published by individuals belonging to the organization suggest that disaster preparation continues to be strongly supported by portions of CUT's membership.[138]

Whether or not factionalization will necessarily take place, it is important to consider this possibility since CUT's own existence came about through mutation from the I AM movement. The history of the group derives from a process of change and adaptation, characteristics that are inherent to social movements in the cultic milieu. This cycle, as Colin Campbell observed, is consistent with the malleable and unstable nature of the beliefs and organizational structures of esoteric movements. The organizations involved in this process tend to be transitory. They come to life, mutate, or die off in the universe of heterodox ideas in which they reside.[139]

The Cultic Milieu and Violence

In our times, the cultic milieu appears to be in a period of efflorescence. The recent spate of activism by groups with apocalyptic ideologies suggests that the calendrical progression to the year 2000, stoked the imagination of some counterculturalists. The symbolism associated with passing into a new period of time may have provoked a minority following of groups in the millennial subculture to become energized. In the last half of the 1990s, there was a sudden increase in the number of cases of apocalyptic groups whose millennial understanding of history and dualistic, cultic-inspired beliefs contributed either to violent confrontation with authorities or to group suicide. It merits attention, of course, that there is often considerable apocalypse-date-setting flexibility within the orbit of groups observing millennial timetables, and that millenarians have never relied on the arrival of the millennial date as a marker to mobilize.[140] In each of the high-profile end-of-century cases, however, the organizations adhered to End of the Age cosmologies connected with a specific time near 2000. The groups included the Order of the Solar Temple, whose members engaged in mass suicides and ritualistic murder at sites in Switzerland, France, and Quebec in phases in October 1994, December 1995, and March 1997; the Japanese separatist sect Aum Shinrikyo; and Heaven's Gate, whose members committed group suicide at their home in Rancho Santa Fe, California, in March 1997.[141]

Like the Church Universal and Triumphant's Royal Teton Ranch community, which anticipated the approach of the End of the Age in March 1990, other collectivities of disaster-focused millennialists may resort to date-setting in anticipation of earthly disaster. The catastrophic millennial beliefs that fuel such activity are perfectly suited for "habitation" in the cultic milieu in which they percolate. This is especially the case when the believers, who have already psychologically "escaped" from the surrounding culture, adopt a physically separate existence. In a segregated community, groups adhering to apocalyptic beliefs can function as self-contained social systems that, as a result of their insular character, promote ideological homogeneity. The fact that the group's cosmology is often indecipherable to outsiders may reinforce the self-imposed barrier used by the community to remain apart. Doctrinal impenetrability allows the group to turn increasingly inward and further lock itself into its own belief structure.[142]

Because we cannot estimate how countercultural beliefs will be psychologically interpreted by catastrophic millenarians, it is impossible to determine precisely whether the start of the calendrical new millennium will spark a period of heightened apocalyptic agitation by groups preparing for their "rebirth" in the perfect age. The Church Universal and Triumphant's absorption with apocalyptic excitement in Montana represents one variation of the catastrophic impulse. The urge for withdrawal and escape define this approach to group perceptions of sudden earthly change, inclinations that tend to steer the

Elizabeth Clare Prophet at a church ceremony in 1997.
Courtesy of the *Calgary Herald*. Photograph by Larry MacDougal.

community of believers away from conflict with the outside world. The alternative option is more troubling. Instead of hunkering down to outlive the disaster, the group's hope for renewal is tied to the destructive event itself, and redemption is dependent upon the realization of the catastrophe. Those adhering to this vision, thus, are far more likely to undertake violence as a means to usher in the new era. This distinction is important because it effectively separates disaster-focused millennialism into either nonviolent or potentially violent forms.[143]

The responsibility for distinguishing between passive millennial groups and End Time believers of a more aggressive character ultimately resides with the internal security agencies of the government. Characterization is made difficult because much remains unknown about the obscure, esoteric beliefs observed by apocalyptists. Furthermore, the insular social networks that act as both repositories and conduits for heterodox ideas are features of an underground counterculture and thus tend to be shielded from the larger society's scrutiny. These obstacles present serious problems for law enforcement groups in their efforts to preemptively counter expressions of violence-prone millennialism. The foremost danger is, nevertheless, to the members of counterculture groups rather than the larger society, when law enforcement agencies abandon dispassionate threat assessments and cautionary tactics. Such a lapse occurred in the unfortunate mishandling of the Waco episode, whose results further convinced some apocalyptists that the government sought to exterminate its opponents.[144]

As we enter the new calender millennium, we may see more cases of disaster-focused millenarian movements that act upon their beliefs. Unlike the Church Universal and Triumphant, whose group-specific millennial outlook led it to a completely nonviolent encounter with the apocalypse, some End Time groups may be moved to adopt violent tactics in the period following the major date transformation. Anticipation about this symbolic event, in a worst case, could result in some millenarians taking action to "trigger" the arrival of the perfect age.[145] It is the specific behavior, the act of inciting the coming glory period for believers, which may put the catastrophic millennial community on a collision course with society. The potential consequences of such outbursts of catastrophic millennial activism oblige scholars and police agencies to expand their efforts at understanding the beliefs of those willing to use violence to usher in the new golden age.[146]

Epilogue

The near-term likelihood of carrying on without the movement's Messenger has expedited CUT's attempts to see through the organizational changes brought about during what officials now call the church's "second life cycle." This euphemism for the period following the earlier shelter cycle involves the further "democratization" of the movement, downsizing the Royal Teton Ranch, and building a congregation of believers focused on the teachings.[1] The objective behind the organization's new plan to rebuild the church is to spread the teachings of the Ascended Masters and Elizabeth Clare Prophet to a wider audience of spiritual seekers. In order to accomplish this task, CUT has resuscitated its practice of holding quarterly conferences at the Royal Teton Ranch and is now using Internet communications to connect its members at overseas study centers with the services taking place at these major meetings.[2]

Although never able to recoup the membership losses it experienced in the years after the failed apocalyptic prediction in 1990, CUT has benefitted financially from its sales of ranch property. In a recent effort at bolstering the church's finances, the organization's board of directors approved the sale in 2000 of a 9,300-acre tract of unused range land it possessed some forty miles north of the Royal Teton Ranch. This North Ranch property was purchased soon after the group relocated to Montana, but it was never a very productive site for farming and often remained completely vacant during the 1990s. The $12.5 million sale to an unnamed buyer provides CUT with a considerable sum for organizational projects, including what its representatives have said might be the establishment of an endowment fund. However, parting with the North Ranch land leaves the church with a much smaller property base in the Paradise Valley region, which currently includes only the eight-thousand-acre Royal Teton Ranch and the three thousand acres it retains in Glastonbury.[3]

In late fall 1999, Elizabeth Clare Prophet was legally declared to be an incapacitated person and two guardians were named to oversee her health care. A conservator was also appointed to handle Prophet's legal and financial affairs. Erin L. Prophet, the church leader's oldest daughter, was named as one of the guardians. A November 1999 open letter to CUT's membership from Erin Prophet on her mother's condition reported on the Messenger's efforts to combat Alzheimer's disease, but made clear that her public appearances are now minimal and that she is no longer giving live dictations.[4] While the Messenger is scheduled to move soon from the Royal Teton Ranch to a care facility in Bozeman, CUT officials say that her departure from the church's headquarters will not initiate the group's withdrawal from Paradise Valley.[5]

News of Elizabeth Clare Prophet's declining health has caused the organization's new leadership to adopt an approach that seeks to allay the concerns of the membership and to frame Prophet's experience in the best light. CUT's presidential triumvirate issued a formal statement in January 2000 that placed the Messenger's illness in the context of a lesson for the group's members. Using the Alzheimer's malady afflicting Prophet as a metaphor for "forgetfulness" among the membership, CUT's chief officers posed the question of whether the faithful would remember "the Path, the Teacher, and the Teachings when all else passes?"[6] In the statement, Prophet was said to be like Christ in that she would remain the same "yesterday, today, and forever."[7] Quite clearly, however, the leaders were preparing CUT's following for the symbolic demise of the old church and the arrival of a new period in the group's history.

NOTES

BIBLIOGRAPHY

INDEX

Notes

1. Escape to the Mountains

1. "Apocalyptic Church Struggling After Armageddon Didn't Happen," *Detroit News,* April 4, 1998.

2. "CUT's New Reality," *Bozeman Daily Chronicle,* March 15, 1998.

3. "Undercover: Delving into the Church's Business Practices," *Calgary Herald,* March 3, 1997.

4. Frederic J. Baumgartner, *Longing for the End: A History of Millennialism in Western Civilization* (New York: St. Martin's, 1999), 249–50.

5. Stuart Wright, "Anatomy of a Government Massacre: Abuse of Hostage-Barricade Protocols during the Waco Standoff," *Terrorism and Political Violence* 11, no. 3 (summer 1999): 47.

6. Philip Jenkins, *Mystics and Messiahs: Cults and New Religions in American History* (New York: Oxford University Press, 2000), 219–20.

7. Murray Steinman, interview by the author, Corwin Springs, Mont., August 8, 1993. At the time of the interview, Steinman was acting as the church's director of public relations.

8. On occasion, CUT inflated these membership figures to the media. See, for example, William Plummer, "Turmoil in a California Camelot," *People* (July 1, 1985): 74–77. In the article, it is estimated that the church had between 75,000 and 150,000 members.

9. "Disease, Dissension Haunt Family," *Bozeman Daily Chronicle,* March 16, 1998.

10. "Former CUT Members Say They Are Messengers," *Bozeman Daily Chronicle,* May 5, 1999, and undated Temple of the Presence advertisement.

11. "1998 Annual Report" published by CUT outlining financial status and organizational planning. The first such report was issued by the church in 1997.

12. "Church Turns Land over to Government," *Salt Lake City Tribune,* September 1, 1999, and *Heart to Heart: Monthly Newsletter of the International Headquarters of the Church Universal and Triumphant,* September 1999.

13. James R. Lewis, "Of Tolerance, Toddlers, and Trailers: First Impressions of the Church Universal and Triumphant," in *The Church Universal and Triumphant in Scholarly Perspective,* ed. James R. Lewis and J. Gordon Melton (Stanford, Calif.: Center for Academic Publication, 1994), xii-xiii.

14. J. Gordon Melton, "The Church Universal and Triumphant: Its Heritage and Thought-world," in *The Church Universal and Triumphant in Scholarly Perspective,* ed. James Lewis and J. Gordon Melton (Stanford, Calif.: Center for Academic Publication, 1994), 20.

15. Ibid., 10.

16. Guy Ballard [Godfre Ray King, pseud.],
Unveiled Mysteries (Mount Shasta, Calif.: Ascended Master Teaching Foundation, 1939), vii.

17. Ibid., viii.

18. Michael Barkun, *Disaster and the Millennium* (New Haven: Yale University Press, 1974), 4.

19. James Rhodes, *The Hitler Movement: A Modern Millenarian Revolution* (Stanford: Hoover Institute Press, 1980), 29.

20. "The Great White Brotherhood as Inner World Government: Basic Cosmic Science," early undated lesson for church members. Probably produced during the group's years in the Washington, D.C., area.

21. Ibid.

22. Catherine Wessinger, "Millennialism with and without the Mayhem," in *Millennium, Messiahs, and Mayhem: Contemporary Apocalyptic Movements,* ed. Thomas Robbins and Susan Palmer (New York: Routledge, 1997), 48.

23. Timothy Weber, *Living in the Shadow of the Second Coming: American Pre-millennialism (1875–1982)* (Grand Rapids: Academie Books, 1983), 9.

24. Wessinger, "Millennialism with and without the Mayhem," 50.

25. See Martha Lee, *Earth First! Environmental Apocalypse* (Syracuse: Syracuse University Press, 1995), 18–20. Lee observes this distinction between millenarian and apocalyptic doctrines.

26. Wessinger, "Millennialism with and without the Mayhem," 50–51.

27. Norman Cohn, *The Pursuit of the Millennium: Revolutionary Millenarians and Mystical Anarchists of the Middle Ages* (New York: Oxford University Press, 1970), 308–10.

28. Ibid., 308.

29. Ibid., 309.

30. Mark and Elizabeth Clare Prophet, *The Lost Teachings of Jesus (Book 4), Good and Evil: Atlantis Revisited* (Livingston, Mont.: Summit University Press, 1986), 5. This volume consists of a series of lectures given by Mark Prophet between 1965 and 1973.

31. Ibid.

32. "Leaders Deny CUT Bought Guns," *Billings Gazette,* February 16, 1995.

33. Mark Prophet, *The Soulless Ones: Cloning a Counterfeit Creation* (Los Angeles: Summit University Press, 1965), 107–11.

34. Colin Campbell, "The Cult, the Cultic Milieu, and Secularization," in *A Sociological Yearbook of Religion in Britain* (London: SCM Press, 1972), 120–23.

35. Ibid.

36. Mark and Elizabeth Clare Prophet, *The Lost Teachings of Jesus (Book 4),* 31–37.

37. Brad Whitsel, "Taking Shelter from the Coming Storm: The Millennial Impulse of the Church Universal and Triumphant's Royal Teton Ranch," *Communal Societies* 19 (1999): 12.

38. James Webb, *The Occult Establishment* (LaSalle, Ill.: Open Court Publishing, 1976), 496.

39. *Pearls of Wisdom* 12, no. 17 (April 27, 1969). Weekly teachings published by the church and mailed to members.

40. *Pearls of Wisdom* 24, no. 36 (August 30, 1981).

2. History and Beliefs of the Church Universal and Triumphant

1. J. Gordon Melton, *New Age Encyclopedia* (Detroit: Gale Research, 1990), xxii.

2. Ibid.

3. Colin Wilson, *The Occult: A History* (New York: Vintage Books, 1973), 280.

4. Melton, *New Age Encyclopedia*, xxii-xxiii.

5. Emanuel Swedenborg, *The True Christian Religion*, vol. 1 (New York: American Swedenborg Printing and Publishing Society, 1952), 8–10.

6. Peter Washington, *Madame Blavatsky's Baboon: A History of the Mystics, Mediums, and Misfits Who Brought Spiritualism to America* (New York: Schocken Books, 1993), 15.

7. Ibid., 16.

8. Winthrop S. Hudson, *Religion in America: An Historical Account of the Development of American Religious Life*, 3d ed. (New York: Charles Scribner's Sons, 1981), 198.

9. Ibid. Among the best-known hoaxes was the acknowledged trickery of the Fox sisters. Taking advantage of some adults who took the girls' furtive joint-cracking as a sign from the deceased, the sisters gained considerable popularity in upstate New York as spiritual mediums. In 1888, however, the girls admitted their fraudulence.

10. Ibid., 289.

11. Melton, *New Age Encyclopedia*, 52.

12. Washington, *Madame Blavatsky's Baboon*, 18.

13. Melton, *New Age Encyclopedia*, xxiv.

14. R. Laurence Moore, "Mormonism, Christian Science, and Spiritualism," in *The Occult in America: New Historical Perspectives*, ed. Howard Kerr and Charles Crow (Urbana: University of Illinois Press, 1983), 143–50. Moore describes the problems faced by Eddy's Church of Christ, Scientist.

15. Hudson, *Religion in America*, 290.

16. J. Gordon Melton, *The Encyclopedia of American Religions*, 2d ed. (Detroit: Garland Publishing, 1989), 121.

17. Ibid.

18. J. Stillson Judah, *The History and Philosophy of the Metaphysical Movements in America* (Philadelphia: Westminster Press, 1967), 96.

19. Robert S. Ellwood, *Alternative Altars: Unconventional and Eastern Spirituality in America* (Chicago: University of Chicago Press, 1979), 105.

20. Wilson, *The Occult*, 330.

21. Ellwood, *Alternative Altars*, 108. Ellwood's book also discusses Blavatsky's early life. Blavatsky's frequently inconsistent claims about her whereabouts during this period have been used by some to discredit her.

22. Melton, *Encyclopedia of American Religions*, 123.

23. Robert S. Ellwood, "The American Theosophical Synthesis," in *The Occult in America: New Historical Perspectives*, ed. Howard Kerr and Charles Crow (Urbana: University of Illinois Press, 1983), 117.

24. Catherine Wessinger, *Annie Besant and Progressive Messianism* (Lewiston, N.Y.: Edwin Mellen Press, 1988), 157–68. Wessinger discusses some of Blavatsky's written works. Blavatsky

claimed that the material in *Isis Unveiled* came from spiritual masters of the Orient who directed her writings.

25. Ellwood, "The American Theosophical Synthesis," 119.

26. Ibid., 118.

27. See Helena Petrovna Blavatsky, *Isis Unveiled* (Pasadena, Calif.: Theosophical University Press, 1972), 2:372–90, for her discussion of the Order of Masons and its possession of "hidden Knowledge" from the East.

28. Melton, *Encyclopedia of American Religions*, 123.

29. Ellwood, *Alternative Altars*, 129.

30. Ibid., 127.

31. Melton, *Encyclopedia of American Religions*, 124.

32. Ibid.

33. Melton, "The Church Universal and Triumphant: Its Heritage and Thoughtworld," 3.

34. Wessinger, *Annie Besant and Progressive Messianism*, 326. According to Bailey, Besant demanded that members pledge loyalty to her.

35. Ibid., 328.

36. See Alice Bailey, *From Intellect to Intuition* (New York: Lucius Publishing Co., 1960), 1–17. Bailey's writings helped popularize the use of the term "New Age" among later alternative religious groups.

37. Melton, *Encyclopedia of American Religions*, 126.

38. Ibid.

39. Bailey, *From Intellect to Intuition*, 4.

40. See Ballard, *Unveiled Mysteries*, iii. Departing from the use of the word "Masters" to describe the spiritual collective (or Brotherhood) believed by Theosophists to guide the evolution of the planet, the I AM movement referred to these entities as "Ascended Masters." Each group, however, perceived these entities as individual beings who once occupied this earth but succeeded in breaking the bonds of human limitation. Thus, they were viewed as more godlike than ordinary beings.

41. For an account of Saint Germain's legendary life, see Wilson, *The Occult*, 315–18.

42. Melton, "The Church Universal and Triumphant: Its Heritage and Thoughtworld," 4.

43. Charles Braden, *These Also Believe: A Study of American Cults and Minority Religious Movements* (New York: Macmillan Co., 1949), 267–69. As taught by the Ballards, the I AM is God. The movement's name comes from the biblical story of Moses who, in his exchange with the burning bush, asked, "Who shall I say sent me?" God's answer was "I am that I am."

44. Ballard, *Unveiled Mysteries*, iv. For an early account of the I AM movement's numerical size, see H. G. McGaughey, "Another One in California, the I AM Movement," *Christian Century* (August 31, 1938): 1038. Ballard claimed in the late-depression years that the movement had over a million members.

45. Gerald B. Bryan, *Psychic Dictatorship in America* (Burbank, Calif.: New Era Press, 1940), 32–33.

46. Ibid. Bryan indicates that Edna Ballard appropriated much of Pelley's written work in her later teachings. For a fuller account of William Dudley Pelley, his writings, and the Silver Legion's philosophy, see John Werly, "The Millenarian Right: William Dudley Pelley and the Silver

Legion of America," Ph.D. diss. (Ann Arbor, Mich.: University Microfilms, 1972).

47. Bryan, *Psychic Dictatorship in America,* 207–15.

48. Braden, *These Also Believe,* 269.

49. J. Gordon Melton, *Encyclopedic Handbook of Cults in America* (New York: Garland, 1986), 48.

50. Ballard, *Unveiled Mysteries,* 17. The Ballards generally referred to this spiritual hierarchy as "the Great White Brotherhood." There is no evidence that the term carried racial connotations.

51. Braden, *These Also Believe,* 173. I AM theology points out that Ascended Masters can dwell on the earthly plane of existence if they so choose.

52. Ibid., 298.

53. Ballard, *Unveiled Mysteries,* v–vi. The group's decrees often took on a political tone. The movement's decrees were used to direct spiritual energies against a variety of foes, including the "unpatriotic" Roosevelt administration.

54. Werly, "The Millenarian Right," 183.

55. Braden, *These Also Believe,* 301.

56. Ballard, *Unveiled Mysteries,* 32–39. Ballard's "tour" with Saint Germain began on Mount Shasta in California. The journey included visits to the Sahara Desert, the Teton Mountains, Yellowstone Park, and ancient sites in Mexico and the Amazon region. Ballard's description of his "travel" bears a close resemblance with later psychic experiences called "astral projection."

57. Ibid., 13.

58. Braden, *These Also Believe,* 275.

59. Ibid., 283.

60. Ibid., 282–83. The Ascended Masters, speaking through Guy Ballard, had previously stated that Ascension (or becoming liberated from the human body) could not take place after the body's death.

61. Melton, *Encyclopedic Handbook of Cults in America,* 47.

62. Ibid.

63. Kenneth Paolini and Talita Paolini, *Four Hundred Years of Imaginary Friends: A Journey into the World of Adepts, Ascended Masters, and Their Messengers* (Livingston, Mont.: Paolini International, 2000), 236–37.

64. Melton, "The Church Universal and Triumphant: Its Heritage and Thoughtworld," 14.

65. Ibid., 14–15.

66. Melton, *Encyclopedic Handbook of Cults in America,* 135.

67. *The History of the Summit Lighthouse* (Livingston, Mont.: Summit University Press, 1994), 3.

68. Ibid., 3–4.

69. Rick Berchiolli, "Civil Religion in the Age of Aquarius: A Sociological Analysis of the Church Universal and Triumphant," unpublished research paper, 1988.

70. Aside from various accounts of Prophet's life provided by the Church Universal and Triumphant's publishing arm, including the videotape *Climb the Highest Mountain: A Profile of the Church Universal and Triumphant* (Livingston, Mont.: Summit University Press, 1993), a brief account of Mark Prophet's early work appears in Melton, *Encyclopedic Handbook of Cults in America,* 135–37.

71. Kenneth Paolini and Talita Paolini, *Four Hundred Years of Imaginary Friends,* 242.

72. Student background statement and financial aid application for Elizabeth Clare Wulf, Antioch College, 1957.

73. "Freshman life statement paper" written by Elizabeth Clare Wulf, Antioch College, 1957.

74. Melton, *Encyclopedic Handbook of Cults in America,* 136.

75. Autobiographical sketch paper written by Elizabeth Clare Wulf, Antioch College, March 1957.

76. Elizabeth Clare Prophet, interview by the author, Corwin Springs, Mont., July 3, 1994.

77. Melton, *Encyclopedic Handbook of Cults in America,* 136.

78. Mark and Elizabeth Clare Prophet, *The Lost Teachings of Jesus (Book 1)* (Livingston, Mont.: Summit University Press, 1986), 95.

79. Elizabeth Clare Prophet, *The Great White Brotherhood in the Culture, History, and Religion of America* (Colorado Springs: Summit University Press, 1976), 24. Sanat Kumara was believed to have descended to earth in the biblical Ancient of Days referred to in the Old Testament Books of Genesis and Daniel. The mission was aimed at preventing humanity's further pursuit of its course of ignorance and wickedness.

80. "I AM Light of the World: Invocations and Decrees for Keepers of the Flame," Summit Lighthouse, Inc., 1968, sec. 7.13A. This publication contains Keepers of the Flame material including decrees and ritual exercises dating from 1962.

81. Ibid., sec. 7.03. This conspiracy is addressed in Elizabeth Clare Prophet, *The Great White Brotherhood in the Culture, History, and Religion of America,* 239–66.

82. Mark Prophet, *The Soulless Ones,* 108. In the book, Prophet refrains from revealing more to the reader about the nature of human-like beings who were not created by God. He suggests that the Keepers of the Flame fraternity would be a more appropriate forum for such discussion.

83. Charles Braden, *These Also Believe: A Study of American Cults and Minority Religious Movements* (New York: Macmillan, 1949), 280.

84. *Keepers of the Flame: A Fraternity of Sons and Daughters of God Dedicated to the Freedom and Enlightenment of Humanity* (Livingston, Mont.: Summit Lighthouse, 1988), 21–26. Pamphlet produced by the Church Universal and Triumphant.

85. Melton, "The Church Universal and Triumphant: Its Heritage and Thoughtworld," 15.

86. Jean Allison, interview by the author, Corwin Springs, Mont., July 2, 1994. The tradition of holding regular, nationwide conferences for members of the Summit Lighthouse was passed on to the Church Universal and Triumphant.

87. *The History of the Summit Lighthouse,* 5.

88. Elizabeth Clare Prophet, *I Believe in the United States of America* (Los Angeles: Summit University Press, 1980). Audiotape recording of a July 4 speech given by Prophet at Camelot to a large gathering of church members.

89. Mark Prophet, *The Soulless Ones,* 107.

90. Ibid.

91. George Hunt Williamson, *Other Tongues, Other Flesh* (Albuquerque, N.Mex.: BE Books, 1990), 16. This is a reprint of Williamson's 1953 book.

92. Peter Arnone, telephone interview by the author, March 4, 1997.

93. Ibid., March 25, 1998.

94. Melton, *Encyclopedic Handbook of Cults in America,* 107.

95. Ibid., 113. As Melton notes, it is difficult to precisely define the philosophical thrust of New Age thought due to its diffuse array of intellectual currents.

96. *Climb the Highest Mountain.*

97. J. Gordon Melton, ed., *The Encyclopedia of American Religions: Religious Creeds* (Detroit: Gale Research, 1992), 747.

98. "The Great White Brotherhood as Inner World Government by the Ascended Master Chananda," early lesson for the Keepers of the Flame fraternity (Colorado Springs: Summit Lighthouse, 1968), 1.

99. Elizabeth Clare Prophet, *The Great White Brotherhood in the Culture, History, and Religion of America,* 59.

100. Michael York, "The Church Universal and Triumphant," *Journal of Contemporary Religion* 10, no. 1 (1995): 72. These beings represent only a small portion of the many Ascended Masters comprising the Great White Brotherhood.

101. 1980 memorandum for the church's administrative staff. The memorandum indicates that the Messenger has balanced 100 percent of her karma.

102. *Pearls of Wisdom* 11, no. 30 (July 28, 1968).

103. "Basic Cosmic Science," undated early lesson by the Ascended Master Chananda.

104. *The History of the Summit Lighthouse,* 5–8.

105. Debra Kantor and Meredith McGuire, "Creative Eclecticism: The Great White Brotherhood of Elizabeth Clare Prophet," paper presented to the Association for the Sociology of Religion, August 1981.

106. Mark Prophet and Elizabeth Clare Prophet, *Climb the Highest Mountain: The Path of the Higher Self* (Los Angeles: Summit University Press, 1972), 407.

107. *The History of the Summit Lighthouse,* 6.

108. Gary Shephard and Lawrence Lilliston, "Children of the Church Universal and Triumphant: Some Preliminary Impressions," in *The Church Universal and Triumphant in Scholarly Perspective,* ed. James Lewis and J. Gordon Melton (Stanford, Calif.: Center for Academic Publication, 1994), 79–80.

109. *Pearls of Wisdom* 22, no. 17 (April 27, 1969).

110. Mark Prophet and Elizabeth Clare Prophet, *Climb the Highest Mountain,* xx–xxvi.

111. Ibid., 96. In a section of the book entitled "The Coming of the Laggards," the Prophets' discuss the origin of this race.

112. Ibid., 124–25.

113. Kantor and McGuire, "Creative Eclecticism." In comparing these early recorded dictations with ones given later, Kantor and McGuire found that Prophet's charisma developed over time. Evidence of Prophet's maturation as a confident speaker can be found in the recorded lectures and dictations she gave several years following Mark Prophet's death. See, for example, Elizabeth Clare Prophet, *I Believe in the United States of America.*

114. Rick Berchiolli, "The Church Universal and Triumphant: The Evolution from World Transformation to Apocalypticism," paper presented at the Annual Meeting of the American Academy of Religion, November 18, 1989, Anaheim, Calif.

115. See Mark and Elizabeth Clare Prophet, *Climb the Highest Mountain,* 285. According to

Summit Lighthouse teachings, the flame represented the divine potential in humankind and was believed to be a manifestation of God.

116. Melton, *New Age Encyclopedia,* 24. For example, in June 1973 Prophet was declared by the church to be the Vicar of Christ.

117. *Royal Teton Ranch News* 6, no. 8 (September-October 1994).

118. Undated church information bulletin for new members, probably dating from the early 1980s.

119. This practice has been a regular aspect of church policy. At CUT's 1994 annual conference, various rituals and sacraments were made available only to members holding Communicant status. Fieldwork by the author, Corwin Springs, Mont., June-July 1994. Also see "The Environment of the Soul," church information brochure for 1994 summer conference.

120. *The History of the Summit Lighthouse,* 6.

121. Ibid.

122. Kantor and McGuire, "Creative Eclecticism." According to church teachings, Mary traveled to England after Jesus' death. She is believed to have carried with her the grail used at the Last Supper. The grail, consequently, became the object of King Arthur's celebrated quest.

123. Anson Shupe and David Bromley, *The New Vigilantes: Deprogrammers, Anti-Cultists, and the New Religions* (Beverly Hills, Calif.: Sage Publications, 1980), 13.

124. David Stupple, "The I AM Sect Today: An Unobituary," *Journal of Popular Culture* 8, no. 4 (1975): 900–902. It is likely, however, that this figure was substantially inflated. More likely, CUT had at this time no more than three to five thousand active members with another ten to fifteen thousand on the organization's mailing list.

125. *The History of the Summit Lighthouse,* 12. For an explanation of the church's understanding of astrology, see Elizabeth Clare Prophet, *The Great White Brotherhood in the Culture, History, and Religion of America,* 173–206.

126. Mark and Elizabeth Clare Prophet, *Climb the Highest Mountain,* 67.

127. See Mark and Elizabeth Clare Prophet, *Climb the Highest Mountain,* 482–88, for the Prophets' discussion of earthly cataclysm.

128. Untitled 1973 church advertising brochure.

129. Ibid.

130. Arnone, telephone interview, March 17, 1997.

131. Kenneth Paolini and Talita Paolini, *Four Hundred Years of Imaginary Friends,* 293–94.

132. Cheri Walsh, CUT staff member and director of library/research department, telephone interview by the author, June 8, 2000.

133. *Pearls of Wisdom* 12, no. 17 (1969).

134. For some insight into this subject, see Mark and Elizabeth Clare Prophet, *Climb the Highest Mountain,* 129–32, 129–32, 584.

135. Ibid., 131.

136. *Pearls of Wisdom* 22, no. 12 (March 24, 1974).

137. Ibid. Evidence of this self-preservationist impulse can be found in CUT literature of the period. Never countenanced as a "retreat" from the struggle against worldly evil, the strategy of

separation was tactical in nature and was aimed at detaching the church from hostile and impure forces believed to threaten the membership.

138. Anonymous former member of the Church Universal and Triumphant, interview by the author, Syracuse, N.Y., October 19, 1993.

139. The best insights into the early Summit Lighthouse's use of enemy construction are found in Mark Prophet, *The Soulless Ones.*

140. Elizabeth Clare Prophet, *From Confidential File 10019 for the Coming Revolution in Higher Consciousness* (Los Angeles: Summit University Press, 1978). Audio recording of a lecture given by Prophet at Camelot.

141. Ibid.

142. Ibid. For the church, the Nephilim were viewed as non-human beings who continued to reincarnate their "evil seed" and thus were responsible for the perpetuation of discord, misery, war, and other earthly problems. Prophet clearly borrowed, and adapted, the term from the references made to the Nephilim in the Old Testament Book of Genesis.

143. Elizabeth Clare Prophet, *I Believe in the United States of America.*

144. Ibid.

145. Elizabeth Clare Prophet, *Vials of the Seven Last Plagues: Prohecies for the 1980s by the Seven Archangels* (Los Angeles: Summit University Press, 1980), 61.

146. Bryan, *Psychic Dictatorship in America,* 75.

147. "Church Buys Ranch for $7 Million," *Los Angeles Times,* September 22, 1981.

148. Elizabeth Clare Prophet, *Prophecy for the 1980s: The Handwriting on the Wall* (Malibu, Calif.: Summit University Press, 1980), 121.

149. Melton, "The Church Universal and Triumphant: Its Heritage and Thoughtworld," 19.

150. "Leader Brings Religion into New Age," *Saint Paul Pioneer Press,* February 27, 1993.

151. "Guru Ma: Leader of a Multi-Million Dollar Church," *Los Angeles Times,* February 11, 1980.

152. Shupe and Bromley, *The New Vigilantes,* 170.

153. Ibid., 29–31. From the time of its organization in the 1970s, the anticult movement has adhered to a concept of "mind control" rejected by both the American Sociological Association and the American Psychological Association. The brainwashing metaphor used by anticultists has its roots in early studies of American prisoners of war from the Korean conflict. Generally viewed today as specious, these studies suggested that blind obedience to authority could easily be shaped in individuals under unusually rigorous environmental conditions.

154. Ibid., 210–18.

155. Susan Palmer, *AIDS as an Apocalyptic Metaphor in North America* (Toronto: University of Toronto Press, 1997), 45–46.

156. Jocelyn DeHaas, "The Mediation of Ideology and Public Image in the Church Universal and Triumphant," in *The Church Universal and Triumphant in Scholarly Perspective,* ed. James Lewis and J. Gordon Melton (Stanford, Calif.: Center for Academic Publication, 1994), 26.

157. Ibid., 29.

158. "Challenging the Media Myth: The Facts about Elizabeth Clare Prophet and the Church

Universal and Triumphant," pamphlet produced by the Church Universal and Triumphant in 1990.

159. "Church Land at Center of Dispute," *Denver Post,* May 27, 1989.

160. Montana state senator Bob Raney, telephone interview by the author, December 16, 1996.

3. Camelot and Group Separatism

1. "Church Members Gun Buying Outlined," *Bozeman Daily Chronicle,* February 27, 1995.

2. Ibid.; "Guru Ma Trial Ends in Biblical Flourish," *Los Angeles Times,* March 20, 1986.

3. Mark Prophet, *The Soulless Ones,* 110–12.

4. "Guru Ma: Leader of a Multi-Million Dollar Church."

5. "Sons and Daughters, Gather Ye Into the Flock," *Los Angles Times,* February 1, 1980.

6. "Officials Deny Rumors, Allegations," *Los Angeles Times,* February 10, 1980. In the interview, leadership members of the group indicated that the church had initiated its survival training during the organization's stay in Colorado.

7. "Dissenters Talk," *Los Angeles Times,* February 7, 1980.

8. Ibid.

9. Marc Galanter, *Cults, Faith, Healing, and Coercion* (New York: Oxford University Press, 1989), 111.

10. Ibid., 112.

11. "Two Religious Learning Centers Planned," *Los Angeles Times,* October 8, 1977.

12. "Sect Channels Energy Through Speech," *Los Angeles Times,* January 1, 1977.

13. Author interview with anonymous member of the Church Universal and Triumphant, Syracuse, N.Y., January 15, 1994.

14. "Go Out and Conduct (Money Making) Business," *Los Angeles Times,* February 1, 1980.

15. Ibid.

16. Thomas Robbins, *Cults, Converts, and Charisma: The Sociology of New Religious Movements* (Beverly Hills, Calif.: Sage Publications, 1988), 6. Jeffrey Kaplan, *Radical Religion in America: Millenarian Movements from the Far Right to the Children of Noah* (Syracuse: Syracuse University Press, 1997), 130–38.

17. Michael Homer, "Protection of Religion Under the First Amendment: Church Universal and Triumphant," in *Church Universal and Triumphant in Scholarly Perspective,* ed. James Lewis and J. Gordon Melton (Santa Barbara, Calif.: Center for Academic Publication, 1994), 126. Randall King was the third husband of Elizabeth Clare Prophet. In order to avoid a bitter, high-profile lawsuit raising sensitive questions about the church and its leadership, CUT settled with King out of court.

18. Ibid.

19. John Hall, *Gone from the Promised Land: Jonestown in American Cultural History* (New Brunswick, N.J.: Transaction, 1989), 138.

20. Galanter, *Cults, Faith, Healing, and Coercion,* 120.

21. Hall, *Gone from the Promised Land,* xiv.

22. Mary McCormick Maaga, *Hearing the Voices of Jonestown* (Syracuse: Syracuse University Press, 1998), 37.

23. J. Gordon Melton, "When Prophets Die: The Succession Crisis in New Religions," in *When Prophets Die: The Post-Charismatic Fate of New Religious Movements,* ed. Timothy Miller (Albany, N.Y.: State University of New York, 1988), 2.

24. "Go Out and Conduct (Money Making) Business."

25. Church literature dated 1973. Lanello Reserves advertised "low-moisture foods" that could be used as an emergency food source. Each package, priced at $312.50, was said to provide enough food for one adult for one year.

26. Ibid.

27. "Why Silver?" undated Lanello Reserves advertisement produced by CUT.

28. Elizabeth Clare Prophet, *Prophecy for the 1980s,* 59–60.

29. Ibid., 61–62.

30. For a description of some of these groups, see James Aho, *The Politics of Righteousness: Idaho Christian Patriotism* (Seattle: University of Washington Press, 1990), 19.

31. Undated brochure (probably from 1973 or 1974) for Lanello Reserves.

32. Transcribed notes from a church senior staff meeting dated February 26, 1980, listed as "instructions from Monroe Shearer." Shearer served as CUT's appointed student dean of Summit University during this time.

33. Although sometimes couched in vague terminology, there are abundant examples of the group's exclusionary self-identity as God's elect. See, for example, *Pearls of Wisdom* 12, no. 18 (May 4, 1969) for an early example of the group's perception of its elite status. For a more recent look at Elizabeth Clare Prophet's view on this subject, see Elizabeth Clare Prophet, *Mother Mary Twentieth-Century Prophecies* (Livingston, Mont.: Summit University Press, 1991). Recorded speech marketed by CUT.

34. *Pearls of Wisdom* 12, no. 18 (May 4, 1969). In the group's perspective, "Lightbearers" were the children of God.

35. *Pearls of Wisdom* 16, no. 20 (May 20, 1973).

36. "Guru Ma Nettles Montana Town," *Los Angeles Times,* March 30, 1986.

37. "Guru Ma: Leader of a Multi-Million Dollar Church."

38. Ibid.

39. Although no concrete numbers are available, it is reasonable to assume (based on press and defector accounts) that approximately three hundred adherents lived on the premises and another three hundred in areas close to the property. See "Church Leaders Say Nay to Allegations," *Los Angeles Times,* February 4, 1980.

40. Literally meaning a "master-student" framework of spiritual edification, CUT's use of this Buddhist ideal can be traced to the early days of the Summit Lighthouse. CUT taught that the relationship was undertaken by the student for the purpose of "balancing" karma, and eventually making the ascension to God. See *Pearls of Wisdom* 39, no. 22 (1996).

41. Elizabeth Clare Prophet, *I Believe in the United States of America.*

42. Michael Barkun, *Religion and the Racist Right* (Chapel Hill: University of North Carolina Press, 1994), 247–48.

43. Ibid.

44. Melton, *Encyclopedia of American Religions,* 121–23.

45. David Stupple, "Mahatmas and Space Brothers: The Ideology of Alleged Contact with Extraterrestrials," *Journal of American Culture* 7, no. 1 (1984): 137.

46. Wessinger, *Annie Besant and Progressive Millennialism,* 33. Wessinger's book offers an understanding of the social vision of the post-Blavatsky leader of the Theosophical Society.

47. Nicholas Goodricke-Clarke, *The Occult Roots of Naziism: Secret Aryan Cults and Their Influence on Nazi Ideology* (New York: New York University Press, 1992), 22.

48. Ibid.

49. Wessinger, *Annie Besant and Progressive Millennialism,* 323. For a discussion of the communitarian and egalitarian themes in Theosophy, see Robert Ellwood, *Religious and Spiritual Groups in America* (Englewood Cliffs, N.J.: Prentice Hall, 1973).

50. S. B. Liljegren, *Bulwer-Lytton's Novels and Isis Unveiled* (Cambridge, Mass.: Harvard University Press, 1957), 1–15.

51. Ibid., 28–35. Liljegren's slim volume is devoted entirely to showing the extent to which Blavatsky was inspired by Bulwer-Lytton's occult novels, particularly *The Last Days of Pompeii* (1834) and *Zanoni* (1834). Bulwer-Lytton, who was a widely read writer of romantic, utopian fiction, incorporated mystical themes (such as astrology and alchemy) in his work. In most of his novels, particularly *Vril: The Power of the Coming Race* (1871), Bulwer-Lytton introduces the reader to unseen secret societies whose powers and knowledge of ancient wisdom allow them to perform astounding feats. In attempting to chart the Nazi's attachment to the occult, Goodricke-Clarke argues that the Theosphical doctrine of "root races" and doctrinal elitism easily found Nazi supporters.

52. The I AM movement's conspiracism was consistent with that of right-wing, populist movements of the period. While Pelley's Silver Legion entertained most of the same beliefs concerning the FDR administration and communism, it differed from the I AM philosophy by attributing to Jews the power behind its perception of a worldwide conspiracy. See Braden, *These Also Believe,* 306. For additional information on Pelley's conspiracy theories, see David Bennett, *The Party of Fear,* 245–46.

53. Braden, *These Also Believe,* 196.

54. John Werly, "The Millenarian Right," 48.

55. Bennett, *The Party of Fear,* 246.

56. Seymour Martin Lipset and Earl Rabb, *The Politics of Unreason* (New York: Harper and Row, 1970), 460–62. Lipset and Rabb use the term as a means to describe a social-psychological state of mind whereby the "afflicted" have a greater stake in the past than in the times in which they live. Although the word "afflicted" conveys disturbingly psycho-pathological overtones that might suggest mental illness, Lipset and Rabb do not use it in this manner.

57. Braden, *These Also Believe,* 296.

58. Ballard, *Unveiled Mysteries,* iv–vii.

59. Werly, "The Millenarian Right," 183–85.

60. Bennett, *The Party of Fear,* 245.

61. Werly, "The Millenarian Right," 174.

62. Lipset and Rabb, *The Politics of Unreason,* 6.

63. Eric Hoffer, *The True Believer: Thoughts on the Nature of Mass Movements* (New York: Harper and Row, 1951), xii.

64. James Webb, *The Occult Underground* (LaSalle, Ill: Open Court Publishing, 1974), 6. This timetable is fluid. Webb indicates that the Romantic revolution was an irregular process.

65. Roland Stromberg, *European Intellectual History Since 1789* (Englewood Cliffs, N.J.: Prentice Hall, 1981), 41–42.

66. Webb, *The Occult Underground,* 7.

67. Goodricke-Clarke, *The Occult Roots of Naziism,* 17. In brief, these doctrines each represented an alternate reality at variance with the Judeo-Christian cosmology of the Mediterranean basin. Neo-Platonism derived from the vision of the universe adopted by Plotinus, a student of Plato. The doctrine is based on an understanding of a dichotomous order of existence, delineated by the divine spheres of the heavenly realm and the mundane order of earth. While the chasm between these separate states of existence was impossible to bridge, human rebirth (or reincarnation) was thought to offer a possibility for divine transcendence. Alchemy, an ancient speculative science best known for attempting to transmute base metals into gold, was similarly concerned with changing the elements of the individual personality to a transcendent state. Studied and practiced by early students of mysticism, alchemy was seen as a divine art capable of elevating humankind from its ordinary condition to a state of godhood. Cabbalism is an ancient mystical system derived from Jewish esotericism. Its historical roots are a matter of debate; however, it is believed to have been a great influence on the mystics, seers, and prophets of the Western esoteric tradition, including Nostradamus. Its complicated system is based upon secret wisdom thought to have been revealed to Moses by God. Neo-Platonism, alchemy, and cabbalism share two basic Gnostic themes: a dualistic perception of good and evil, and a belief that the earthly world is corrupt and impure. For additional discussion of these concepts, see A. T. Mann, *Millennium Prophecies: Predictions for the Year 2000* (Rockport, Maine: Element Books, 1992), 62–63. Elizabeth Clare Prophet has written extensively on these subjects in *Saint Germain and Alchemy* (Livingston, Mont.: Summit University Press, 1993).

68. John Saliba, *Understanding New Religious Movements* (Grand Rapids, Mich.: William B. Eerdman Publishing, 1995), 39.

69. Ibid., 39–40.

70. Melton, *Encyclopedia of American Religions,* 350. For a sympathetic treatment of the Knights Templar, a secret society reportedly emerging in Europe in the 1300s, see Michael Biagent and Richard Leigh, *The Temple and the Lodge* (New York: Arcade Publishing, 1989).

71. Prophet accepted as fact the mythological history of these secret societies. See Elizabeth Clare Prophet, *Lecture on Gnosticism* (Livingston, Mont.: Summit University Press, 1986). Recording of speech given by Prophet at Camelot on July 6, 1986.

72. See, for example, Nesta H. Webster, *Secret Societies and Subversive Movements* (Palmdale, Calif.: Omni Publications, 1924), and Edith Starr Miller (Lady Queensborough), *Occult Theocracy* (Los Angeles: Christian Book Club of America, 1933), for critical accounts of secret and occult groups by writers who credit such organizations with shaping world history to group-desired ends through conspiracies. Also see Robert Hieronimus, *America's Secret Destiny: Spiritual Vision and the Founding of a Nation* (Rochester, Vt.: Destiny Books, 1989), for a sympathetic account of occult-based secret societies, particularly the Freemasons and Rosicrucians.

73. Edmond Mazet, "Freemasonry and Esotericism," in *Modern Esoteric Spirituality: An Encyclopedic History of the Religious Quest,* ed. Antoine Faivre and Jacob Needleman (New York: Crossroads, 1992), 250–51. Freemasonry, as opposed to Rosicrucianism, began as a craft guild in fourteenth-century Europe. In its earliest form, Freemasonry had no esoteric/occult orientation since its purpose was to organize and initiate craftsmen into a special community of laborers. The movement adopted an esoteric character when its early emphasis upon the building trade was displaced by the interests of an increasingly upper-class membership in practices of a secretive and occult nature.

74. The central belief in Rosicrucianism was that man was evolving toward the godhead and that reincarnation permitted this course to divinity to take place. See Melton, *Encyclopedia of American Religions,* 350. The Freemasons were not organized around explicit religious principles, although the group (in line with its humanitarian convictions) stressed the spiritual development of its members.

75. Mazet, "Freemasonry and Esotericism," 270. Scholarly accounts of Freemasonry attribute much of the movement's esoteric content to the Knights Templar, a mysterious secret society of the Middle Ages that is believed to have been the inspiration for Freemasonry.

76. Bennett, *The Party of Fear,* 23–24.

77. Arkon Daraul, *A History of Secret Societies* (New York: Citadel Press, 1994), 220–32.

78. Goodricke-Clarke, *The Occult Roots of Naziism,* 29.

79. Crane Brinton, *The Anatomy of Revolution* (New York: Vintage Books, 1965), 40–41.

80. Edward Tiryakian, "Toward the Sociology of Esoteric Culture," *American Journal of Sociology* 78, no. 3 (1972): 505.

81. Hieronimus, *America's Secret Destiny,* 22–35. This account of the early history of the United States reflects the author's belief that the Founders were influenced by the esoteric tradition and particularly by the philosophies of the Freemasons, Rosicrucians, and Illuminati.

82. Goodricke-Clarke, *The Occult Roots of Naziism,* 20–25. See also Dusty Sklar, *The Nazis and the Occult* (New York: Dorset Press, 1977), 27–36.

83. Tiryakian, "Toward the Sociology of Esoteric Culture," 306.

84. Barkun, *Religion and the Racist Right,* 248–49. Barkun's analysis of the conspiratorial mind-set of the radical Christian Identity groups finds an easy application to conspiracists of all types.

85. Ellwood, *Religious and Spiritual Groups in America,* 95–97. Ellwood argues that the movement played an important role in gaining India's independence from Great Britain.

86. Webb, *The Occult Establishment,* 226–27. Webb alleges that the Blavatsky-led early Theosophists were involved with promoting racist and conspiracy theories. According to Webb, during the 1880s the Theosophical Publishing House in London reprinted various anti-Semitic tracts.

87. Bryan, *Psychic Dictatorship in America,* 220–26. According to Bryan, the group routinely prayed for the destruction of its enemies.

88. Werly, "The Millenarian Right," 197. Also see Sara Diamond, *Roads to Dominion: Right-Wing Movements and Political Power in the United States* (New York: Guilford Press, 1995), 22.

89. Carroll Quigley, *Tragedy and Hope: A History of the World in Our Time* (New York: Macmillan Co., 1966), 952–53. Quigley, whose revelations about the CFR are often cited by con-

spiracists on the right as proof of the existence of a world-controlling conspiracy, argues that the CFR and its predecessor organizations wielded power that "can hardly be exaggerated." Quigley, however, was most certainly not an opponent of the CFR.

90. Bennett, *The Party of Fear,* 344.

91. Dennis King, *Lyndon LaRouche and the New American Fascism* (New York: Doubleday, 1989), 60. See also Daniel Pipes, *Conspiracy: How the Paranoid Style Flourishes and Where It Comes From* (New York: Free Press, 1997), 11–12.

92. King, *Lyndon LaRouche and the New American Fascism,* 103. Also see Ronald Johnson, *The Architects of Fear* (Boston: Houghton Mifflin, 1983), 187–88.

93. "The Real Story Behind the Trilateral Commission: The 1980s Plot to Destroy the Nation," pamphlet produced by Citizens for LaRouche, March 1980.

94. Elizabeth Clare Prophet, *I Believe in the United States of America,* and Elizabeth Clare Prophet, *Planet Earth: The Future Is to the Gods* (Los Angeles: Summit University Press, 1981). The latter is a speech given to a church audience in Philadelphia in September 1980. For evidence of LaRouche's published work appearing in CUT literature, see Elizabeth Clare Prophet, *Prophecy for the 1980s,* 141.

95. Elizabeth Clare Prophet, *Planet Earth.*

96. "A Prayer Vigil for the World," prayer probably from the organization's 1984 decree book. In this prayer, "psychotronics" (or mind control) is specifically mentioned as a strategy used by the Nephilim to influence the thinking of American political officeholders and citizens.

97. Elizabeth Clare Prophet, *I Believe in the United States of America.*

98. Johnson, *The Architects of Fear,* 195.

99. Diamond, *Roads to Dominion,* 261–62.

100. Frank Mintz, *The Liberty Lobby and the American Right: Race, Conspiracy, and Culture* (Westport, Conn.: Greenwood Press, 1985), 60–63, discusses some of these far-right groups.

101. Elizabeth Clare Prophet, *Planet Earth.*

102. Ibid.

103. Elizabeth Prophet's theory does not differ from Mark Prophet's original statement concerning the reasons for the existence of world evil as explained in his 1966 book *The Soulless Ones.* However, she has elaborated on some of her late husband's arguments. For her views on the extraterrestrial origins of evil, see Elizabeth Clare Prophet, *Forbidden Mysteries of Enoch: Fallen Angels and the Origins of Evil* (Livingston, Mont.:Summit Univ. Press, 1992) 1–15.

104. "More Violet Flame," internal staff document dated November 21, 1981.

105. Ballard, *Unveiled Mysteries,* x.

106. C. E. Ashworth, "Flying Saucers, Spoon-Bending, and Atlantis," *Sociological Review* 28, no. 3 (1980): 357.

107. Zechariah Sitchin, *The Twelfth Planet* (New York: Avon Books, 1976), 372–78.

108. See Sitchin, *The Twelfth Planet.* In 1980, Prophet frequently mentioned Sitchin's research in her lectures. Sitchin's work continues to be popular among UFO enthusiasts who reject more conventional explanations of human development on earth. For two decades he has been routinely featured as a speaker at alternative science and UFO society meetings.

109. "Freedom 1982," 84.16–84.18. Decree book prayer entitled "Judgment of the Conspiracy of Watchers."

110. George C. Andrews, "An Explosive Exchange," in *Extraterrestrial Friends and Foes,* ed. George C. Andrews (Lilburn, Ga.: Illuminati Press, 1993), 227–29.

111. Elizabeth Clare Prophet, *Prophecy for the 1980s,* 106–14. Prophet also discusses in this passage the possibility that the new scientific technologies of psychotronic energy, genetic manipulation, and subliminal thought reform might reduce societies to robot populations exploited by a "technocratic priest class."

112. *Pearls of Wisdom* 24, no. 35 (August 30, 1981).

113. Elizabeth Clare Prophet, *Prophecy for the 1980s,* 121.

114. "Guru Ma Nettles Montana Town." This observation was also confirmed by my October 22, 1993, interview of an anonymous former member of CUT's staff. It is likely that the "earth changes" concept observed by the church was derived from the prophecies of the Kentucky-born psychic Edgar Cayce (1877–1945). Predicting global cataclysmic geological disturbances, Cayce believed that the present shape of the continents would be changed beyond recognition around the turn of the twenty-first century. Interestingly, Cayce predicted that large portions of the American northwest (including all of geographical Montana) would not be affected by the catastrophe. See Mann, *Millennium Prophecies,* 84–92.

115. *Pearls of Wisdom* 24, no. 35 (August 30, 1981).

116. Ibid.

4. The Road to Armageddon

1. "Church Buys Ranch for $7 Million."

2. "Church Members' Gun-Buying Outlined."

3. *Pearls of Wisdom* 24, no. 36 (September 6, 1981).

4. Mark Prophet and Elizabeth Clare Prophet, *Climb the Highest Mountain,* 476.

5. Mark Prophet and Elizabeth Clare Prophet, *Lords of the Seven Rays* (Livingston, Mont.: Summit University Press, 1986), 51.

6. Ibid., 45.

7. Hall, *Gone from the Promised Land,* 205.

8. Elizabeth Clare Prophet, *I Believe in the United States of America.*

9. "Montanans Wary of Church's Plans for Promised Land," *Los Angeles Times,* January 25, 1987.

10. *Elizabeth Clare Prophet Interviews Tomas Schuman* (Los Angeles: Summit University Press, 1984). Videotape of Tomas Schuman's lecture at Camelot.

11. "Invocation to the Hierarchy of the Ruby Ray," prayer from the church's 1984 decree/prayer manual, 110.04.

12. Cheri Walsh, interview by the author, July 3, 1994.

13. Ibid., May 9, 2000. Walsh had severed her twenty-five year ties with CUT by the time of this interview.

14. This message would appear a few months later in *Pearls of Wisdom.* During the group's years in Montana, many of the most important messages received by Prophet came from the Ascended Master Saint Germain.

15. *Pearls of Wisdom* 28, no. 50 (December 15, 1985).

16. Hall, *Gone from the Promised Land,* 138. The use of the term "other-worldly sect" has been used by Hall to describe utopian communities harboring apocalyptic beliefs and interpreting the outside as threatening and inherently evil. For Hall, Jonestown represented such a community. In the group's view, its enemies are to be ultimately defeated by the community of the elect.

17. Mark Prophet and Elizabeth Clare Prophet, *Saint Germain on Alchemy* (Livingston, Mont.: Summit University Press, 1985), 136–39.

18. See, for example, Jean Rosenfeld, "Pai Marire: Peace and Violence in a New Zealand Millenarian Tradition," *Terrorism and Political Violence* 7, no. 3 (1995): 86.

19. Bennett, *The Party of Fear,* 2.

20. *Pearls of Wisdom* 29, no. 9 (March 2, 1986).

21. Elizabeth Clare Prophet, *Prophecy for the 1980s,* 66.

22. Ibid., 114.

23. Charles Strozier, *Apocalypse: On the Psychology of Fundamentalism in America* (Boston: Beacon Press, 1994), 231.

24. Ibid.

25. Melton, *New Age Encyclopedia,* xiii.

26. Wessinger, "Millennialism with and without the Mayhem," 49–51.

27. *Pearls of Wisdom* 16, no. 21 (May 27, 1973).

28. Melton, *New Age Encyclopedia,* 59.

29. *Pearls of Wisdom* 16, no. 21 (May 27, 1973).

30. Ibid.

31. "A Prayer Vigil for Washington, D.C.," undated mid-1980s church prayer most likely from CUT's decree/prayer manual.

32. "Dynamic Decree," undated mid-1980s church prayer most likely from CUT's decree/prayer manual.

33. *Elizabeth Clare Prophet Interviews Tomas Schuman.* This program was underway in the early 1970s when the group was in Colorado and involved the sale of survival equipment to church members. Prophet briefly mentioned the church's preparations for "emergency events" in this 1984 videotaped interview of Soviet defector Tomas Schuman.

34. Mark and Elizabeth Clare Prophet, *The Lost Teachings of Jesus: Atlantis Revisited* (Livingston, Mont.: Summit University Press, 1986), 9. This volume consists of a series of lectures delivered by Mark Prophet between 1965 and 1973.

35. Ibid.

36. Ibid., 15.

37. For a discussion of the significance of George Washington's prophecy for American right-wing movements, see Kaplan, *Radical Religion in America,* 52–53.

38. Mark and Elizabeth Clare Prophet, *Saint Germain on Alchemy,* 149.

39. Elizabeth Clare Prophet, *Freedom 1988: Fourth of July Address* (Livingston, Mont.: Summit University Press, 1988). This is a videotaped speech delivered by Prophet at the Royal Teton Ranch.

40. Elizabeth Clare Prophet, *The Astrology of the Four Horsemen: How You Can Heal Yourself and Planet Earth* (Livingston, Mont.: Summit University Press, 1991), 435.

41. Elizabeth Clare Prophet, *Planet Earth.*

42. Ibid.

43. See Edward Bulwer-Lytton (Lord Lytton), *The Coming Race* (New York: George Routledge and Sons, 1871), 1–8. Also see Walter Kaffon-Minkel, *Subterranean Worlds: 100,000 Years of Dragons, Dwarfs, the Dead, Lost Races, and UFOs from Inside the Earth* (Port Townsend, Wash.: Loompanics, 1989), 258–63.

44. Mark Prophet, *The Soulless Ones,* 105–6.

45. Ibid., 106. In the book, Prophet states that Bulwer-Lytton revealed truths concerning the malevolent intentions of non-human beings.

46. Liljegren, *Bulwer-Lytton's Novels and Isis Unveiled,* 27.

47. Ballard, *Unveiled Mysteries,* 114–22.

48. See Blavatsky, *Isis Unveiled.* According to Blavatsky, concealed underground realms existed in various parts of the world. She alleged that these sites contained the lost wisdom of the ancients and were connected by tunnels that stretched for miles under the earth.

49. Elizabeth Clare Prophet, *Lecture on Gnosticism.*

50. Ibid.

51. Ibid.

52. This sentiment is made clear in the videotaped interview, *Elizabeth Clare Prophet Interviews Tomas Schuman.*

53. For a discussion of Prophet's impression of urban California's crisis condition, see Elizabeth Clare Prophet, *Prophecy for the 1980s,* 94–95.

54. "Buyers Clearing Out Reminders of Secretive Cult as It Heads for New Home in Montana," *Los Angeles Times,* November 29, 1986.

55. See John Pietrangelo, *Lambs to Slaughter: My Fourteen Years with Elizabeth Clare Prophet and the Church Universal and Triumphant* (self-published, 1994). Pietrangelo was a former staff member at the church's headquarters at Colorado Springs and Camelot.

56. Correspondence with Cheri Walsh, May 27, 2000.

57. "Guru Ma: Leader of a Multi-Million Dollar Church."

58. Author interview with anonymous member of ranch staff, July 3, 1994.

59. Galanter, *Cults, Faith, Healing, and Coercion,* 31.

60. "Guru Ma Trial Ends in a Biblical Flourish."

61. For general insights into this concept, see Dick Anthony and Thomas Robbins, "Religious Totalism, Violence, and Exemplary Dualism: Beyond the Extrinsic Model," *Terrorism and Political Violence* 7, no. 3 (1995): 15–16. For a more detailed understanding of the brainwashing theory, see Robert J. Lifton, *Chinese Thought Reform and the Psychology of Totalism* (New York: Norton, 1961). Lifton is often mistakenly assumed to have implied that thought reform did not require any willingness on the part of the individual.

62. Author interview with anonymous staff member at the Royal Teton Ranch, July 3, 1994.

63. "Basic Cosmic Science," early Summit Lighthouse student lesson probably dating from the mid-1960s.

64. Ibid.

65. *Pearls of Wisdom* 31, no. 38 (1988).

66. Ibid.

67. Kathy Schmook, "Apocalypse on the Yellowstone," *Edging West* (June-July 1995): 30.

68. See *Elizabeth Clare Prophet Interviews Tomas Schuman.*

69. Murray Steinman, public relations director of the Church Universal and Triumphant, interview by the author, July 31, 1995.

70. Paul Boyer, *By the Bomb's Early Light* (New York: Pantheon, 1985), 356–57.

71. Ibid., 359–60.

72. *To Deploy or Not to Deploy* (Livingston, Mont.: Summit University Press, 1987). Videotaped panel discussion held at the Royal Teton Ranch and moderated by Elizabeth Clare Prophet.

73. *Pearls of Wisdom* 32, no. 27 (July 2, 1989).

74. Elizabeth Clare Prophet, *I Believe in the United States of America.*

75. See Col. Archibald Roberts, *The Anatomy of a Revolution* (Fort Collins, Colo.: Betsy Ross Press, 1968).

76. Arnone, telephone interview, March 4, 1997.

77. Author correspondence with Col. Archibald Roberts, April 30, 1997.

78. For Sutton's account of Western technological assistance to the Soviet Union, see his three-volume work, *Western Technology and Soviet Economic Development* (Stanford, Calif.: Hoover Institute, 1973). Also see Anthony Sutton, *America's Secret Establishment* (Billings, Mont.: Liberty House, 1986). The latter gives Sutton's analysis of the Skull and Bones Club at Yale.

79. Catherine McNicol-Stock, *Rural Radicals: Righteous Rage in the American Grain* (Ithaca, N.Y.: Cornell University Press, 1997), 70.

80. *East Minus West Equals Zero* (Livingston, Mont.: Summit University Press, 1988). Videotaped discussion between Elizabeth Clare Prophet and Antony Sutton at the Royal Teton Ranch.

81. Sutton, *America's Secret Establishment,* 119.

82. *We Have Built Ourselves an Enemy* (Livingston, Mont.: Summit University Press, 1988). Videotape of Antony Sutton presentation at the Royal Teton Ranch.

83. Ibid. For additional discussion, see Anthony Sutton, *The Two Faces of George Bush* (Dresden, N.Y.: Wiswell Ruffin House, 1988), 12–24.

84. Ibid.

85. Elizabeth Clare Prophet, *Prophecy for the 1980s,* 112–13.

86. *We Have Built Ourselves an Enemy.*

87. Ibid.

88. Elizabeth Clare Prophet, *I Believe in the United States of America.*

89. Webster, *Secret Societies and Subversive Movements,* xii.

90. Ibid., 404–5.

91. Mintz, *The Liberty Lobby and the American Right,* 144–49.

92. Daniel [pseud.], interview by the author, Royal Teton Ranch, July 1, 1994.

93. Bennett, *The Party of Fear,* 315. These concerns dominated the thinking of the John Birch Society. See, for example, Gary Allen, *None Dare Call It Conspiracy* (Boring, Ore.: CPA Books, 1971).

94. *Pearls of Wisdom* 29, no. 9 (March 2, 1986).

95. Diamond, *Roads to Dominion,* 253.

96. See Alan Cantwell, M.D., "Paranoid/Paranoia: Media Buzzwords to Silence the Politically

Incorrect," *Steamshovel Press* 14 (fall 1995): 17. It is worth noting that Cantwell is the author of three books on AIDS. The best known, *AIDS and the Doctors of Death* (Los Angeles: Aries Rising Press, 1991), alleges that the AIDS virus was introduced into homosexual males through government-administered hepatitis-B vaccines.

97. *The AIDS Conspiracy* (Livingston, Mont.: Summit University Press, 1988). Videotape recording of Elizabeth Clare Prophet's moderated panel discussion on AIDS at the Royal Teton Ranch.

98. Ibid.

99. Ibid.

100. See Michael Kelly, "The Road to Paranoia," *New Yorker* (June 19, 1995): 60–69. Kelly uses the term in his discussion of the ideological cross-fertilization of conspiracy theories from the right and left.

101. For insights into this aspect of CUT's philosophy, see Mark and Elizabeth Clare Prophet, *Climb the Highest Mountain*, 584–87.

102. *The UFO Connection* (Livingston, Mont.: Summit University Press, 1988). Videotape of the panel discussion on UFOs at the Royal Teton Ranch.

103. Stupple, "Mahatmas and Space Brothers," 131–33.

104. See George Adamski, *Inside the Space Ships* (New York: Abelard-Schuman, 1955), 105. For a comprehensive examination of the themes adopted by writers in the UFO community, see John Saliba, "UFO Contactee Phenomena from a Sociopsychological Perspective," in *The Gods Have Landed: New Religions from Other Worlds,* ed. James Lewis (Albany, N.Y.: State University of New York Press, 1995), 207–50.

105. Undated decree entitled "Judgment of the Conspiracy of Watchers," probably from a church decree/prayer manual.

106. *The UFO Connection.*

107. Phil Cousineau, *UFOs: A Manual for the Millennium* (New York: Harper Collins, 1995), 20–21.

108. See, for example, Brad Steiger, *Project Blue Book* (New York: Ballantine Books, 1976), 10.

109. *The UFO Connection.*

110. Linda Mouton-Howe, "A Hall of Mirrors with a Quicksand Floor," in *Extraterrestrial Friends and Foes,* ed. George Andrews (Lilburn, Ga.: Illuminet Press, 1993), 166–68.

111. *The UFO Connection.* Stanton Friedman later said that he felt Elizabeth Clare Prophet had her own "religious agenda" at the forum. Friedman indicated that the panelists were uncomfortable with Prophet's efforts to steer the discussion in a theological direction. In Friedman's view, Prophet was not knowledgeable about contemporary UFO research. Author communication with Stanton Friedman, February 20, 2000.

112. Ibid.

113. *Pearls of Wisdom* 32, no. 27 (July 2, 1989).

114. Elizabeth Clare Prophet, *The Astrology of the Four Horsemen,* 419.

115. Schmook, "Apocalypse on the Yellowstone," 32.

116. Anonymous church member and Glastonbury resident, interview by the author, Emigrant, Mont., August 13, 1993.

117. "Weapons Seizure Grand Jury Probe of New Age Sect," *San Francisco Chronicle,* August 17, 1989.

118. "CUT Documents Show Church's Long History of Arms Purchases," *Livingston Enterprise,* March 5, 1990.

119. Ibid.

120. "Weapons Seizure Grand Jury Probe of New Age Sect," *San Francisco Chronicle,* August 17, 1989.

121. "CUT Documents Show Church's Long History of Arms Purchases."

122. Ibid.

123. "Trouble in Paradise: A Doomsday Prophet Wears Out Her Welcome," *Maclean's* (May 7, 1990): 33–35. Typical of the sensationalistic media treatment given to CUT in the wake of the gun-buying scheme, the *MaClean's* article alleges, among other things, that the Royal Teton Ranch was home to racist skinheads.

124. *Focus* (October 1996): 4. *FOCUS* was a short-lived monthly newsletter published by Peter Arnone, a former CUT staff member. The publication, which was critical of the church and its leader, was discontinued in 1997.

125. "Bomb Shelters in the Mountains: Sect Gets Ready for Dark Days," *San Francisco Chronicle,* July 24, 1989.

126. "Leader of a cult? 'No' she insists," *Chicago Tribune,* March 5, 1993.

127. "New Leader Brings New Methods," *Bozeman Daily Chronicle,* March 15, 1998.

128. Arnone, telephone interview, March 4, 1997.

129. Telephone interview by author with anonymous former staff member, December 5, 1998.

130. Brenda Wilson [pseud.], former CUT staff member, author communication, July 13, 2000.

131. Ibid.

132. "Sect Orders Members in Bomb Shelters," *Los Angeles Times,* March 17, 1990.

133. Communication with anonymous former CUT staff member, December 5, 1998.

134. Ibid.

135. Neroli Duffy, senior CUT staff member, interview by the author, Royal Teton Ranch, July 3, 1994.

136. "Sect Orders Members in Bomb Shelters," *Los Angeles Times,* March 17, 1990.

137. "1990s Could Be the Decade the World Will End—Just Ask Guru Ma," *Chicago Tribune,* December 31, 1989.

138. "Sect Orders Members in Bomb Shelters."

139. Montana state senator Bob Raney, telephone interview by the author, December 16, 1996.

140. Ibid.

141. Ibid.

142. "Thousand Plan Life Below After Doomsday," *New York Times,* March 15, 1990. Also see "Doomsday Reason to Throw Big Party," *Denver Post,* April 24, 1990.

143. Mark and Elizabeth Clare Prophet, *Climb the Highest Mountain,* 407.

144. This declared purpose for the Royal Teton Ranch is discussed in *Pearls of Wisdom* 24, no. 35 (August 30, 1981).

5. The Apocalyptic Nonevent

1. "Prophet Visits San Francisco to Give Divine Word," *San Francisco Chronicle,* April 27, 1991.

2. Ibid.

3. "Space in Shelters Sells for a Song as World Fails to End," *Denver Post,* May 17, 1990.

4. Anonymous interview, August 13, 1993.

5. Author telephone interview with anonymous former CUT member, March 4, 1997. This person, who left the church after the survivalist mobilization, indicated that a number of the members who left Montana in the spring and summer in 1990 did so because of their loss of faith in the Messenger.

6. I base this claim on information received from an anonymous former CUT member. Author interview, February 7, 1994.

7. "The Shelter: Church Has Refuge in Woods," *Calgary Herald,* May 2, 1997. The Cranbrook shelter was discovered by reporters from the *Calgary Herald* who located the facility through public property records.

8. Author interview with anonymous CUT member from New York State who attended the summer 1994 conference at the Royal Teton Ranch, July 1, 1994. It should be noted that a few CUT members have produced their own books on shelter design and survival techniques. See, for example, Philip L. Hoage, *No Such Thing as Doomsday: Underground Shelters, Earth Changes, Wars, and Other Threats* (Emigrant, Mont.: Yellowstone River Publishing, 1996).

9. "Doomsday Good Reason to Throw Big Party."

10. "Church Members Gun-Buying Outlined."

11. Duffy, interview, Royal Teton Ranch, July 3, 1994.

12. "Critics Ignorant and Uninformed Says Montana Church Leader," *Denver Post,* July 13, 1990.

13. Leon Festinger, Henry Riecken, and Stanley Schacter, *When Prophecy Fails* (Minneapolis: University of Minnesota Press, 1956), 30–34.

14. Ibid., 27.

15. Ibid., 28.

16. Ibid.

17. Ibid., 28–30.

18. "Leader of a Cult? 'No,' She Insists," *Chicago Tribune,* March 5, 1993.

19. "Challenging the Media Myth." The pamphlet explains how the church's "predictions" for nuclear war were inaccurately reported upon by the media.

20. Elizabeth Clare Prophet, *Mother Mary's Twentieth-Century Prophecies.*

21. Michael Cuneo, "Catholic Apocalypticism" in *Millennium, Messiahs, and Mayhem,* ed. Thomas Robbins and Susan Palmer (New York: Routledge, 1997), 176–81.

22. Francis Alban, *Fatima Priest* (Pound Ridge, N.Y.: Good Counsel Publications, 1997), 8–10. The Catholic Church, which addressed the Fatima message as being "worthy of belief,"

ended these speculations in May 2000 when it revealed that "the third secret of Fatima" prophesied the 1981 assassination attempt on Pope John Paul II. See "Third Secret of Fatima: No Apocalypse Now," Reuters newswire, June 26, 2000 (accessible at <http://www.dailynews.yahoo.com>).

23. Elizabeth Clare Prophet, *Mother Marys Twentieth-Century Prophecies.*

24. Ibid.

25. "World Close to Nuclear War in 1990," *Arizona Republic,* March 22, 1993.

26. *Pearls of Wisdom* 36, no. 43 (September 26, 1993).

27. Ibid.

28. "Challenging the Media Myth." Also see "Waco Standoff's Unwelcome Limelight," *Washington Post,* March 20, 1993.

29. David Snow and Richard Machalek, "On the Presumed Fragility of Unconventional Beliefs," *Journal of the Society for the Scientific Study of Religion* 21, no. 1 (1982): 23.

30. Ibid.

31. Elizabeth Clare Prophet, *The Astrology of the Four Horsemen,* 430–35. As Prophet indicates, Saint Germain's November 1986 warning stressed the need for the membership to prepare both for the catastrophic event and its aftermath.

32. Michael Barkun, "Millennial Violence in Contemporary America," in *Millennialism, Persecution, and Violence: Historical Cases,* ed. Catherine Wessinger (Syracuse: Syracuse University Press, 2000), 355.

33. See Galanter, *Cults, Faith, Healing, and Coercion,* 112–14. Although Galanter does not specifically address millenarian movements, the socio-cultural characteristics of the cultic groups he examines share these general traits with historical examples of apocalyptic millennial groups.

34. Dick Anthony and Thomas Robbins, "Religious Totalism, Exemplary Dualism, and the Waco Tragedy," in *Millennium, Messiahs, and Mayhem,* ed. Thomas Robbins and Susan Palmer (New York: Routledge, 1997), 268.

35. Hall, *Gone from the Promised Land,* 176.

36. Ibid., 299.

37. John Hall and Philip Schuyler, "Apostasy, Apocalypse, and Religious Violence," in *The Politics of Religious Apostasy: The Role of Apostates in the Transformation of Religious Movements,* ed. David Bromley (Westport, Conn.: Praeger, 1998), 145–51.

38. Thomas Robbins, "Religious Movements and Violence: A Friendly Critique of the Interpretive Approach," *Nova Religio* 1, no. 1 (1997): 15.

39. Ibid., 17.

40. For an example of the interpretive approach to millenarian violence, see Kaplan, *Radical Religion in America,* 164–73. This theory has been used to explain at least two recent cases in which apocalyptic survivalists clashed with the forces of the state. See, for example, Michael Barkun, "The Millennial Dream," in *From the Ashes: Making Sense of Waco,* ed. James Lewis (Lanham, Md.: Rowman and Littlefield, 1994), 51–53. Also see James Aho, *This Thing of Darkness: A Sociology of the Enemy* (Seattle: University of Washington Press, 1994), 50–57.

41. Mark Mullins, "Aum Shinrikyo as an Apocalyptic Movement," in *Millennium, Messiahs, and Mayhem,* ed. Thomas Robbins and Susan Palmer (New York: Routledge, 1997), 316.

42. Ian Reader, *A Poisonous Cocktail? Aum Shinrikyo's Path to Violence* (Copenhagen: Nordic Institute of Asian Studies, 1996), 67. As Reader notes, Aum also attributed other "enemies" with a

role in the world conspiracy. Jews and Freemasons were, at times, also thought to be plotting against the sect.

43. Ibid., 23–30. Reader indicates that Aum had approximately 10,000 members in Japan in 1995. About 1,200 of the group's most committed members lived in Aum communities that were separated from the larger society. It is believed that Aum may have also had up to 30,000 members in Russia.

44. David Kaplan and Andrew Marshall, *The Cult at the End of the World* (New York: Crown Publishers, 1996), 85.

45. Reader, *A Poisonous Cocktail?* 70.

46. Kaplan and Marshall, *The Cult at the End of the World,* 84.

47. Reader, *A Poisonous Cocktail?* 70.

48. Robert Robins and Jerrold Post, *Political Paranoia: The Psychopolitics of Hatred* (New Haven: Yale University Press, 1997), 130.

49. Ibid., 139.

50. Mark Juergensmeyer, "Terror Mandated by God," *Terrorism and Political Violence* 9, no. 2 (1997): 18. It requires attention that the March 20, 1995, attack on the Tokyo subway was not the first time that Aum attempted an act of millennial mass terrorism. After the arrest of Asahara and numerous Aum officials in Japan following the subway incident, group members confessed to carrying out no fewer than nine other attempted acts of terrorism. The first of these was in April 1990 and involved an effort by Aum members to spray botulinum toxin from trucks circulating through Tokyo. Again, in 1993, group members engineered a sprayer device attached to a vehicle and attempted to release anthrax spores into the air in Tokyo. These and several other pre-March 20, 1995, terrorist attempts failed. See Jessica Stern, *The Ultimate Terrorists* (Cambridge, Mass.: Harvard University Press, 1999), 63–64.

51. "Environmentalists, Sect Wage Battle," *Chicago Tribune,* June 10, 1988.

52. Anthony and Robbins, "Religious Totalism, Violence, and Exemplary Dualism," 35.

53. "Leaders Deny CUT Bought Guns."

54. *Pearls of Wisdom* 22, no. 12 (1974).

55. "Feds Rule to Release CUT Documents," *Livingston Enterprise,* January 17, 1995.

56. Walsh, interview, July 1, 1994, Royal Teton Ranch.

57. Ibid.

58. Hall, *Gone from the Promised Land,* 299. Hall uses this term to describe a group fighting a violent Manichaean struggle with forces believed to represent the agents of evil.

59. See Elizabeth Clare Prophet, *Prophecy for the 1980s,* 120.

6. Post-Prophetic Failure and Decline

1. Shephard and Lilliston, "Children of the Church Universal and Triumphant," 91.

2. Church member Davies Andersen, interview by the author, Royal Teton Ranch, July 4, 1994.

3. "CUT's Theology Hasn't Changed," *Bozeman Daily Chronicle,* March 18, 1998.

4. FBI records on Church Universal and Triumphant, 0055–2372343. Obtained through the Freedom of Information Act (FOIA). The slim FOIA file on CUT reveals that reports about the

group's business operations occasionally made their way into the bureau's Los Angeles field office, but that no further investigation was conducted.

5. "Undercover: Delving into the Church's Business Practices," *Calgary Herald,* March 3, 1997.

6. Ibid.

7. "Leaders Deny CUT Bought Guns."

8. "IRS Settles with CUT over Status," *Billings Gazette,* January 4, 1994.

9. "Montana Sect Cleared in IRS Tax Ruling," *Washington Times,* May 9, 1994.

10. "Critics Dismayed with CUT Deal," *Livingston Enterprise,* June 7, 1994.

11. "Church Retains Tax Status," *Bozeman Daily Chronicle,* June 3, 1994.

12. "Leader of a Cult? 'No' She Insists."

13. Stephen Kent and Theresa Krebs, "When Scholars Know Sin," *Skeptic* 6, no. 3 (1998): 35.

14. FBI records on the Church Universal and Triumphant, 0055–2372342, obtained through the Freedom of Information Act (FOIA). The FBI did, however, collect open-source information on the arrest of Vernon Hamilton and received several letters from both Montana residents and political officeholders in the Park County region expressing concern about CUT's survivalist mobilization.

15. "Waco Standoff's Unwelcome Light."

16. This special issue of *Syzygy* was marketed in book form. See James Lewis and J. Gordon Melton, eds., *Church Universal and Triumphant in Scholarly Perspective.*

17. Bruce Sowards, Michael Walser, and Rick Hoyle, "Personality and Intelligence Measurement of the Church Universal and Triumphant," in *Church Universal and Triumphant in Scholarly Perspective,* ed. James Lewis and J. Gordon Melton (Stanford, Calif.: Center for Academic Publication, 1993), 66.

18. Robert Balch and Stephan Langdon, "How the Problem of Malfeasance Gets Overlooked in the Studies of New Religions: An Examination of the Church Universal and Triumphant," in *Wolves within the Fold: Religious Leadership and Abuses of Power,* ed. Anson Shupe (New Brunswick, N.J.: Rutgers University Press, 1998), 192.

19. Ibid., 199.

20. Elizabeth Clare Prophet, interview by the author, Royal Teton Ranch, July 3, 1994.

21. York, "The Church Universal and Triumphant," 74–75.

22. Elizabeth Clare Prophet, interview, Royal Teton Ranch, July 3, 1994.

23. "Motzko Sues CUT," *Livingston Enterprise,* December 20, 1995.

24. "Tenant Owes for Rent," *Livingston Enterprise,* August 22, 1996.

25. *Royal Teton Ranch News* (January 1994): 8.

26. Ibid., 3.

27. Ibid. For a general overview of the various types of antigovernment and tax-protest groups in the American northwest, see James Aho, *The Politics of Righteousness,* 17–19.

28. "Motzko Sues CUT."

29. "CUT Settles Standoff Suit," *Livingston Enterprise,* December 8, 1998.

30. Arnone, telephone interview, March 17, 1997.

31. "A Special Dispensation," 14–15. This lengthy pamphlet was produced by the church in 1995.

32. Ibid., 21.

33. "CUT Decentralizing Power?" *Religion Watch* (November 1996): 3.

34. "Go Out and Conduct (Money Making) Business." Only one of the ten members of the church's board of directors in 1980 (Edward Francis) was still functioning in that capacity in 1996.

35. "Sixth CUT Leader Steps Down from Board," *Livingston Enterprise*, January 24, 1996.

36. "Ex-CUT Members Get Aid," *Billings Gazette*, March 7, 1996.

37. "Prophet Gives Up Position," *Billings Gazette*, June 11, 1996.

38. "With World Still Intact, Sect Draws More Critics," *New York Times*, March 2, 1997.

39. "CUT Decentralizing Power?"

40. "CUT Leaders Admit Group Living Beyond Its Means," *Bozeman Daily Chronicle*, March 17, 1997. CUT's financial figures were made public in a report issued to church members in early 1997. The report, which was the first of its kind to be produced and distributed by the organization, documented that the chief source of revenues were member contributions, sale of publications, conference fees, and income from property rentals. CUT's plans for a new, decentralized management structure were also discussed. See "Building a New Culture: Handbook for Individual and Organizational Change," 1997 pamphlet produced by the Church Universal and Triumphant.

41. "Trouble in Paradise," *Bozeman Daily Chronicle*, November 24, 1996. While this stipend amounted to $15 per month in the 1970s, CUT officials claimed that the figure was about $1250 per month after the staff population was reduced on the Royal Teton Ranch. A health-care plan was also provided to full-time staff in the wake of the downsizing initiative.

42. "Rightsizing: CUT Offers Staff Members Incentive to Leave," *Livingston Enterprise*, November 11, 1996.

43. "Trouble in Paradise."

44. Author interview with an anonymous resident of CUT's Glastonbury settlement, Emigrant Point, Mont., July 1, 1994.

45. "CUT to End Policy of Limited Housing to Members Only," *Bozeman Daily Chronicle*, March 21, 1997.

46. Ibid.

47. "Prophet, Francis Announce Divorce," *Livingston Enterprise*, November 25, 1996.

48. Berchiolli, "Civil Religion in the Age of Aquarius."

49. Untitled news release issued by CUT, November 22, 1996.

50. "Prophet, Francis Announce Divorce."

51. "Church Goes to South America," *Calgary Herald*, March 3, 1997.

52. *Royal Teton Ranch News* (spring-summer 1996): 5. Among the cities listed on Prophet's itinerary were: Buenos Aires, Porto Alegre, Santos, Sao Paulo, Bogota, Quito, and Medellin. This was not Prophet's first speaking venture in South America. Shortly after Mark Prophet's death in 1973, the Messenger traveled to the continent to give lectures and recruit new members.

53. *Pearls of Wisdom* 39, no. 31 (August 4, 1996).

54. *Royal Teton Ranch News* (spring-summer 1996): 5–7.

55. Ibid.

56. *Pearls of Wisdom* 38, no. 18 (May 5, 1996). In this particular dictation from one of the As-

cended Masters, Prophet stated that aliens from other worlds were endangering the safety of the people of the Americas.

57. CUT news release, August 21, 1997.

58. "Leader of a Cult? 'No,' She Insists."

59. The short-lived *Heart to Heart* program was ended in 1999. For information on the program, see CUT's web site, <http://www.tsl.org/radioshow/index.html>. Most of the programs were devoted to interviews with New Age writers, musicians, and practitioners of New Age therapies and holistic health care.

60. Bill Ardorfer, "A Heaven's Gate Recruiting Session in Colorado," *Skeptical Inquirer* (July-August 1997): 23.

61. Bill Ardorfer, "Art Bell, Heaven's Gate, and Journalistic Integrity," *Skeptical Inquirer* (July-August 1997): 23.

62. "Odyssey to Suicide," *New York Times,* April 28, 1997.

63. "The Art Bell Interview with Elizabeth Clare Prophet" (Central Point, Ore.: Chancellor Broadcasting, 1997), April 17, 1997. Audiotaped interview Art Bell conducted with Prophet on the radio program *Coast to Coast with Art Bell.*

64. Ibid.

65. Rodney Perkins and Forrest Jackson, *Cosmic Suicide: The Tragedy and Transcendence of Heaven's Gate* (Dallas, Tex.: Pentaradial Press, 1997), 78.

66. "The Art Bell Interview with Elizabeth Clare Prophet." For a more complete treatment of Sitchin's theory, see Sitchin, *The Twelfth Planet.*

67. Elizabeth Clare Prophet, interview, Royal Teton Ranch, July 3, 1994.

68. Ibid.

69. Ibid.

70. CUT minister Gene Voessler, interview by the author, Royal Teton Ranch, July 1, 1994.

71. Church staff member Paul Haugen, interview by the author, Royal Teton Ranch, July 2, 1994. Other interviewees stressed that the growth of the New Age movement had corrupted the image of the church.

72. "All of Us Can Walk and Talk with God," *Daily Aztec* (San Diego State University newspaper), April 10, 1997.

73. "Practical Spirituality: A Six Day Conference on Living a Spiritual Life," CUT advertising brochure for its June 30-July 5, 1997, conference in San Diego.

74. "Soul Evolution: A Fusion of Mind and Spirit," CUT advertising brochure for its 1995 summer conference at the Royal Teton Ranch.

75. "Environment of the Soul," CUT advertsing brochure for its 1994 summer conference at the Royal Teton Ranch. CUT's 1994 and 1995 summer conferences featured several well-known speakers from the New Age and human potential orbit. Among those making presentations at the meetings were Margaret Paul, Bettie Youngs, Martin Rossman, and Lana Israel.

76. Author field notes. These are examples of some of the New Age-derived themes discussed in classes at CUT's 1994 summer conference.

77. Author field notes, Royal Teton Ranch, July 4, 1994.

78. It is commonly recognized that the former Soviet Union devoted much spending to its

development of a civil defense system to protect citizens from nuclear attack. See Michio Kaku and Daniel Axelrod, *To Win a Nuclear War: The Pentagon's Secret War Plans* (Boston: South End Press, 1987), 294.

79. Author field notes, Royal Teton Ranch, July 3, 1994.

80. Richard Abanes, *End Time Visions* (New York: Four Walls, Eight Windows, 1998), 187–201.

81. Author field notes, Royal Teton Ranch, July 1, 1994.

82. Elizabeth Clare Prophet, interview, Royal Teton Ranch, July 3, 1994.

83. Ibid.

84. Elizabeth Clare Prophet, *The Astrology of the Four Horsemen,* 363.

85. "Freedom 1988," church promotional bulletin. These issues were highlighted at CUT's 1988 summer conference.

86. Elizabeth Clare Prophet, interview, Royal Teton Ranch, July 3, 1994.

87. Ibid.

88. Sun Tzu, *The Art of War,* trans. Lionel Giles (London: Luzac and Co., 1910), 3.

89. Elizabeth Clare Prophet, interview, Royal Teton Ranch, July 3, 1994.

90. Ibid.

91. Evidence of this can be found in the dictations given by Elizabeth Clare Prophet during her summer tour of South America. See, for example, *Pearls of Wisdom* 39, no. 18 (March 5, 1996). In this dictation, Prophet delivered a message stating that "enemies of world freedom" are out to destroy the United States. She went further to state that this threat came from karma attached to the peoples of "the Near and Far East and the Indian subcontinent."

92. News release from the Church Universal and Triumphant, August 8, 1997.

93. *Pearls of Wisdom* 40, no. 17 (April 27, 1997).

94. Ibid.

95. Ibid.

96. Ibid.

97. *The AIDS Conspiracy* (Livingston, Mont.: Summit University Press, 1988); *The UFO Connection* (Livingston, Mont.: Summit University Press, 1988). Videotapes produced by CUT.

98. Author interview with anonymous staff member, Royal Teton Ranch, June 30, 1994. This subject indicated that the church has become more sensitive to this issue since the revocation of its tax exemption.

99. Edward Francis, interview by the author, Royal Teton Ranch, July 4, 1994.

100. Ibid.

101. Mark and Elizabeth Clare Prophet, *Climb the Highest Mountain* (Livingston, Mont.: Summit University Press, 1986), 584–85.

102. Francis, interview, Royal Teton Ranch, July 4, 1994.

103. Timothy Miller, "The Historical Communal Roots of Ultraconservative Groups: Early American Communes That Have Shaped Today's Far Right," in *Rejected and Suppressed Knowledge: The Radical Right and the Cultic Milieu,* ed. Jeffrey Kaplan and Helene Loow (Stockholm: National Council of Crime Prevention, 2003).

104. Elizabeth Clare Prophet, *On the Edge: Challenges on the Cusp of the Twenty-first Century*

(Livingston, Mont.: Summit University Press, 1995). Videotaped speech given by Prophet on the Royal Teton Ranch.

105. In recent days, a number of New Age Ascended Master groups have begun to attract former CUT members. Two such organizations are the Universal Church, located in Centreville, Virginia, and the Temple of the Presence, based in Chelsea, Vermont. See "The Foundation of Higher Spiritual Learning," July 8, 1992, literature brochure from the Universal Church; untitled recruitment information dated February 21, 1996, from the Temple of the Presence.

106. "CUT Looks to Future," *Bozeman Daily Chronicle*, March 18, 1998.

107. "CUT Lays Off More Employees," *Bozeman Daily Chronicle*, August 28, 1998.

108. Ibid.

109. "Church's Loss Near Yellowstone Will Become Wildlife's Gain," *New York Times*, March 24, 1998.

110. "Elizabeth Clare Prophet Announces Plans to Retire," Church Universal and Triumphant news release, January 1, 1999.

111. "Apocalyptic Church Struggling after Armageddon Didn't Happen," *Detroit News*, April 4, 1998.

112. "CUT Spiritual Leader Announces She Has Alzheimer's Disease," CUT news release, November 25, 1998.

113. "CUT Cuts Work Force in Half—Again," *Bozeman Daily Chronicle*, November 3, 1999.

114. "Land Agreement Closes," *Heart to Heart Newsletter*, October 1999. This monthly news publication replaced the *Royal Teton Ranch News* as the church's official newsletter in 1997.

115. "Church Turns Land Over to Government."

116. "Yellowstone Land Swap Will Protect Bison, Geysers," *Pittsburgh Post Gazette*, August 23, 1999.

117. Melton, "The Church Universal and Triumphant: Its Heritage and Thoughtworld," 12–14.

118. Stupple, "The I AM Sect Today," 901.

119. Ibid., 903. The I AM temples continue to function in a number of American cities.

120. Max Weber, *The Theory of Social and Economic Organization* (New York: Free Press, 1964), 363–64.

121. Lorne Dawson, *Comprehending Cults: The Sociology of New Religious Movements* (New York: Oxford University Press, 1998), 139–42.

122. "CUT Shifts Focus," *Bozeman Daily Chronicle*, April 3, 1999.

123. "Church, Family Will Share Guardianship of CUT Leader," *Bozeman Daily Chronicle*, April 14, 1999.

124. "CUT's New Reality."

125. Paula [pseud.], interview by the author, Glastonbury settlement, Emigrant Point, Mont., June 30, 1994.

126. "Cleirbaut: Church Here to Stay," *Bozeman Daily Chronicle*, March 15, 1998.

127. *Heart to Heart*, November 1999, 3.

128. Elizabeth Clare Prophet, Patricia Spadaro, and Murray Steinman, *Saint Germain's Prophecy for the New Millennium* (Livingston, Mont.: Summit University Press, 1999), 166–70.

129. *Pearls of Wisdom* 39, no. 42 (October 20, 1996).

130. Church Universal and Triumphant 1998 annual report, 13.

131. "Glastonbury Blaze Damages Shelter," *Livingston Enterprise,* December 22, 1999.

132. "Building Community," *Heart to Heart,* April 1998, 1.

133. Church Universal and Triumphant 1998 annual report, 15.

134. "Treasurer's Corner," *Heart to Heart,* April 1998, 7.

135. "Cleirbaut: Church Here to Stay."

136. Promotional literature and recruitment information from the Temple of the Presence, April 1996; organizational statement from the Universal Church, July 8, 1992.

137. "Former CUT Members Say They Are Messengers."

138. See Philip Hoag, *No Such Thing As Doomsday* (Livingston, Mont.: Yellowstone River Publishing, 1996). Hoag's book offers tips on shelter construction and emergency prepartions for a future catastrophe. The book seems to be marketed specifically to a CUT audience.

139. Campbell, "The Cult, the Cultic Milieu, and Secularization," 122.

140. Barkun, "Millennial Violence in Contemporary America," 353.

141. See John Hall and Philip Schuyler, "The Mystical Apocalypse of the Solar Temple," in *Millennialism, Messiahs, and Mayhem: Contemporary Apocalyptic Movements,* ed. Thomas Robbins and Susan Palmer (New York: Routledge, 1997), 285–311; Reader, *A Poisonous Cocktail?* 71–89; Winston Davis, "Heaven's Gate: A Study of Religious Obedience," *Nova Religio* 3, no. 2, 241–67.

142. Robins and Post, *Political Paranoia,* 113–40. The authors' analysis of the Jonestown and Aum Shinrikyo cases brings to attention these details of each group's thoughtworld.

143. Elsewhere I have discussed this distinction. See Brad Whitsel, "The Turner Diaries and Cosmotheism: William Pierce's Theology of Revolution," *Nova Religio* 1, no. 2 (1998): 183–97.

144. Mark Hamm, *Apocalypse in Oklahoma* (Boston: Northeastern University Press, 1996), 7.

145. Whitsel, "The Turner Diaries and Cosmotheism," 193.

146. The Japanese apocalyptic sect Aum Shinrikyo represents the clearest recent example of a group that set strategic plans to trigger the arrival of an anticipated glory period for its members. See Mullins, "Aum Shinrikyo as an Apocalyptic Movement," 314–27.

Epilogue

1. "CUT Heads into Second Life Cycle," *Bozeman Daily Chronicle,* March 14, 1998.

2. "Spiritual Guidance for a Changing World," CUT brochure, 2000.

3. "CUT Reportedly Finds Buyer for North Ranch," *Bozeman Daily Chronicle,* January 4, 2001.

4. "Letter from Mother's Co-Guardians," November 1, 1999. This statement was distributed to CUT members.

5. "Within Year CUT Leader Moving to Bozeman," *Livingston Enterprise,* January 27, 2000.

6. "Reflections on Mother," January 1, 2000. Letter written by CUT presidents and distributed to membership.

7. Ibid.

Bibliography

Books, Dissertations, and Book Chapters

Abanes, Richard. *End Time Visions.* New York: Four Walls, Eight Windows, 1998.

Adamski, George. *Inside the Space Ships.* New York: Abelard-Schuman, 1955.

Aho, James. *The Politics of Righteousness: Idaho Christian Patriotism.* Seattle: Univ. of Washington Press, 1990.

———. *This Thing of Darkness: A Sociology of the Enemy.* Seattle: Univ. of Washington Press, 1994.

Alban, Francis. *Fatima Priest.* Pound Ridge, N.Y.: Good Counsel, 1997.

Allen, Gary. *None Dare Call It Conspiracy.* Boring, Ore.: CPA Books, 1971.

Andrews, George C. "An Explosive Exchange." In *Extraterrestrial Friends and Foes,* edited by George C. Andrews, 227–29. Lilburn, Ga.: Illuminati Press, 1993.

Anthony, Dick, and Thomas Robbins. "Religious Totalism, Exemplary Dualism, and the Waco Tragedy." In *Millennium, Messiahs, and Mayhem,* edited by Thomas Robbins and Susan Palmer, 261–84. New York: Routledge, 1997.

Bailey, Alice. *From Intellect to Intuition.* New York: Lucius Publishing Company, 1960.

Balch, Robert, and Stephan Langdon. "How the Problem of Malfeasance Gets Overlooked in the Studies of New Religions: An Examination of the Church Universal and Triumphant." In *Wolves Within the Fold: Religious Leadership and Abuses of Power,* edited by Anson Shupe, 191–211. New Brunswick, N.J.: Rutgers Univ. Press, 1998.

Ballard, Guy [Godfre Ray King, pseud.]. *Unveiled Mysteries.* Mount Shasta, Calif.: Ascended Master Teaching Foundation, 1939.

Barkun, Michael. *Disaster and the Millennium.* New Haven: Yale Univ. Press, 1974.

———. "Millennial Violence in Contemporary America." In *Millennialism, Persecution, and Violence: Historical Cases,* edited by Catherine Wessinger, 340–53. Syracuse: Syracuse Univ. Press, 2000.

———. "Reflections afer Waco: Millennialists and the State." In *From the Ashes: Making Sense of Waco,* edited by James R. Lewis, 41–49. Lanham, Md.: Rowman and Littlefield, 1994.

———. *Religion and the Racist Right.* Chapel Hill: Univ. of North Carolina Press, 1994.

Baumgartner, Frederic J. *Longing for the End: A History of Millennialism in Western Civilization.* New York: St. Martin's Press, 1999.

Biagent, Michael, and Richard Leigh. *The Temple and the Lodge.* New York: Arcade Publishing, 1989.

Blavatsky, Helena Petrovna. *Isis Unveiled,* vol. 2. Wheaton, Ill.: Theosophical Univ. Press, 1972.

Boyer, Paul. *By the Bomb's Early Light.* New York: Pantheon, 1985.

Braden, Charles. *These Also Believe: A Study of American Cults and Minority Religious Movements.* New York: Macmillan, 1949.

Brinton, Crane. *The Anatomy of Revolution.* New York: Vintage Books, 1965.

Bryan, Gerald B. *Psychic Dictatorship in America.* Burbank, Calif.: New Era Press, 1940.

Bulwer-Lytton, Edward (Lord Lytton). *The Coming Race.* New York: George Routledge and Sons, 1871.

Campbell, Colin. "The Cult, the Cultic Milieu, and Secularization." In *A Sociological Yearbook of Religion in Britain.* London: SCM Press, 5: 119–36.

Cohn, Norman. *The Pursuit of the Millennium: Revolutionary Millenarianism and Mystical Anarchists of the Middle Ages.* New York: Oxford Univ. Press, 1970.

Cousineau, Phil. *UFOs: A Manual for the Millennium.* New York: HarperCollins, 1995.

Cuneo, Michael. "Catholic Apocalypticism." In *Millennium, Messiahs, and Mayhem,* edited by Thomas Robbins and Susan Palmer, 176–94. New York: Routledge, 1997.

Daraul, Arkon. *A History of Secret Societies.* New York: Citadel Press, 1994.

Dawson, Lorne. *Comprehending Cults: The Sociology of New Religious Movements.* New York: Oxford Univ. Press, 1998.

DeHaas, Jocelyn. "The Mediation of Ideology and Public Image in the Church Universal and Triumphant." In *The Church Universal and Triumphant in Scholarly Perspective,* edited by James Lewis and J. Gordon Melton, 21–37. Stanford, Calif.: Center for Academic Publication, 1994.

Diamond, Sara. *Roads to Dominion: Right-Wing Movements and Political Power in the United States.* New York: Guilford Press, 1995.

Ellwood, Robert S. *Alternative Altars: Unconventional and Eastern Spirituality in America.* Chicago: Univ. of Chicago Press, 1971.

———. "The American Theosophical Synthesis." In *The Occult in America: New Historical Perspectives,* edited by Howard Kerr and Charles Crow, 110–38. Urbana: Univ. of Illinois Press, 1983.

———. *Religious and Spiritual Groups in America.* Englewood Cliffs, N.J.: Prentice Hall, 1973.

Festinger, Leon, Henry Reicken, and Stanley Schacter. *When Prophecy Fails.* Minneapolis: Univ. of Minnesota Press, 1956.

Galanter, Marc. *Cults, Faith, Healing, and Coercion.* New York: Oxford Univ. Press, 1989.

Goodricke-Clarke, Nicholas. *The Occult Roots of Nazism: Secret Aryan Cults and Their Influence on Nazi Ideology.* New York: New York Univ. Press, 1992.

Hall, John. *Gone from the Promised Land: Jonestown in American Cultural History.* New Brunswick, N.J.: Transaction, 1989.

Hall, John, and Philip Schuyler. "Apostasy, Apocalypse, and Religious Violence." In *The Politics of Religious Apostasy: The Role of Apostates in the Transformation of Religious Movements,* edited by David Bromley, 145–60. Westport, Conn.: Praeger, 1998.

———. "The Mystical Apocalypse of the Solar Temple." In *Millennium, Messiahs, and Mayhem: Contemporary Apocalyptic Movements,* edited by Thomas Robbins and Susan Palmer, 285–311. New York: Routledge, 1997.

Hamm, Mark. *Apocalypse in Oklahoma.* Boston: Northeastern Univ. Press, 1996.

Hieronimus, Robert. *America's Secret Destiny: Spiritual Vision and the Founding of a Nation.* Rochester, Vt.: Destiny Books, 1989.

Hoag, Philip. *No Such Thing as Doomsday: Underground Shelters, Earth Changes, Wars, and Other Threats.* Emigrant, Mont.: Yellowstone River Publishing, 1996.

Hoffer, Eric. *The True Believer: Thoughts on the Nature of Mass Movements.* New York: Harper and Row, 1951.

Homer, Michael. "Protection of Religion Under the First Amendment: Church Universal and Triumphant." In *The Church Universal and Triumphant in Scholarly Perspective,* edited by James Lewis and J. Gordon Melton, 119–37. Stanford, Calif.: Center for Academic Publication.

Hudson, Winthrop S. *Religion in America,* 3d ed. New York: Charles Scribner's Sons, 1981.

Jenkins, Philip. *Mystics and Messiahs: Cults and New Religions in American History.* New York: Oxford Univ. Press, 2000.

Johnson, Ronald. *The Architects of Fear.* Boston: Houghton Mifflin, 1983.

Judah, J. Stillson. *The History and Philosophy of the Metaphysical Movements in America.* Philadelphia: Westminster Press, 1967.

Kaffon-Minkel, Walter. *Subterranean Worlds: 100,000 Years of Dragons, Dwarfs, the Dead, Lost Races, and UFOs from Inside Earth.* Port Townsend, Wash.: Loompanics, 1989.

Kaku, Michio, and Daniel Axelrod. *To Win a Nuclear War: The Pentagon's Secret War Plans.* Boston: South End Press, 1987.

Kaplan, David, and Andrew Marshall. *The Cult at the End of the World.* New York: Crown, 1996.

Kaplan, Jeffrey. *Radical Religion in America.* Syracuse: Syracuse Univ. Press, 1997.

King, Dennis. *Lyndon LaRouche and the New American Fascism.* New York: Doubleday, 1989.

Lee, Martha. *Earth First! Environmental Apocalypse.* Syracuse: Syracuse Univ. Press, 1995.

Lewis, James. "Of Tolerance, Toddlers, and Trailers: First Impressions of the Church Universal and Triumphant." In *The Church Universal and Triumphant in Scholarly Perspective,* edited by James Lewis and J. Gordon Melton, vii-viv. Stanford, Calif.: Center for Academic Publication, 1994.

Liljegren, S. B. *Bulwer-Lytton's Novels and Isis Unveiled.* Cambridge, Mass.: Harvard Univ. Press, 1957.

Lipset, Seymour Martin, and Earl Rabb. *The Politics of Unreason.* New York: Harper and Row, 1970.

Maaga, Mary McCormick. *Hearing the Voices of Jonestown.* Syracuse: Syracuse Univ. Press, 1998.

Mann, A. T. *Millennium Prophecies: Predictions for the Year 2000.* Rockport, Maine: Element Books, 1992.

Mazet, Edmond. "Freemasonry and Esotericism." In *Modern Esoteric Spirituality,* edited by Antoine Faivre and Jacob Needleman, 240–76. New York: Crossroads, 1992.

McNicol-Stock, Catherine. *Rural Radicals: Righteous Rage in the American Grain.* Ithaca, N.Y.: Cornell Univ. Press, 1997.

Melton, J. Gordon. "The Church Universal and Triumphant: Its Heritage and Thought-world." In *The Church Universal and Triumphant in Scholarly Perspective,* edited by James Lewis and J. Gordon Melton, 1–20. Stanford, Calif.: Center for Academic Publication, 1994.

———. *The Encyclopedia of American Religions,* 2d ed. Detroit: Gale Research, 1989.

———. *The Encyclopedia of American Religions: Religious Creeds.* Detroit: Gale Research, 1992.

———. *Encyclopedic Handbook of Cults in America.* New York: Garland, 1986.

———. *New Age Encyclopedia.* Detroit: Gale Research, 1990.

———. "When Prophets Die: The Succession Crisis in New Religions." In *When Prophets Die: The Post-Charismatic Fate of New Religious Movements,* edited by Timothy Miller, 2–15. Albany: State Univ. of New York Press, 1998.

Miller, Edith Starr [Lady Queensborough, pseud.]. *Occult Theocracy.* Los Angeles: Christian Book Club of America, 1933.

Miller, Timothy. "The Historical Communal Roots of Ultraconservative Groups: Early American Communes That Have Shaped Today's Far Right." In *Rejected and Suppressed Knowledge: The Radical Right and the Cultic Milieu,* edited by Jeffrey Kaplan and Helene Loow. Stockholm: National Council of Crime Prevention, 2003.

Mintz, Frank. *The Liberty Lobby and the American Right: Race, Conspiracy, and Culture.* Westport, Conn.: Greenwood Press, 1985.

Moore, R. Laurence. "Mormonism, Christian Science, and Spiritualism." In *The Occult in America: New Historical Perspectives,* edited by Howard Kerr and Charles Crow, 143–50. Urbana: Univ. of Illinois Press, 1983.

Moulton-Howe, Linda. "A Hall of Mirrors with a Quicksand Floor." In *Extraterrestrial Friends and Foes,* edited by George C. Andrews, 164–68. Lilburn, Ga.: Illuminet Press, 1993.

Mullins, Mark. "Aum Shinrikyo as an Apocalyptic Movement." In *Millennium, Messiahs, and Mayhem,* edited by Thomas Robbins and Susan Palmer, 313–24. New York: Routledge, 1997.

Palmer, Susan. *AIDS as an Apocalyptic Metaphor in North America.* Toronto: Univ. of Toronto Press, 1997.

Paolini, Kenneth, and Talita Paolini. *Four Hundred Years of Imaginary Friends: A Journey into the World of Adepts, Ascended Masters, and Their Messengers.* Livingston, Mont.: Paolini International, 2000.

Perkins, Rodney, and Forrest Jackson. *Cosmic Suicide: The Tragedy and Transcendence of Heaven's Gate.* Dallas: Pentaradial Press, 1997.

Pietrangelo, John. *Lambs to Slaughter: My Fourteen Years with Elizabeth Clare Prophet and the Church Universal and Triumphant.* Self-published, 1994.

Pipes, Daniel. *Conspiracy: How the Paranoid Style Flourishes and Where It Comes From.* New York: Free Press, 1997.

Prophet, Elizabeth Clare. *The Astrology of the Four Horsemen.* Livingston, Mont.: Summit Univ. Press, 1991.

———.*Forbidden Mysteries of Enoch: Fallen Angels and the Origins of Evil* (Livingston, Mont.:Summit Univ. Press, 1992)

———. *The Great White Brotherhood in the Culture, History, and Religion of America.* Colorado Springs: Summit Univ. Press, 1976.

———. *Prophecy for the 1980s: The Handwriting on the Wall.* Malibu, Calif.: Summit Univ. Press, 1980.

———. *Saint Germain and Alchemy.* Livingston, Mont.: Summit Univ. Press, 1993.

———. *Vials of the Seven Last Plagues: Prophecies for the 1980s by the Seven Archangels.* Los Angeles: Summit Univ. Press, 1980.

Prophet, Elizabeth Clare, Patricia Spadaro, and Murray Steinman. *Saint Germain's Prophecy for the New Millennium.* Livingston, Mont.: Summit Univ. Press, 1999.

Prophet, Mark. *The Soulless Ones: Cloning a Counterfeit Creation.* Los Angeles: Summit Univ. Press, 1965.

Prophet, Mark and Elizabeth Clare. *Climb the Highest Mountain: The Path of the Higher Self.* Los Angeles: Summit Univ. Press, 1972; Livingston, Mont.: Summit University Press, 1986.

———. *Lords of the Seven Rays.* Livingston, Mont.: Summit Univ. Press, 1986.

————. *The Lost Teachings of Jesus (Book One)*. Livingston, Mont.: Summit Univ. Press, 1986.

————. *The Lost Teachings of Jesus (Book Four), Good and Evil: Atlantis Revisited*. Livingston, Mont.: Summit Univ. Press, 1986.

Quigley, Carroll. *Tragedy and Hope: A History of the World in Our Time*. New York: Macmillan Co., 1966.

Reader, Ian. *A Poisonous Cocktail? Aum Shinrikyo's Path to Violence*. Copenhagen: Nordic Institute of Asian Studies, 1996.

Rhodes, James. *The Hitler Movement: A Modern Millenarian Revolution*. Stanford, Calif.: Hoover Institute Press, 1980.

Robbins, Thomas. *Cults, Converts, and Charisma: The Sociology of New Religious Movements*. Beverly Hills, Calif.: Sage Publications, 1988.

Roberts, Archibald. *The Anatomy of a Revolution*. Fort Collins, Colo.: Betsy Ross Press, 1968.

Robins, Robert, and Jerrold Post. *Political Paranoia: The Psychopolitics of Hatred*. New Haven: Yale Univ. Press, 1997.

Saliba, John. "UFO Contactee Phenomena from a Sociological Perspective." In *The Gods Have Landed: New Religions from Other Worlds*, edited by James Lewis, 207–50. Albany: State Univ. of New York Press, 1995.

————. *Understanding New Religious Movements*. Grand Rapids, Mich.: William B. Eerdman, 1995.

Shephard, Gary, and Lawrence Lilliston. "Children of the Church Universal and Triumphant: Some Preliminary Impressions." In *The Church Universal and Triumphant in Scholarly Perspective*, edited by James Lewis and J. Gordon Melton, 67–95. Stanford, Calif.: Center for Academic Publication, 1994.

Shupe, Anson, and David Bromley. *The New Vigilantes: Deprogrammers, Anti-Cultists, and the New Religions*. Beverly Hills, Calif.: Sage Publications, 1980.

Sitchin, Zechariah. *The Twelfth Planet*. New York: Avon Books, 1976.

Sklar, Dusty. *THe Nazis and the Occult*. New York: Dorset Press, 1977.

Sowards, Bruce, Michael J. Walser, and Rick Hoyle. "Personality and Intelligence Measurement of the Church Universal and Triumphant." In *Church Universal and Triumphant in Scholarly Perspective*, edited by James Lewis and J. Gordon Melton, 55–66. Stanford, Calif.: Center for Academic Publication, 1993.

Steiger, Brad. *Project Blue Book*. New York: Ballantine Books, 1976.

Stern, Jessica. *The Ultimate Terrorists*. Cambridge, Mass.: Harvard Univ. Press, 1999.

Stromberg, Roland. *European Intellectual History Since 1789*. Englewood Cliffs, N.J.: Prentice Hall, 1981.

Strozier, Charles. *Apocalypse: On the Psychology of Fundamentalism in America*. Boston: Beacon Press, 1994.

Sutton, Anthony. *America's Secret Establishment.* Billings, Mont.: Liberty House, 1986.

———. *The Two Faces of George Bush.* Dresden, N.Y.: Wiswell Ruffin House, 1988.

———. *Western Technology and Soviet Economic Development.* 3 vols. Stanford, Calif.: Hoover Institute, 1973.

Swedenborg, Emmanuel. *The True Christian Religion.* Vol. 1. New York: American Swedenborg Printing and Publishing Society, 1952.

Tzu, Sun. *The Art of War.* Translated by Lionel Giles. London: Luzac and Co., 1910.

Washington, Peter. *Madame Blavatsky's Baboon: A History of the Mystics, Mediums, and Misfits Who Brought Spiritualism to America.* New York: Schocken Books, 1993.

Webb, James. *The Occult Establishment.* LaSalle, Ill: Open Court, 1976.

———. *The Occult Underground.* LaSalle, Ill: Open Court, 1974.

Weber, Max. *The Theory of Social and Economic Organization.* New York: Free Press, 1964.

Weber, Timothy. *Living in the Shadow of the Second Coming: American Premillennialism (1875–1982).* Grand Rapids: Academie Books, 1983.

Webster, Nesta. *Secret Societies and Subversive Movements.* Palmdale, Calif.: Omni Publications, 1924.

Werly, John. "The Millenarian Right: William Dudley Pelley and the Silver Legion of America." Ph.D. dissertation. Ann Arbor: University Microfilms, 1972.

Wessinger, Catherine. *Annie Besant and Progressive Messianism.* Lewistown, N.Y.: Edwin Mellen Press, 1988.

Wessinger, Catherine. "Millennialism with and without the Mayhem." In *Millennium, Messiahs, and Mayhem: Contemporary Apocalyptic Movements,* edited by Thomas Robbins and Susan Palmer, 47–59. New York: Routledge, 1997.

Wilson, Colin. *The Occult: A History.* New York: Vintage Books, 1973.

Journal Articles

Anthony, Dick, and Thomas Robbins. "Religious Totalism, Violence, and Exemplary Dualism: Beyond the Extrinsic Model." *Terrorism and Political Violence* 7, no. 3 (1995): 10–50.

Ashworth, C. E. "Flying Saucers, Spoon-Bending, and Atlantis." *Sociological Review* 28, no. 2 (1980): 353–76.

Berchiolli, Rick. "Civil Religion in the Age of Aquarius: A Sociological Analysis of the Church Universal and Triumphant." Unpublished research paper, 1988.

Davis, Winston. "Heaven's Gate: A Study of Religious Obedience." *Nova Religio* 3, no. 2 (1999): 241–67.

Juergensmeyer, Mark. "Terror Mandated by God." *Terrorism and Political Violence* 9, no. 2 (1997): 16–23.

Kantor, Debra, and Meredith McGuire. "Creative Eclecticism: The Great White Brotherhood of Elizabeth Clare Prophet." Paper given at the Annual Meeting of the Association for the Sociology of Religion, August 1981.

Kent, Stephen, and Theresa Krebs. "When Scholars Know Sin." *Skeptic* 6, no. 3 (1998): 35.

Robbins, Thomas. "Religious Movements and Violence: A Friendly Critique of the Interpretive Approach." *Nova Religio* 1, no. 1 (1997): 13–29.

Rosenfeld, Jean. "Pai Marire: Peace and Violence in a New Zealand Millenarian Tradition." *Terrorism and Political Violence* 7, no. 3 (1995): 83–108.

Snow, David, and Richard Machalek. "On the Presumed Fragility of Unconventional Beliefs." *Journal of the Society for the Scientific Study of Religion* 21, no. 1 (1982): 15–25.

Stupple, David. "The I AM Sect Today: An Unobituary." *Journal of Popular Culture* 8, no. 4 (1975): 898–905.

———. "Mahatmas and Space Brothers: The Ideology of Alleged Contact with Extraterrestrials." *Journal of American Culture* 7, no. 1 (1984): 131–38.

Tiryakian, Edward. "Toward the Sociology of Esoteric Culture." *American Journal of Sociology* 78, no. 3 (1972): 491–511.

Whitsel, Brad. "Taking Shelter from the Coming Storm: The Millennial Impulse of the Church Universal and Triumphant." *Communal Societies* 19 (1999): 1–23.

Whitsel, Brad. "The Turner Diaries and Cosmotheism: William Pierce's Theology of Revolution." *Nova Religio* 1, no. 2 (1998): 183–97.

Wright, Stuart. "Anatomy of a Government Massacre: Abuse of Hostage-Barricade Protocols during the Waco Standoff." *Terrorism and Political Violence* 11, no. 2 (summer 1999): 39–68.

York, Michael. "The Church Universal and Triumphant." *Journal of Contemporary Religion* 10, no. 1 (1995): 71–82.

Newspapers, Periodicals, and Other Materials

"All of Us Can Walk and Talk with God." *Daily Aztec* (San Diego State University student newspaper), April 10, 1997.

"Apocalyptic Church Struggling after Armageddon Didn't Happen." *Detroit News,* April 14, 1998.

Ardorfer, Bill. "Art Bell, Heaven's Gate, and Journalistic Integrity." *Skeptical Inquirer,* July-August 1997, 23.

———. "A Heaven's Gate Recruiting Session in Colorado." *Skeptical Inquirer,* July-August 1997, 23.

Autobiographical sketch paper, written by Elizabeth Clare Wulf, Antioch College, March 1957.

Bell, Art. "The Art Bell Interview with Elizabeth Clare Prophet." Audiotape interview on *The Art Bell Show: Coast to Coast with Art Bell.* Program #970410C, April 17, 1997.

Berchiolli, Rick. "The Church Universal and Triumphant: The Evolution from World Transformation to Apocalypticism." Paper presented at the annual meeting of the American Academy of Religion, Anaheim, Calif., November 18, 1989.

"Bomb Shelters in the Mountains: Sect Gets Ready for Dark Days." *San Francisco Chronicle,* July 24, 1989.

"Buyers Clearing Out Reminders of Secretive Cult As It Heads for New Home in Montana." *Los Angeles Times,* November 29, 1986.

"Church Buys Ranch for $7 Million." *Los Angeles Times,* September 22, 1981.

"Church, Family Will Share Guardianship of CUT Leader." *Bozeman Daily Chronicle,* April 4, 1999.

"Church Goes to South America." *Calgary Herald,* March 3, 1997.

"Church Land at Center of Dispute." *Denver Post,* May 27, 1989.

"Church Leaders Say Nay to Allegations." *Los Angeles Times,* February 4, 1980.

"Church Members Gun Buying Outlined." *Bozeman Daily Chronicle,* February 27, 1995.

"Church Retains Tax Status." *Bozeman Daily Chronicle,* June 3, 1994.

"Church Turns Land Over to Government." *Salt Lake City Tribune,* September 1, 1999.

"Church's Loss Near Yellowstone Will Become Wildlife's Gain." *New York Times,* March 24, 1998.

"Cleirbaut: Church Here to Stay." *Bozeman Daily Chronicle,* March 15, 1998.

"Critics Dismayed with CUT Deal." *Livingston Enterprise,* June 7, 1994.

"Critics Ignorant and Uninformed Says Montana Church Leader." *Denver Post,* July 13, 1990.

"CUT Cuts Work Force in Half Again." *Bozeman Daily Chronicle,* November 3, 1999.

"CUT Decentralizing Power?" *Religion Watch,* November 1996, 3.

"CUT Documents Show Church's Long History of Arms Purchases." *Livingston Enterprise,* March 5, 1990.

"CUT Heads into Second Life Cycle." *Bozeman Daily Chronicle,* March 14, 1998.

"CUT Lays Off More Employees." *Bozeman Daily Chronicle,* August 28, 1998.

"CUT Leaders Admit Group Living Beyond Its Means." *Bozeman Daily Chronicle,* March 17, 1997.

"CUT Looks to Future." *Bozeman Daily Chronicle,* March 18, 1998.

"CUT Reportedly Finds Buyer for North Ranch." *Bozeman Daily Chronicle,* January 4, 2001.

"CUT Settles Standoff Suit." *Livingston Enterprise,* December 8, 1998.

"CUT Shifts Focus." *Bozeman Daily Chronicle,* April 3, 1999.

"CUT to End Policy of Limited Housing to Members Only." *Bozeman Daily Chronicle,* March 21, 1997.

"CUT's New Reality." *Bozeman Daily Chronicle,* March 15, 1998.

"CUT's Theology Hasn't Changed." *Bozeman Daily Chronicle,* March 18, 1998.

"Disease, Dissension Haunted Family." *Bozeman Daily Chronicle,* March 16, 1998.

"Dissenters Talk." *Los Angeles Times,* February 7, 1980.

"Doomsday Good Reason to Throw Big Party." *Denver Post,* April 24, 1990.

"Environmentalists, Sect Wage Battle." *Chicago Tribune,* June 10, 1988.

"Ex-CUT Members Get Aid." *Billings Gazette,* March 7, 1996.

Federal Bureau of Investigation File, F.O.I. #0055–2372343. Washington, D.C.: FBI.

"Feds Rule to Release CUT Documents." *Livingston Enterprise,* January 17, 1995.

"Former CUT Members Say They Are Messengers." *Bozeman Daily Chronicle,* May 5, 1999.

"Freshman Life Statement Paper," written by Elizabeth Clare Wulf, Antioch College, 1957.

"Glastonbury Blaze Damages Shelter." *Livingston Enterprise,* December 22, 1999.

"Go Out and Conduct (Money Making) Business." *Los Angeles Times,* February 1, 1980.

"Guru Ma: Leader of a Million Dollar Church." *Los Angeles Times,* February 11, 1980.

"Guru Ma Nettles Montana Town." *Los Angeles Times,* March 30, 1986.

"Guru Ma Trial Ends in Biblical Flourish." *Los Angeles Times,* March 20, 1986.

"IRS Settles with CUT over Status." *Billings Gazette,* January 4, 1994.

Kelly, Michael. "The Road to Paranoia." *New Yorker* (June 19, 1995): 60–69.

"Leader Brings Religion into New Age." *Saint Paul Pioneer Press,* February 27, 1993.

"Leader of a Cult? 'No,' She Insists." *Chicago Tribune,* March 5, 1993.

"Leaders Deny CUT Bought Guns." *Billings Gazette,* February 16, 1995.

McGaughey, H. G. "Another One in California, the I AM Movement." *Christian Century* (August 31, 1938): 1038.

"Montana Sect Cleared in IRS Tax Ruling." *Washington Times,* May 9, 1994.

"Montanans Wary of Church's Plan for Promised Land." *Los Angeles Times,* January 25, 1987.

"Motzko Sues CUT." *Livingston Enterprise,* December 20, 1995.

"New Leader Brings New Methods." *Bozeman Daily Chronicle,* March 15, 1998.

"1990s Could Be the Decade World Will End." *Chicago Tribune,* December 31, 1989.

"Odyssey to Suicide." *New York Times,* April 28, 1997.

"Officials Deny Rumors, Allegations." *Los Angeles Times,* February 10, 1980.

Plummer, William. "Turmoil in a California Camelot." *People,* July 1, 1985, 74–77.

"Prophet, Francis to Announce Divorce." *Livingston Enterprise,* November 25, 1996.

"Prophet Gives Up Position." *Billings Gazette,* June 11, 1996.

"Prophet Visits San Francisco to Give Divine Word." *San Francisco Chronicle,* April 27, 1991.

"Real Story Behind the Trilateral Commission, The." Pamphlet produced by Citizens for LaRouche, March 1980.

"Sect Channels Energy Through Speech." *Los Angeles Times,* January 1, 1977.

"Sect Orders Members in Shelter." *Los Angeles Times,* March 17, 1990.

"Shelter: Church Has Refuge in Woods, The." *Calgary Herald,* May 2, 1997.

"Sixth CUT Leader Steps Down from Board." *Livingston Enterprise,* January 24, 1996.

Schmook, Kathy Grizzard. "Apocalypse on the Yellowstone." *Edging West,* June-July 1995, 28–33.

"Sons and Daughters, Gather Ye into the Flock." *Los Angeles Times,* February 11, 1980.

"Space in Shelters Sells for a Song as World Fails to End." *Denver Post,* May 17, 1990.

Student background statement and financial aid application for Elizabeth Clare Wulf, Antioch College, 1957.

"Tenant Owes for Rent." *Livingston Enterprise,* August 22, 1996.

"Thousand Plan Life Below after Doomsday." *New York Times,* March 15, 1990.

"Trouble in Paradise." *Bozeman Daily Chronicle,* November 24, 1996.

"Trouble in Paradise: A Doomsday Prophet Wears Out Her Welcome." *Maclean's: Canada's News Magazine,* May 7, 1990, 33–35.

"Two Religious Learning Centers Planned." *Los Angeles Times,* October 8, 1977.

"Undercover: Delving into the Church's Business Practice." *Calgary Herald,* March 3, 1997.

"Waco Standoff's Unwelcome Limelight." *Washington Post,* March 20, 1993.

"Weapons Seizure Grand Jury Probe of New Age Sect." *San Francisco Chronicle,* August 17, 1989.

"With World Still Intact, Sect Draws More Critics." *New York Times,* March 2, 1997.

"Within Year CUT Leader Moving to Bozeman." *Livingston Enterprise,* January 27, 2000.

"World Close to Nuclear War in 1990." *Arizona Republic,* March 22, 1993.

"Yellowstone Land Swap Will Protect Bisons, Geysers." *Pittsburgh Post Gazette,* August 23, 1999.

Church Universal and Triumphant Material and Ephemera

The AIDS Conspiracy. 1988 videotape produced by the Church Universal and Triumphant.

"Basic Cosmic Science." Undated early instructional lesson.

"Building a New Culture: Handbook for Individual and Organizational Change." 1997 pamphlet produced by the Church Universal and Triumphant, 14–15.

"Building Community." *Heart to Heart: Monthly Newsletter of the Church Universal and Triumphant* (April 8, 1998): 1.

"Challenging the Media Myth: The Facts about the Church Universal and Triumphant." 1990 pamphlet produced by the Church Universal and Triumphant.

"Church Universal and Triumphant 1998 Annual Report." 1998.

"Church Universal and Triumphant News Release." August 21, 1997.

Climb the Highest Mountain: A Profile of the Church Universal and Triumphant. 1993 videotape produced by the Church Universal and Triumphant.

"CUT Spiritual Leader Announces She Has Alzheimer's Disease." Church Universal and Triumphant news release, November 25, 1998.

"Dynamic Decree." Undated mid-1980s Church Universal and Triumphant decree.

East Minus West Equals Zero. 1988 videotape produced by the Church Universal and Triumphant.

"Elizabeth Clare Prophet Announces Plans to Retire." Church Universal and Triumphant news release, January 1, 1999.

Elizabeth Clare Prophet Interviews Tomas Schuman. 1984 videotape produced by the Church Universal and Triumphant.

"Environment of the Soul, The." Church Universal and Triumphant information brochure from June 25-July 4, 1994, summer conference.

"Foundation of Higher Spiritual Learning, The." Brochure produced by the Universal Church, July 8, 1992.

"Freedom 1982." Statement probably from the Church Universal and Triumphant 1984 Decree Book.

"Freedom 1988." Church Universal and Triumphant promotional bulletin.

FOCUS (October 1996): 4. Short-lived anti-Church Universal and Triumphant newsletter.

"Great White Brotherhood as Inner World Government, The: Basic Cosmic Science." Early undated lesson for church members.

"Great White Brotherhood as Inner World Government by the Ascended Master Chananda, The." 1968 instructional lesson for the Keepers of the Flame fraternity.

Heart to Heart: Monthly newsletter of the International Headquarters of the Church Universal and Triumphant (September 1998): 1.

History of the Summit Lighthouse, The. Livingston, Mont.: Summit Univ. Press, 1994. Short booklet produced by the Church Universal and Triumphant.

I AM Light of the World: Invocations and Decrees for Keepers of the Flame. The Summit Lighthouse, Inc., 1968.

"Invocation to the Hierarchy of the Ruby Ray." Prayer from the Church Universal and Triumphant's 1984 decree book.

"Judgment of the Conspiracy of Watchers." Undated Church Universal and Triumphant decree.

"Keeper of the Flame: A Fraternity of Sons and Daughters Dedicated to the Freedom and Enlightenment of Humanity." 1988 pamphlet produced by the Church Universal and Triumphant.

"Land Agreement Closes." *Heart to Heart: Monthly Newsletter of the Church Universal and Triumphant* (November 1999): 3.

"Letter from Mother's Co-Guardians." Statement issued to Church Universal and Triumphant members, dated January 27, 2000.

Memorandum for the Church Universal and Triumphant administrative staff, 1980.

"More Violet Flame." Internal Church Universal and Triumphant staff document dated November 21, 1981.

Pearls of Wisdom 11, no. 30 (July 28, 1968); 12, no. 17 (April 27, 1969); 12, no. 18 (May 4, 1969); 16, no. 20 (May 20, 1973); 16, no. 21 (May 27, 1973); 22, no. 12 (March 24, 1974); 22, no. 17 (Undated); 24, no. 35 (August 1981); 24, no. 36 (August 30, 1981); 28, no. 50 (December 15, 1985); 29, no. 9 (March 2, 1986); 31, no. 38 (1988); 32, no. 27 (July 2, 1989); 36, no. 43 (September 26, 1993); 39, no. 18 (March 5, 1996); 39, no. 22 (1996); 39, no. 31 (August 4, 1996); 39, no. 42 (Oct. 20, 1996); 40, no. 17 (April 27, 1997).

"Practical Spirituality: A Six-Day Conference on Living a Spiritual Life." Church Universal and Triumphant information brochure for 1997 conference.

"Prayer Vigil for the World, A." Undated decree.

"Prayer Vigil for Washington, D.C., A." Undated mid-1980s Church Universal and Triumphant decree.

Prophet, Elizabeth Clare. *Freedom 1988: Fourth of July Address.* 1988 videotape produced by the Church Universal and Triumphant.

———. *From Confidential File 10019 for the Coming Revolution in Higher Consciousness.* 1978 audiotape recording produced by the Church Universal and Triumphant.

———. *I Believe in the United States of America.* 1980 audiotape recording produced by the Church Universal and Triumphant.

———. *Lecture on Gnosticism.* 1986 audiotape recording produced by the Church Universal and Triumphant.

———. *Mother Mary Twentieth-Century Prophecies.* 1991 audiotape recording produced by the Church Universal and Triumphant.

———. *On the Edge: Challenges on the Cusp of the Twenty-first Century.* 1995 videotape produced by the Church Universal and Triumphant.

———. *Planet Earth: The Future Is to the Gods.* 1981 audiotape recording produced by the Church Universal and Triumphant.

"Reflections on Mother." Statement written by Church Universal and Triumphant officers and distributed to members, January 1, 2000.

Royal Teton Ranch News (September-October 1994); spring-summer 1996): 5.

"Soul Evolution: A Fusion of Mind and Spirit." Church Universal and Triumphant information brochure for 1995 summer conference.

"Special Dispensation, A." Church Universal and Triumphant pamphlet, 1995.

"Spiritual Guidance for a Changing World." Church Universal and Triumphant brochure, 2000.

Temple of the Presence advertisement, undated.

Temple of the Presence promotional literature. April 1996.

Transcribed notes from Church Universal and Triumphant senior staff meeting, February 26, 1980.

"Treasurer's Corner." *Heart to Heart: Monthly Newsletter of the Church Universal and Triumphant* (April 1998): 7.

To Deploy or Not to Deploy. 1987 videotape produced by the Church Universal and Triumphant.

UFO Connection, The. 1988 videotape produced by the Church Universal and Triumphant.

Universal Church organizational statement. July 8, 1992.

Untitled brochure for Lanello Reserves produced by the Church Universal and Triumphant. Undated.

Untitled Church Universal and Triumphant advertising brochure. 1973.

Untitled Church Universal and Triumphant information bulletin for new members, probably dating from the early 1980s.

Untitled Church Universal and Triumphant literature pertaining to Lanello Reserves. 1973.

Untitled Temple of the Presence pamphlet, February 21, 1996.

We Have Built Ourselves an Enemy. 1988 videotape produced by the Church Universal and Triumphant.

"Why Silver?" Undated Lanello Reserves advertisement produced by the Church Universal and Triumphant.

Selected Interviews and Correspondence

All interviews were conducted by the author.

Allison, Jean. Royal Teton Ranch, Corwin Springs, Mont. July 2, 1994.

Anderson, Davies. Royal Teton Ranch, Corwin Springs, Mont. July 1, 1994.

Anonymous Church Universal and Triumphant staff member. Royal Teton Ranch, Corwin Springs, Mont. June 30, 1994.

Anonymous Church staff member. Royal Teton Ranch, Corwin Springs, Mont. July 3, 1994.

Anonymous former member of the Church Universal and Triumphant. Syracuse, N.Y. Oct. 19, 1993; Oct. 22, 1993.

Anonymous former Church staff member. Telephone interview. December 5, 1998.

Anonymous former staff member of the Church Universal and Triumphant. Telephone interviews. March 4, 1997; February 7, 1994.

Anonymous member of the Church Universal and Triumphant. Emigrant Point, Mont. July 1, 1994.

Anonymous Church member. Royal Teton Ranch, Corwin Springs, Mont. July 1, 1994.

Anonymous Church member. Royal Teton Ranch, Corwin Springs, Mont. July 1, 1994.

Anonymous Church member. Syracuse, N.Y. January 15, 1994.

Anonymous Church member. residing at Glastonbury. Emigrant, Mont. August 13, 1993.

Arnone, Peter. Telephone interviews. March 4, 1997; March 17, 1997; March 25, 1998.

Daniel [pseud.]. Royal Teton Ranch, Corwin Springs, Mont. July 1, 1994.

Duffy, Neroli. Royal Teton Ranch, Corwin Springs, Mont. July 3, 1994.

Francis, Edward. Royal Teton Ranch, Corwin Springs, Mont. July 4, 1994.

Friedman, Stanton. Correspondence with author. February 20, 2000.

Haugen, Paul. Royal Teton Ranch, Corwin Springs, Mont. July 2, 1994.

Paula [pseud.]. Emigrant Point, Mont. June 30, 1994.

Prophet, Elizabeth Clare. Royal Teton Ranch, Corwin Springs, Mont. July 3, 1994.

Raney, Bob (Montana state representative). Telephone interview. December 16, 1996.

Roberts, Archibald (Col.). Correspondence with author. April 30, 1997.

Steinman, Murray. Corwin Springs, Mont. August 8, 1993.

———. Telephone interviews. July 31, 1995; August 2, 1995.

Voessler, Gene. Royal Teton Ranch, Corwin Springs, Mont. July 1, 1994.

Walsh, Cheri. Correspondence with author. May 27, 2000.

———. Royal Teton Ranch, Corwin Springs, Mont. July 3, 1994.

———. Telephone interviews. May 9, 2000; June 8, 2000.

Wilson, Brenda [pseud.]. Correspondence with author. July 13, 2000.

Index

Freemasonry: Blavatsky's view of, 20–21; development of, 178nn. 73–75; occult nature of, 65–66; paranoia about, 188n. 42; political influence of, 178n. 81; revolutionary activity of, 67

Friedman, Stanton, 102, 103, 184n. 111

full moon meditation, 23

fusionism, 101, 184n. 100

genetic manipulation: AIDS epidemic as, 102; counterfeit beings from, 46, 72–73; Moulton-Howe on, 104; E. C. Prophet's revelations on, 180n. 111; soulless automations from, 32

Germain, Saint: Guy Ballard's tour with, 26, 169n. 56; on catastrophic event, 187n. 31; dwelling place of, 47; I AM movement and, 23; Geraldine Innocente and, 27; on CUT's move to Montana, 81–82, 180n. 14; on nuclear threat, 105; E. C. Prophet and, 31; on underground shelters, 86–87, 93

Glastonbury community: apocalypticism at, 104–5; apocalyptic mobilization and, 109–11; cost of shelter in, 159; Mandell shooting at, 135–36; nuclear fears and, 113; present readiness of, 155; sale of properties at, 138; separatism and, 91; underground shelters at, 105

Gnosticism, 64–65, 88–89, 177n. 67

god concept, 24–25, 34–35

Godfre, Goddess of Liberty, 35

God-government, 93–94

golden age of renewal: AIDS as threat to, 100; catastrophe and, 83–84; exclusivity of, 11; foundation of belief in, 14; CUT's move to Montana and, 78–79, 82; survivalist tendencies and, 6; underlying concepts, 8

golden age renewal, 62

gold/silver hoarding, 56–57, 109

Goodricke-Clarke, 176n. 51

Gordon, Kate, 151

government: AIDS crisis suspicions, 101–2; concerns about CUT activities, 131, 133, 186–87n. 22; CUT distrust of, 56–57; as enemy of CUT, 11; financial investigation of CUT by, 2–3, 131–33, 134, 190nn. 40–41; Jonestown suicides and, 55, 124–25; lawsuit against Edna Ballard, 26; purchase of Royal Tetons land, 149, 151; and alleged secrecy concerning UFO activity, 102–4; Waco standoff and, 3–4, 132–33

Graham, Daniel, 95–96

Great White Brotherhood, 35, 94, 169n. 50, 171n. 100. *See also* Ascended Masters

Hall, John, 82

Hamilton, Vernon, 106, 128

Heart to Heart, 140, 190n. 59

Heaven's Gate suicides, 141, 157

Hoag, Philip, 194n. 138

hoaxes, 18, 167n. 9

Hoffer, Eric, 63

Hopkins, Budd, 102

human ascendance, 11, 95, 169n. 60

human transcendence, 34, 65, 78–79

human transformation, 34, 36, 83

I AM Activity: anticommunism of, 43; Ascended Masters and, 168n. 40, 169n. 50; conspiracism of, 69, 176n. 52; cultic milieu concept and, 60, 61–63; current status, 193n. 119; CUT as splinter of, 15; decline of, 152; esoteric expression in, 63; extraterrestrial beings, belief in, 32–33, 102–3; God of, 168n. 43; history of, 23–28; human ascendance concept in, 11; influence on M. Prophet, 7–8, 12–13; membership of, 168n. 44; One Hundred Percenters of, 31; significance of Tetons to, 47; teachings on extraterrestrials, 74